Real World Camera Raw
with Adobe Photoshop CS2

Real World Camera Raw with Adobe Photoshop CS2

Industrial-Strength Production Techniques

Bruce Fraser

Peachpit Press

Adobe

Real World Camera Raw with Adobe Photoshop CS2

Bruce Fraser

Copyright ©2005 by Bruce Fraser

Peachpit Press
1249 Eighth Street
Berkeley, CA 94710
510/524-2178
Fax: 510/524-2221

Find us on the World Wide Web at www.peachpit.com.

Peachpit Press is a division of Pearson Education.
Real World Camera Raw with Adobe Photoshop CS2 is published in association with Adobe Press.

Interior design by Stephen F. Roth/Open House
Cover Design: Aren Howell
Cover Illustration: Ben Fishman, Artifish, Inc.

ISBN 0-321-33409-4
9 8 7 6 5 4 3 2

Printed and bound in the United States of America

Overview

The Big Picture

Contents

What's Inside

Preface

Real World Raw

If you're reading this book because you want to be told that digital really is better than film, look elsewhere. The term "digital photography" may still be in current use, but sooner rather than later, it will be replaced by the simple term "photography." If you want to be told that shooting digital raw is better than shooting JPEG, you'll have to read between the lines—what this book does is to explain how raw *differs* from JPEG, and how you can exploit those differences.

But if you're looking for solid, tested, proven techniques for dealing with hundreds or thousands of raw images a day—moving them from the camera to the computer, making initial selects and sorts, optimizing the raw captures, enriching them with metadata, and processing them into deliverable form—this is the book for you. My entire reason for writing this book was to throw a lifebelt to all those photographers who find themselves drowning in gigabytes of data.

The combination of Photoshop CS2, Bridge, and the Camera Raw plug-in offers a fast, efficient, and extremely powerful workflow for dealing with raw digital captures, but the available information tends to be short on answers to questions such as the following.

▶ What special considerations should I take into account when shooting digital raw rather than film or JPEG?

▶ What edits should I make in Camera Raw?

▶ How and where are my Camera Raw settings saved?

▶ How can I fine-tune Camera Raw's color performance to better match my camera's behavior?

▶ How can I set up Bridge to speed up making initial selects from a day's shoot?

▶ How can I make sure that every image I deliver contains copyright and rights management notices?

▶ How do I make sure that all the work I do in Bridge, ranking or flagging images, entering keywords and other metadata, and sorting in a custom order, doesn't suddenly disappear?

▶ What are my alternatives to editing each individual image by hand?

▶ How can I automate the conversion of raw images to deliverable files?

Raw shooters face these questions, and many others, every day. Unfortunately, the answers are hard to find in the gazillion Photoshop books out there—much less Photoshop's own manuals—and when they're addressed at all they tend to be downplayed in favor of whizzy filter effects. This book answers these questions, and the other daily workflow issues that arise, head-on, and focuses on everything you need to do *before* you get your images open in Photoshop.

Teach a Man to Fish

The old saw goes, "Give a man a fish, and you give him a meal; teach a man to fish, and you give him a living." By that reckoning, my goal is to make you, gentle reader, a marine biologist—teaching you not only how to fish, but also to understand fish, how they think, where they hang out, and how to predict their behavior.

Digital capture is the future of photography, but if you're on a deadline and suddenly find that all your raw images are mysteriously being processed at camera default settings rather than the carefully optimized ones you've applied, or your images insist on displaying in order of filename rather than the custom sort order you spent an hour constructing, you can easily be forgiven for contemplating a return to rush processing at your friendly local lab and sorting on a light table with a grease pencil.

My hope is that you'll turn to this book instead.

You Are the Lab

One of the best things about shooting raw is the freedom it confers in imposing your preferred interpretation on your images. The concomitant downside is that if you don't impose your preferred interpretation on the images, you'll have to settle for one imposed by some admittedly clever software that is nonetheless a glorified adding machine with no knowledge of tone and color, let alone composition, aesthetics, or emotion.

With raw capture, you have total control, and hence total responsibility. A great many photographers wind up converting all their raw images at default settings and then try to fix everything in Photoshop, because Photoshop is something they know and understand. You'd be hard pressed to find a bigger Photoshop fan than I am—I've been living and breathing Photoshop for almost 15 years—but the fact is that Camera Raw lets you do things that you simply cannot do in Photoshop. If you don't use Camera Raw to optimize your exposure and color balance, you'll wind up doing a lot more work in Photoshop than you need to, and the quality of the results will almost certainly be less than you'd obtain by starting from an optimized raw conversion rather than a default one.

Drowning in Data

If you had to edit every single image by hand, whether in Photoshop or in Camera Raw, you'd quickly find that digital is neither faster nor cheaper than film. A day's shoot may produce six or seven gigabytes of image data, and it all has to get from the camera to the computer before you can even start making your initial selects. Building an efficient workflow is critical if you want to make the digital revolution survivable, let alone enjoyable. So just about every chapter in this book contains key advice on building a workflow that lets you work smarter rather than harder.

Making Images Smarter

We're already living science fiction, and the future arrived quite a while ago. One of the most-overlooked aspects of digital imaging is the opportunities offered by metadata. Your camera already embeds a great deal of potentially useful information in the image—the date and time of shooting, the ISO speed, the exposure and aperture settings, the focal length, and so on—but Bridge makes it easy to enrich your images still further with keywords and other useful metadata and lets you protect your intellectual property by embedding copyright and rights management.

Metadata is a means of adding value to your images. Camera metadata provides unambiguous image provenance, while keywords make it much likelier that your images will be selected by clients you've yet to meet. An image with no metadata is simply a collection of pixels, while an image that has been enriched by metadata is a digital asset that can keep earning for a lifetime.

Starting Out Right

The reason for doing a lot of work in Camera Raw and Bridge is simple. If you do the work correctly right at the start of the workflow, you never have to do it again later. When you attach your preferred Camera Raw setting to a raw image, those settings will be used every time you open that raw image, with no further work required on your part. And any metadata you apply to the raw image will automatically be embedded in every converted image you create from that raw image unless you take steps to remove it (and yes, I'll show you how to do that too). Not only do you have to do the work only once, you greatly reduce the likelihood that it will be undone later.

Understanding and Hubris

If it took somewhat less nerve for me to write the second edition of this book than it did the first, it's partly because the first edition was greeted with an enthusiasm that surprised me, and partly because my friend and colleague Jeff Schewe has informed me that it's time for me to relinquish the mantle of world's worst photographer. But I'm free of delusions of adequacy when it comes to my photography, and it still takes a certain amount of hubris for me to advise photographers who are hugely more skilled than I am on how to ply their trade.

With a very few exceptions (which are noted on the pages on which they appear), all the images in the book are my own. One of the two most common complaints about the first edition was that many of the images didn't illustrate well the points I was trying to make. I'm much better at making problem images than are the great photographers whose work graced the pages of the first edition, and I was perhaps reluctant to take the kinds of liberties with their images that I cheerfully do with my own. The images are solely intended to illustrate the process—this is not a book about my photography!

I may still be among the world's worst photographers, but I've been lucky enough to enjoy a close and fruitful relationship with the wonderful group of people who have made Photoshop the incredibly powerful tool it has become, and in the process I've had the opportunity to look longer and deeper at its inner workings than most people who use it to earn their livelihood.

Some of those inner workings are probably what my friend and colleague Fred Bunting likes to term "more interesting than relevant," but others—such as where and how your ranking or flagging information, your hand-tuned image settings, and your color-correct previews get stored— are pieces of vital information for anyone who entrusts their work to the tools discussed by this book. If conveying that information helps much better photographers than I to realize their vision, I consider the effort worthwhile.

How the Book Is Organized

A significant problem I faced in writing this book is that everything in the workflow affects everything else in the workflow, so some circularity is inherent. But the second most-common complaint about the first edition was that it had more redundancy than seemed necessary. I've tried to address that in this second edition.

The first two chapters look at the technical underpinnings of digital raw capture. Chapter 1, *Digital Camera Raw*, looks at the fundamental nature of raw images—what they are, and the advantages and pitfalls of shooting them. Chapter 2, *How Camera Raw Works*, looks at the specific advantages that Camera Raw offers over other raw converters.

Chapter 3, *Raw System Overview*, provides a road map for the remainder of the book by showing the roles of the three major components in the system, Photoshop, Bridge, and the Camera Raw plug-in.

Chapter 4, *Camera Raw Controls*, describes the many features offered by the Camera Raw plug-in, which has grown to the point where it's almost an application in its own right. Chapter 5, *Hands-On Camera Raw*, explores how to use these features quickly and effectively to evaluate and edit raw captures.

Chapter 6, *Adobe Bridge*, looks at the features in Bridge that are particularly relevant to a raw workflow—Bridge is a surprisingly deep application that serves the entire Adobe Creative Suite, not just Photoshop. Chapter 7, *It's All About the Workflow*, doesn't evangelize a specific workflow, because my needs may be very different from yours. Instead, it introduces some basic workflow principles, then looks at the various ways in which you can use Bridge to perform common tasks, so that you can build the workflow that works for you.

Chapter 8, *Mastering Metadata*, looks at the inner workings of the various metadata schemes used by Camera Raw and Bridge, and shows you how to make them work for you. Finally, Chapter 9, *Exploiting Automation*, show you how to leverage the work done in Camera Raw and Bridge to produce converted images that require minimal work in Photoshop and contain the metadata you want them to.

A Word to Windows Users

This book applies to both Windows and Macintosh. But I've been using Macs for over 20 years, so all the dialog boxes, menus, and palettes are illustrated using screen shots from the Macintosh version. Similarly, when discussing the many keyboard shortcuts in the program, I cite the Macintosh versions. In almost every case, the Command key translates to the Ctrl key and the Option key translates to the Alt key. In the relatively few exceptions to this rule, I've spelled out both the Macintosh and the Windows versions explicitly. I apologize to all you Windows users for the small inconvenience, but because Photoshop is so close to being identical on both platforms, I picked the one I know and ran with it.

The Pace of Innovation

I received the first beta version of Camera Raw 3.1 long after Chapters 4 and 5 had already been through copyedit and indexing. In addition to support for some interesting new cameras, Camera Raw 3.1 adds significant enhancements to a DNG-based workflow. Camera Raw 3.1 doesn't ship with Photoshop CS2, but it will probably be available for download by the time you read this, so if you download it and are puzzled by the discrepancies between its preferences and the ones shown in Chapters 4 and 5, look at the sidebar "Working with DNG" on pages 206–207.

Downloads

For those of you who may find such an exercise helpful, I've made the raw files of the images that I evaluated and processed in Chapter 5, *Hands-On Camera Raw*, available for download should you wish to go through the steps yourself. You can find them at www.realworldcameraraw.com. The login is RWCR2, and the password, in tribute to Mel Brooks, is swordfish.

Thank You!

I owe thanks to the many people who made this book possible. First, Thomas Knoll, both for creating Photoshop and Camera Raw, and for taking the time to review chapters while they were under construction and correcting a number of egregious errors. Jeff Schewe made many useful suggestions, and called me on explanations that made no sense. Thanks also to the inimitable Russell Preston Brown, who convinced Peachpit Press that this book was needed and that I was the person to write it. Any errors or inadequacies that remain in the book are despite their best efforts and are solely my responsibility.

I couldn't have done this without the Peachpit Dream Team. Rebecca Gulick, my editor extraordinaire, somehow just makes things happen when and how they need to while appearing absolutely unflappable; production virtuoso Lisa Brazieal turned my virtual creation into a manufactured reality;

Liz Welch painstakingly combed the manuscript for typos and inconsistencies, and patiently helped me translate my native language into American English. Steve Rath provided the comprehensive index to make sure that everyone can find the information they need.

Stephen Johnson, Michael Kieran, and Larry Baca contributed to this book in entirely mysterious ways, mostly by being great human beings and even better friends. Thanks to my partners in Pixel Genius LLC—Martin Evening, Seth Resnick, Andrew Rodney, Jeff Schewe, and Mike Skurski—for forging a brotherhood that does business in a way that makes MBAs blanch but keeps our customers happy, and for being the finest bunch of people with whom it has ever been my pleasure and privilege to work. Thanks also to the Pixel Mafia—you know who you are!

Last but by no stretch of the imagination least, I thank my lovely wife, Angela, for putting up with the stresses and strains that go with an author's life, for being my best friend and partner, and for making my life such a very happy one.

Bruce Fraser
San Francisco, April 2005

Digital Camera Raw

Exploiting the Digital Negative

Perhaps the greatest challenge that faces shooters who have made, or are in the process of making, the transition to digital is just dealing with the gigabytes of captured data. You can make some gross judgments about the image from a camera's on-board LCD display; but to separate the hero images from the junk, you have to copy the images from the camera media to a computer with a decent display, which is a major challenge for those of you who are used to getting rush-processed chromes back from the lab and sorting them on the light table.

Digital raw files present a further bottleneck, since they require processing before you can even see a color image. This book tells you how to deal with raw images quickly and efficiently, so that you can exploit the very real advantages of raw capture over JPEG, yet still have time to have a life. The key is in unlocking the full power of three vital aspects of Adobe Photoshop CS2—the Adobe Camera Raw plug-in, the standalone Bridge application, and Photoshop actions. Together, these three features can help you build an efficient workflow based on raw captures, from making the initial selects, through rough editing for client approval, to final processing of selected images.

In this first chapter, though, we'll focus on raw captures themselves, their fundamental nature, their advantages, and their limitations. So the first order of business is to understand just what a raw capture is.

What Is a Digital Raw File?

Fundamentally, a digital raw file is a record of the raw sensor data from the camera, accompanied by some camera-generated *metadata* (literally, data about data). I'll discuss metadata in great detail in Chapter 8, *Mastering Metadata*, but for now, all you need to know is that the camera metadata supplies information about the way the image was captured, including ISO setting, shutter speed and aperture value, white balance setting, and so on.

Different camera vendors may encode the raw data in different ways, apply various compression strategies, and in some cases even apply encryption, so it's important to realize that "digital camera raw" isn't a single file format. Rather, it's a catch-all term that encompasses Canon .CRW and CR2, Minolta .MRW, Nikon .NEF, Olympus .ORF, and all the other raw formats on the ever-growing list that's readable by Adobe Camera Raw. But all the various flavors of raw files share the same basic properties and offer the same basic advantages. To understand these, you need to know a little something about how digital cameras work.

The Camera Sensor

A raw file is a record of the sensor data, so let's look at what the sensor in a digital camera actually captures. A number of different technologies get lumped into the category of "digital camera," but virtually all the cameras supported by the Camera Raw plug-in are of the type known as "mosaic sensor" or "color filter array" cameras ("virtually all" because versions 2.2 and later of Camera Raw also support the Sigma cameras based on Foveon's X3 technology—see "The Foveon X3 Difference," later in this chapter). The first key point is that striped-array raw files are grayscale!

Color filter array cameras use a two-dimensional area array to collect the photons that are recorded in the image. The array is made up of rows and columns of photosensitive detectors—typically using either CCD (charge-coupled device) or CMOS (complementary metal oxide semiconductor) technology—to form the image. In a typical setup, each element of the array contributes one pixel to the final image (see Figure 1-1).

Figure 1-1
An area array

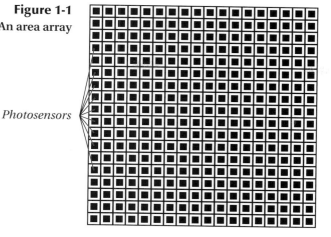

Photosensors

Each photosensor contributes one pixel to the image.

But the sensors in the array, whether CCD or CMOS, just count photons—they produce a charge proportional to the amount of light they receive—without recording any color information. The color information is produced by color filters that are applied over the individual elements in the array in a process known as "striping"—hence the term "striped array." Most cameras use a Bayer pattern arrangement for the color filter array, alternating green, red, green, blue filters on each consecutive element, with twice as many green as red and blue filters (because our eyes are most sensitive in the green region). See Figure 1-2.

Figure 1-2
Bayer pattern

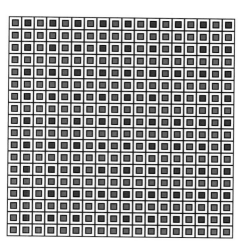

In a Bayer Pattern color filter array, each photosensor is filtered so that it captures only a single color of light: red, green, or blue. Twice as many green filters are used as red or blue because our eyes are most sensitive to green light.

Other color filter array configurations are possible—some cameras use a cyan, magenta, yellow arrangement instead of the GRGB configuration in the classic Bayer pattern, while still others may use four colors in an attempt to improve color fidelity. But unless you plan on designing your own cameras, you needn't worry about the details of this or that filter setup.

Raw Files Are Grayscale

No matter what the filter arrangement, the raw file simply records the luminance value for each pixel, so the raw file is a grayscale image. It contains color *information*—the characteristics of the color filter array are recorded, so raw converters know whether a given pixel in the raw file represents red, green, or blue luminance (or whatever colors the specific camera's filter array uses)—but it doesn't contain anything humans can interpret as color.

Obtaining a color image from the raw file is the job of a raw converter such as Camera Raw. The raw converter interpolates the missing color information for each pixel from its neighbors, a process called *demosaicing*, but it does much more, too. Besides interpolating the missing color information, raw converters control all of the following.

▶ **White balance.** The white balance indicates the color of the light under which the image was captured. Our eyes automatically adapt to different lighting situations—to oversimplify slightly, we interpret the brightest thing in the scene as white, and judge all the other colors accordingly. Cameras—whether film or digital—have no such adaptation mechanism, as anyone who has shot tungsten film in daylight has learned the hard way, so digital cameras let us set a white balance to record the color of the light.

But the on-camera white balance setting has no effect on the raw capture. It's saved as a metadata tag, and applied by the raw converter as part of the conversion process.

▶ **Colorimetric interpretation.** Each pixel in the raw file records a luminance value for either red, green, or blue. But "red," "green," and "blue" are pretty vague terms. Take a hundred people and ask them to visualize "red." If you could read their minds, you'd almost certainly see a hundred different shades of red.

Many different filter sets are in use with digital cameras. So the raw converter has to assign the correct, specific color meanings to the "red," "green," and "blue" pixels, usually in a colorimetrically defined color space such as CIE XYZ, which is based directly on human color perception, and hence represents color unambiguously.

▶ **Tone mapping.** Digital raw captures have linear gamma (gamma 1.0), a very different tonal response from that of either film or the human eye. The raw converter applies tone-mapping to redistribute the tonal information so that it corresponds more closely to the way our eyes see light and shade. I discuss the implications of linear capture on exposure in the section "Exposure and Linear Capture," on the next page.

▶ **Noise reduction, antialiasing, and sharpening.** When the detail in an image gets down to the size of individual pixels, problems can arise. If the detail is only captured on a red-sensing pixel or a blue-sensing pixel, its actual color can be difficult to determine. Simple demosaicing methods also don't do a great job of maintaining edge detail, so raw converters perform some combination of edge-detection, antialiasing to avoid color artifacts, noise reduction, and sharpening.

All raw converters perform each of these tasks, but each one may use different algorithms to do so, which is why the same image can appear quite different when processed through different raw converters.

The Foveon X3 Difference

Foveon X3 technology, embodied in the Sigma SD-9 and SD-10 SLR cameras, is fundamentally different from striped-array cameras.

The Foveon X3 direct image sensor captures color by exploiting the fact that blue light waves are shorter than green light waves, which in turn are shorter than red ones. It uses three layers of photosensors on the same chip.

The front layer captures the short blue waves, the middle layer captures the green waves, while only the longest red waves penetrate all the way to the third layer, which captures red.

The key benefit claimed by the X3 sensor is that it captures full color data, red, green, and blue, for every pixel in the image. As a result, .X3F files—Foveon X3 raws—don't require demosaicing. But they do need all the other operations a raw converter carries out—white balance, colorimetric interpretation, gamma correction, and detail control—so Camera Raw is as applicable to files from Foveon X3-equipped cameras as it is to those from the more common striped array cameras.

Exposure and Linear Capture

One final topic is key to understanding digital capture in general, not just digital raw. Digital sensors, whether CCD or CMOS, respond to light quite differently than does either the human eye or film. Most human perception, including vision, is nonlinear.

If we place a golf ball in the palm of our hand, then add another one, it doesn't feel twice as heavy. If we put two spoonfuls of sugar in our coffee instead of one, it doesn't taste twice as sweet. If we double the acoustic power going to our stereo speakers, the resulting sound isn't twice as loud. And if we double the number of photons reaching our eyes, we don't see the scene as twice as bright—brighter, yes, but not twice as bright.

This built-in compression lets us function in a wide range of situations without driving our sensory mechanisms into overload—we can go from subdued room lighting to full daylight without our eyeballs catching fire! But the sensors in digital cameras lack the compressive nonlinearity typical of human perception. They simply count photons in a linear fashion. If a camera uses 12 bits to encode the capture, producing 4,096 levels, then level 2,048 represents half the number of photons recorded at level 4,096. This is the meaning of linear capture—the levels correspond exactly to the number of photons captured. So if it takes 4,096 photons to make the camera record level 4,096, it takes 3,248 photons to make the same camera record level 3,248 and 10 photons to make it register level 10.

Linear capture has important implications for exposure. When a camera captures six stops of dynamic range (which is fairly typical of today's digital SLRs), half of the 4,096 levels are devoted to the brightest stop, half of the remainder (1,024 levels) are devoted to the next stop, half of the remainder (512 levels) are devoted to the next stop, and so on. The darkest stop, the extreme shadows, is represented by only 64 levels—see Figure 1-3.

Figure 1-3   Linear capture

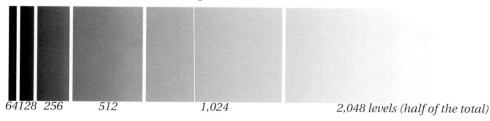

64 128 256   512   1,024   2,048 levels (half of the total)

We see light very differently. Human vision can't really be modeled accurately using a gamma curve, but gamma curves are so easy to implement, and come sufficiently close, that the working spaces we use to edit images almost invariably use a gamma encoding of somewhere between 1.8 and 2.2. Figure 1-4 shows approximately how we see the same six stops running from black to white.

Figure 1-4   Gamma-encoded gradient

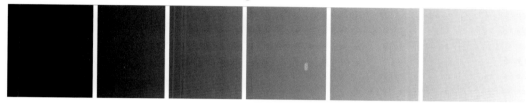

One of the major tasks raw converters perform is to convert the linear capture to a gamma-encoded space to make the captured levels more closely match the way human eyeballs see them. In practice, though, the tone-mapping from linear to gamma-encoded space is considerably more complex than simply applying a gamma correction—when we edit raw images, we typically move the endpoints, adjust the midtone, and tweak the contrast, so the tone-mapping curve from linear to gamma-encoded space is much more complex than can be represented by a simple gamma formula. If we want our images to survive this tone-mapping without falling apart, good exposure is critical.

Exposure

Correct exposure is at least as important with digital capture as it is with film, but correct exposure in the digital realm means keeping the highlights as close to blowing out, without actually doing so, as possible. If you fall prey to the temptation to underexpose images to avoid blowing out the highlights, you'll waste a lot of the bits the camera can capture, and you'll run a significant risk of introducing noise in the midtones and shadows. If you overexpose, you *may* blow out the highlights, but one of the great things about the Camera Raw plug-in is its ability to recover highlight detail (see the sidebar, "How Much Highlight Detail Can I Recover?" in Chapter 2, *How Camera Raw Works*), so if you're going to err on one side or the other, it's better to err on the side of *slight* overexposure.

Figure 1-5 shows what happens to the levels in the simple process of conversion from a linear capture to a gamma-corrected space. These illustrations use 8 bits per channel to make the difference very obvious, so the story they tell is somewhat worse than the actual behavior of a 10-bit, 12-bit, or 14-bit per channel capture, but the principle remains the same.

Figure 1-5   Exposure and tone-mapping

With a correct exposure, this range of data…

…gets stretched down into the midtones, forcing more bits into the shadow areas, where our eyes are more sensitive.

If you underexpose by one stop, you've only captured this much data…

…which must get stretched to cover the entire tonal range before the highlight range is stretched again to darken the midtones.

Note that the on-camera histogram shows the histogram of the conversion to JPEG: a raw histogram would be a strange-looking beast, with all the data clumped at the shadow end, so cameras show the histogram of the image after processing using the camera's default settings. Most cameras apply an S-curve to the raw data to give the JPEGs a more film-like response, so the on-camera histogram often tells you that your highlights are blown when in fact they aren't. Also, the response of a camera set to ISO 100 may be more like ISO 125 or ISO 150 (or, for that matter, ISO 75). It's worth spending some time determining your camera's real sensitivity at different speeds, then dialing in an appropriate exposure compensation to ensure that you're making the best use of the available bits.

Why Shoot Raw?

The answer to the above question is simply, control over the interpretation of the image. When you shoot JPEG, the camera's on-board software carries out all the tasks listed earlier to produce a color image, then compresses it using JPEG compression. Some cameras let you set parameters for this conversion—typically, a choice of sRGB or Adobe RGB as color space, a sharpness value, and perhaps a tone curve or contrast setting—but unless your shooting schedule is atypically leisurely, you probably can't adjust these parameters on an image-by-image basis, so you're locked into the camera's interpretation of the scene. JPEGs offer fairly limited editing headroom—large moves to tone and color tend to exaggerate the 8-by-8-pixel blocks that form the foundation of JPEG compression—and while JPEG does a pretty good job of preserving luminance data, it really clobbers the color, leading to problems with skin tones and gentle gradations.

When you shoot raw, however, *you* get to control the scene interpretation through all the aforementioned aspects of the conversion. With raw, the *only* on-camera settings that have an effect on the captured pixels are the ISO speed, shutter speed, and aperture. Everything else is under your control when you convert the raw file. You can reinterpret the white balance, the colorimetric rendering, the tonal response, and the detail rendition (sharpening and noise reduction) with a great deal of freedom, and, within the limits explained in the previous section, "Exposure and Linear Capture," you can even reinterpret the basic exposure itself, resetting the white and black points.

Using All the Bits

Most of today's cameras capture at least 12 bits per channel per pixel, for a possible 4,096 levels in each channel. More bits translates directly into editing headroom, but the JPEG format is limited to 8 bits per channel per pixel: So when you shoot JPEG, you trust the camera's built-in conversions to throw away one-third of your data in a way that does justice to the image.

When you shoot raw, though, you have, by definition, captured everything the camera can deliver, so you have much greater freedom in shaping the overall tone and contrast for the image. You also produce a file that can withstand a great deal more editing in Photoshop than can an 8-bit per channel JPEG.

Edits in Photoshop are "destructive"—when you use a tool such as Levels, Curves, Hue/Saturation, or Color Balance, you change the actual pixel values, creating the potential for either or both of two problems:

▶ Posterization can occur when you stretch a tonal range. Where the levels were formerly adjacent, they're now stretched apart, so instead of a gradation from, for example, level 100 through 101, 102, 103, 104, to 105, the new values may look more like 98, 101, 103, 105, 107. On its own, such an edit is unlikely to produce visible posterization—it usually takes a gap of four or five levels before you see a visible jump instead of a smooth gradation—but subsequent edits can widen the gaps, inducing posterization.

▶ Detail loss can occur when you compress a tonal range. Where the levels were formerly different, they're now compressed into the same value, so the differences, which represent potential detail, are tossed irrevocably into the bit-bucket, never to return.

Figure 1-6 shows how the compression and expansion of tonal ranges can affect pixel values. Don't be overly afraid of losing levels—it's a normal and necessary part of image editing, and its effect can be greatly reduced by bringing correctly exposed images into Photoshop as 16-bit/channel files rather than 8-bit/channel ones—but simply be aware of the destructive potential of Photoshop edits.

White Balance Control

I'll go into much more detail on how Camera Raw's white balance controls actually work in Chapter 2, *How Camera Raw Works*. For now, I'll make the key point that adjusting the white balance on a raw file is fundamentally different from attempting to do so on an already-rendered image in Photoshop.

As Figure 1-6 shows, Photoshop edits are inherently destructive—you wind up with fewer levels than you started out with. But when you change the white balance as part of the raw conversion process, the edit is much less destructive, because instead of changing pixel values by applying curves, you're gently scaling one or two channels to match the third. There may be very few free lunches in this world, but white balance control in Camera Raw is a great deal cheaper, in terms of losing data, than anything you can do to the processed image in Photoshop.

Figure 1-6
Destructive editing

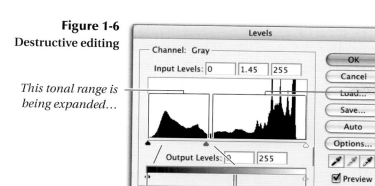

This tonal range is being expanded…

This tonal range is being compressed…

…to this range, spreading the pixels out and making them more different, so detail is more apparent.

…to this range, making the pixels more similar (and in some cases, identical), so detail is less visible or completely lost.

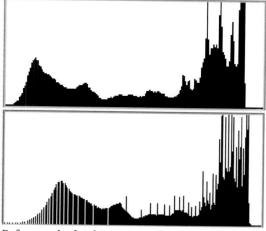

Before-and-after histograms show the loss of levels. The top histogram shows the state of the unedited image; the bottom one shows the state of the image after editing. The gaps indicate lost levels where the tonal range was stretched, and the spikes indicate lost differences where the tonal range was compressed.

Colorimetric Interpretation

When you shoot JPEG, you typically have a choice between capturing images in either sRGB or Adobe RGB (1998). Yet the vast majority of today's cameras can capture colors that lie outside the gamut of either of these spaces, especially in the case of saturated yellows and cyans, and those colors get clipped when you convert to sRGB or Adobe RGB.

Raw converters vary in their ability to render images into different color spaces, but Adobe Camera Raw offers four possible destinations. One of these, ProPhoto RGB, encompasses all colors we can capture, and the vast majority of colors we can see—if you see serious color clipping on a conversion to ProPhoto RGB, you're capturing something other than visible light!

Figure 1-7 shows a totally innocuous image rendered to ProPhoto RGB, and plotted against the gamuts of sRGB and Adobe RGB. Notice just how much of the captured color lies outside the gamut of both spaces.

Figure 1-7
Color spaces and clipping

The gamut plots below, produced using Chromix ColorThink, plot color in Lab space. You're looking at a side elevation of the color space, with the Lightness axis running vertically. The a* axis, from red to green, runs almost straight toward you out of the page; the b* axis, from blue to yellow, runs from left to right.

Even an innocuous image like the one at right can contain colors that lie well outside the range that either Adobe RGB (1998) or sRGB can represent.

The image above plotted (as squares) against the color gamut of Adobe RGB (1998) (shaded solid)

These dark yellows and oranges lie outside the gamut of Adobe RGB (1998) or sRGB

The image above plotted (as squares) against the color gamut of sRGB (shaded solid)

Exposure

As with white balance adjustments, exposure adjustments performed as part of the raw conversion are relatively lossless (unless you clip highlights to white or shadows to black), unlike tonal adjustments made in Photoshop on the rendered image (see Figure 1-3). In practice, however, you have rather less freedom to adjust exposure than you do white balance.

The main limitation on exposure adjustments is that when you try to open up significantly underexposed images, you'll probably see noise or posterization in the midtones and shadows. It's not that the edit is destructive—you just didn't capture enough shadow information in the first place.

Completely blown highlights are also beyond recovery, but Camera Raw goes a good bit further than other raw converters in rescuing highlight detail even when only one channel contains data. Depending on the camera and the white balance chosen, you may be able to recover one or more stops of highlight detail. Nevertheless, good exposure is still highly desirable—see the section "Exposure and Linear Capture," earlier in this chapter.

Detail and Noise

When you shoot JPEG, the sharpening and noise reduction are set by the on-camera settings (most cameras let you make a setting for sharpness, but few do for noise reduction). When you shoot raw, you have control over both sharpening and noise reduction—Camera Raw even lets you handle luminance noise and color noise separately.

This confers several advantages. You can tailor the noise reduction to different ISO speeds, apply quick global sharpening for rough versions of images, or convert images with no sharpening at all so that you can apply more nuanced localized sharpening to the rendered image in Photoshop.

Raw Limitations

While raw offers significant advantages over JPEG, it also has some limitations. For the majority of work, I believe that the advantages outweigh the disadvantages, but I'd be remiss if I didn't point out the downsides. So in the interests of full disclosure, let's look at the limitations of raw.

Processing Time

Perhaps the biggest limitation is also the main strength of raw files—you gain a huge amount of control in the conversion process, but you have to take the time to process the raw file to obtain an image. Camera Raw lets you convert raw images very efficiently, particularly once you learn to use it in conjunction with Photoshop's automation features, but each image still takes some time—a few seconds—to process.

If you digest and implement all the techniques, tips, and tricks offered in this book, you'll find that the bulk of the time spent on raw conversions is computer time—you can set up batch conversions and go do something more interesting while the computer crunches the images. But any way you slice it, raw files aren't as immediately available as JPEGs, and they require one more step in the workflow.

File Size

Raw files are larger than JPEGs—typically somewhere between two and four times as large. Storage is cheap and getting cheaper every year, but if you need to fit the maximum number of images on a camera's storage card, or you need to transmit images as quickly as possible over a network or the Web, the larger size of raw files may be an issue.

In most cases, a modicum of planning makes file size a non-issue—just make sure you have enough storage cards, and leave yourself enough time for file transmission.

Tip: Two small cards are better than one large one. High-capacity Compact Flash cards command premium prices compared to lower-capacity ones—a 4GB card costs more than double the price of a 2GB one, which in turn costs more than double the price of a 1GB one. But using two smaller cards rather than one bigger one lets you hand off the first card to an assistant who can then start copying the files to the computer, archiving them, and perhaps even doing rough processing, while you continue to shoot with the second card. Multiple smaller, cheaper cards give you much more flexibility than one big one.

Longevity

There's one other issue with raw files. Currently, many camera vendors use proprietary formats for raw files, raising a concern about their long-term readability. Hardware manufacturers don't have the best track record when it comes to producing updated software for old hardware—I have cupboards full of ancient orphaned weird junk to prove it—so it's entirely legitimate to raise the question of how someone will be able to read the raw files you capture today in 10 or 100 years time.

Adobe's commitment to making Camera Raw a universal converter for raw images is clear. At the same time, it's no secret that some camera vendors are less than supportive of Adobe's efforts in this regard. If you're concerned about long-term support for your raw files, you need to make your camera vendor aware of the fact. You can also support Adobe's .DNG initiative, which offers an open, documented file format for raw captures, and, if necessary, use your wallet to vote against vendors who resist such initiatives. I'll discuss .DNG in much more detail in Chapter 7, *It's All About the Workflow.*

Adobe Camera Raw

If you've read this far, I hope I've convinced you of the benefits of shooting raw. In the remainder of this chapter, let's examine the reasons for making Adobe Camera Raw the raw converter of choice.

Universal Converter

Unlike the raw converters supplied by the camera vendors, Camera Raw doesn't limit its support to a single brand of camera. Adobe has made a commitment to add support for new cameras on a regular basis, and so far, they seem to be doing a good job. So even if you shoot with multiple cameras from different vendors or add new cameras regularly, you have to learn only one user interface and only one set of controls. This translates directly into savings of that most precious commodity, time.

Industrial-strength Features

Camera Raw is one of the most full-featured raw converters in existence. It offers fine control over white balance, exposure, noise reduction, and sharpness, but unlike most other raw converters, it also has controls for eliminating chromatic aberration (digital capture is brutal at revealing lens flaws that film masks) and for fine-tuning the color response for individual camera models.

Thanks to the magic of metadata, Camera Raw can identify the specific camera model on which an image was captured. You can create Calibration settings for each camera model, which Camera Raw then applies automatically. Of course, you can also customize all the other Camera Raw settings and save them as Camera Defaults—so each camera model can have its own set of custom settings.

Integration with Photoshop

As soon as you point Adobe Bridge at a folder full of raw images, Camera Raw goes straight to work, generating thumbnails and previews so that you can make your initial selects quickly.

Bridge's automation features let you apply custom settings on a per-image basis, then call Photoshop to batch-convert images to Web galleries, PDF presentations, or virtual contact sheets. And when it's time to do serious selective manual editing on selected images, Camera Raw delivers them right into Photoshop, where you need them.

The Digital Negative

If you've digested this chapter, you'll doubtless have concluded that, like most analogies, the one that equates digital raw with film negative isn't perfect—for one thing, raw capture doesn't offer the kind of exposure latitude we expect from negative film. But in a great many other respects, it holds true.

Both offer a means for capturing an unrendered image, providing a great deal of freedom in how you render that image post-capture. Both allow you to experiment and produce many different renderings of the same image, while leaving the actual capture unchanged.

In the next chapter, *How Camera Raw Works*, we'll look at some of the technological underpinnings of Camera Raw. If you're the impatient type who just wants to jump in with both feet, feel free to skip ahead to Chapter 4, *Camera Raw Controls*, where you'll learn what the various buttons and sliders do, and Chapter 5, *Hands-On Camera Raw*, where you'll learn to use them to interpret your images. But if you want to understand *why* these buttons and sliders work the way they do, and why you should use them rather than try to fix everything in Photoshop, it's worth setting aside part of a rainy afternoon to understanding just what Camera Raw actually does.

2 How Camera Raw Works

What Lies Under the Hood

Despite the title of this chapter, I promise to keep it equation-free and relatively nontechnical. Camera Raw offers functionality that at a casual glance may seem to replicate that of Photoshop. But the important ways in which raw files differ from more conventional Photoshop fare, which we spent the last chapter examining, dictate that just about everything you can do in Camera Raw, you *should* do in Camera Raw.

To understand why this is so, it helps to know a little about how Camera Raw performs its magic. If you're the type who would rather learn by doing, feel free to skip ahead to Chapter 4, *Camera Raw Controls*, where you'll be introduced to the nitty-gritty of actually using all the controls in Camera Raw; but if you take the time to digest the contents of this chapter, you'll have a much better idea of what the controls actually do, and hence a better understanding of how and when to use them.

To use Camera Raw effectively, you must first realize that computers and software applications like Photoshop and Camera Raw don't know anything about tone, color, truth, beauty, or art. They're really just glorified and incredibly ingenious adding machines that juggle ones and zeroes to order. I won't go into the intricacies of binary math except to note that there are 10 kinds of people in this world, those who understand binary math and those who don't! You don't need to learn to count in binary or hexadecimal, but you do need to understand some basic stuff about how numbers can represent tone and color.

Digital Image Anatomy

Digital images are made up of numbers. The fundamental particle of a digital image is the pixel—the number of pixels you capture determines the image's size and aspect ratio. It's tempting to use the term *resolution*, but doing so often confuses matters more than it clarifies them. Why?

Pixels and Resolution

Strictly speaking, a digital image in its pure Platonic form doesn't have resolution—it simply has pixel dimensions. It only attains the attribute of resolution when we realize it in some physical form—displaying it on a monitor, or making a print. But resolution isn't a *fixed* attribute.

If we take as an example a typical six-megapixel image, it has the invariant property of pixel dimensions, specifically, 3,072 pixels on the long side of the image, 2,048 pixels on the short one. But we can display and print those pixels at many different sizes. Normally, we want to keep the pixels small enough that they don't become visually obvious, so the pixel dimensions essentially dictate how large a print we can make from the image. As we make larger and larger prints, the pixels become more and more visually obvious until we reach a size at which it just isn't rewarding to print.

Just as it's possible to make a 40-by-60-inch print from a 35mm color neg, it's possible to make a 40-by-60-inch print from a six-megapixel image, but neither of them is likely to look very good. With the 35mm film, you end up with grain the size of golf balls, and with the digital capture, each pixel winds up being just under 1/50th of an inch square—big enough to be obvious.

Different printing processes have different resolution requirements, but in general, you need not less than 100 pixels per inch, and rarely more than 360 pixels per inch to make a decent print. So the effective size range of our six-megapixel capture is roughly from 20 by 30 inches downward, and 20 by 30 is really pushing the limits. The basic lesson is that you can print the same collection of pixels at many different sizes, and as you do so, the resolution—the number of pixels per inch—changes, but the number of pixels does not. At 100 pixels per inch, our 3072-by-2048-pixel image will yield a 30.72-by-20.48-inch print. At 300 pixels per inch, the same image will make a 10.24-by-6.83-inch print. So resolution is a fungible quality—you can spread the same pixels over a smaller or larger area.

To find out how big an image you can produce at a specific resolution, divide the pixel dimensions by the resolution. Using pixels per inch (ppi) as the resolution unit and inches as the size unit, if you divide 3,072 (the long pixel dimension) by 300, you obtain the answer 10.24 inches for the long dimension and if you divide 2,048 (the short pixel dimension) by the same quantity, you get 6.826 inches for the short dimension. At 240 ppi, you get 12.8 by 8.53 inches. Conversely, to determine the resolution you have available to print at a given size, divide the pixel dimensions by the size, in inches. The result is the resolution in pixels per inch. For example, if you want to make a 10-by-15-inch print from your six-megapixel, 3,072-by-2,048-pixel image, divide the long pixel dimension by the long dimension in inches, or the short pixel dimension by the short dimension in inches. In either case, you'll get the same answer, 204.8 pixels per inch.

Figure 2-1 shows the same pixels printed at 50 pixels per inch, 150 pixels per inch, and 300 pixels per inch.

Figure 2-1
Image size and resolution

50 ppi   *150 ppi*   *300 ppi*

But each individual pixel is defined by a set of numbers, and these numbers also impose limitations on what you can do with the image, albeit more subtle limitations than those dictated by the pixel dimensions.

Bit Depth, Dynamic Range, and Color

We use numbers to represent a pixel's tonal value—how light or dark it is—and its color—red, green, blue, yellow, or any of the myriad gradations of the various rainbow hues we can see.

Bit Depth. In a grayscale image, each pixel is represented by some number of bits. Photoshop's 8-bit/channel mode uses 8 bits to represent each pixel, and its 16-bit/channel mode uses 16 bits to represent each pixel. An 8-bit pixel can have any one of 256 possible tonal values, from 0 (black) to 255 (white), or any of the 254 intermediate shades of gray. A 16-bit pixel can have any one of 32,769 possible tonal values, from 0 (black) to 32,768 (white), or any of the 32,767 intermediate shades of gray. If you're wondering why 16 bits in Photoshop gives you 32,769 shades instead of 65,536, see the sidebar "High-Bit Photoshop," later in this chapter (if you don't care, skip it).

So while pixel dimensions—the number of pixels—describe the two-dimensional height and width of the image, the bits that describe each pixel produce a third dimension that describes how light or dark each pixel is—hence the term *bit depth*.

Dynamic Range. Some vendors try to equate bit depth with dynamic range. This is largely a marketing ploy, because while there *is* a relationship between bit depth and dynamic range, it's an indirect one.

Dynamic range in digital cameras is an analog limitation of the sensor. The brightest shade the camera can capture is limited by the point at which the current generated by a sensor element starts spilling over to its neighbors—a condition often called "blooming"—and produces a featureless white blob. The darkest shade a camera can capture is determined by the more subjective point at which the noise inherent in the system overwhelms the very weak signal generated by the small number of photons that hit the sensor—the subjectivity lies in the fact that some people can tolerate a noisier signal than others.

One way to think of the difference between bit depth and dynamic range is to imagine a staircase. The dynamic range is the height of the staircase. The bit depth is the number of steps in the staircase. If we want our staircase to be reasonably easy to climb, or if we want to preserve the illusion of a continuous gradation of tone in our images, we need more steps in a taller staircase than we do in a shorter one, and we need more bits to describe a wider dynamic range than a narrower one. But more bits, or a larger number of smaller steps, doesn't increase the dynamic range, or the height of the staircase.

High-Bit Photoshop

If an 8-bit channel consists of 256 levels, a 10-bit channel consists of 1,024 levels, and a 12-bit channel consists of 4,096 levels, doesn't it follow that a 16-bit channel should consist of 65,536 levels?

Well, that's certainly one way that a 16-bit channel could be constructed, but it's not the way Photoshop does it. Photoshop's implementation of 16 bits per channel uses 32,769 levels, from 0 (black) to 32,768 (white). One advantage of this approach is that it provides an unambiguous midpoint between white and black, which is very useful in imaging operations such as blending modes, that a channel comprising 65,536 levels lacks.

To those who would claim that Photoshop's 16-bit color is really more like 15-bit color, I simply point out that it takes 16 bits to represent, and by the time capture devices that can actually capture more than 32,769 levels are at all common, we'll all have moved on to 32-bit floating point channels rather than 16-bit integer ones.

Color. RGB color images are comprised of three 8-bit or 16-bit grayscale images, or *channels*, one representing shades of red, the second representing shades of green, and the third representing shades of blue. Red, green, and blue are the primary colors of light, and combining them in different proportions allows us to create any color we can see. So an 8-bit/channel RGB image can contain any of 16.7 million unique color definitions (256 x 256 x 256), while a 16-bit/channel image can contain any of some 35 *trillion* unique color definitions.

Either of these may sound like a heck of a lot of colors, and indeed, they are. Estimates of how many unique colors the human eye can distinguish vary widely, but even the most liberal estimates are well shy of 16.7 million and nowhere close to 35 trillion. Why then do we need all this data?

We need it for two quite unrelated reasons. The first one, which isn't particularly significant for the purposes of this book, is that 8-bit/channel RGB contains 16.7 million color *definitions*, not 16.7 million perceivable colors. Many of the color definitions are redundant: Even on the very best display, you'd be hard pressed to see the difference between RGB values of 0,0,0, and 0,0,1 or 0,1,0 or 1,0,0, or for that matter between 255,255,255 and 254, 255, 255 or 255, 254, 255 or 255, 255, 254. Depending on the specific flavor of RGB you choose, you'll find similar redundancies in different parts of the available range of tone and color.

The second reason, which is *extremely* significant for the purposes of this book, is that we need to edit our images—particularly our digital raw images, for reasons that will become apparent later—and every edit we make has the effect of reducing the number of unique colors and tone levels in the image. A good understanding of the impact of different types of edits is the best basis for deciding where and how you apply edits to your images.

Gamma and Tone Mapping

To understand the key difference between shooting film and shooting digital, you need to get your head around the concept of gamma encoding. As I explained in Chapter 1, digital cameras respond to photons quite differently from either film or our eyes. The sensors in digital cameras simply count photons and assign a tonal value in direct proportion to the number of photons detected—they respond linearly to incoming light.

Human eyeballs, however, do not respond linearly to light. Our eyes are much more sensitive to small differences in brightness at low levels than at high ones. Film has traditionally been designed to respond to light approximately the way our eyes do, but digital sensors simply don't work that way.

Gamma encoding is a method of relating the numbers in the image to the perceived brightness they represent. The sensitivity of the camera sensor is described by a gamma of 1.0—it has a linear response to the incoming photons. But this means that the captured values don't correspond to the way humans see light. The relationship between the number of photons that hit our retinas and the sensation of lightness we experience in response is approximated by a gamma of somewhere between 2.0 and 3.0 depending on viewing conditions. Figure 2-2 shows the approximate difference between what the camera sees and what we see.

Figure 2-2
Digital capture and
human response

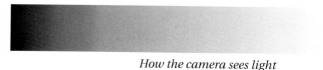

How the camera sees light

How the human eye sees light

I promised that I'd keep this chapter equation-free—if you want more information about the equations that define gamma encoding, a Google search on "gamma encoding" will likely turn up more than you ever wanted to know—so I'll simply cut to the chase and point out the practical implications of the linear nature of digital capture.

Digital captures devote a large number of bits to describing differences in highlight intensity to which our eyes are relatively insensitive, and a relatively small number of bits to describing differences in shadow intensity to which our eyes are very sensitive. As you're about to learn, all our image-editing operations have the unfortunate side effect of reducing the number of bits in the image. This is true for all digital images, whether scanned from film, rendered synthetically, or captured with a digital camera, but it has specific implications for digital capture.

With digital captures, darkening is a much safer operation than lightening, since darkening forces more bits into the shadows, where our eyes are sensitive, while lightening takes the relatively small number of captured bits that describe the shadow information and spreads them across a wider tonal range, exaggerating noise and increasing the likelihood of posterization. With digital, you need to turn the old rule upside down—you need to expose for the highlights, and develop for the shadows!

Image Editing and Image Degradation

Just about anything you do to change the tone or color of pixels results in some kind of data loss. If this sounds scary, rest assured that it's a normal and necessary part of digital imaging. The trick is to make the best use of the available bits you've captured to produce the desired image appearance, while preserving as much of the original data as possible. Why keep as much of the original data as possible if you're going to wind up throwing it away later? Very simply, it's all about keeping your options open.

The fact is, you don't need a huge amount of data to represent an image. But if you want the image to be editable, you need a great deal more data than you do to simply display or print it. Figure 2-3 shows two copies of the same image. They appear very similar visually, but their histograms are very different. One contains a great deal more data than the other.

Figure 2-3
Levels and appearance

This image was produced by making corrections in Camera Raw, producing a 16-bit-per-channel image in Photoshop.

This image was produced by converting at Camera Raw default settings, producing an 8-bit-per-channel image that was further edited in Photoshop.

The two images shown above appear quite similar, but the histograms shown to the right of each image reveal a significant difference. The lower image contains a great deal less data than the upper one. Careful examination may reveal subtle differences in hue and detail, but the biggest difference is the amount of editing headroom each image offers.

Despite the vast difference in the amount of data they contain, it's hard to see any significant differences between the two images—you may be able to see that the one with more data shows more details on the chest feathers, but it's a pretty subtle difference. Figure 2-4 shows what happens when a fairly gentle curve edit is applied to the images shown in Figure 2-3. The difference is no longer subtle!

Figure 2-4
Levels and editing
headroom

*Here you see the images from Figure
2-3 after application of a fairly gentle
S-curve (to increase contrast slightly)
to both images. The differences
between the data-rich (upper) and
data-poor (lower) versions are now
much more obvious. The data-poor
version shows much less detail, and
displays both exaggerated contrast
and unwanted hue shifts.*

The difference between the two images is in the way they were edited.
The one with the larger amount of data made full use of Camera Raw to
convert the raw file into a 16-bit/channel image in Photoshop. Additional
edits were done in 16-bit/channel mode. The one with the smaller amount
of data was converted to an 8-bit/channel image at camera default settings,
and the edits were performed in 8-bit/channel mode in Photoshop.

Losing Data and Limiting Options

The sad truth is that every edit you make limits the options that are available to you afterward. You can keep many more options open by making
full use of Camera Raw controls and by converting to a 16-bit/channel
image rather than an 8-bit one. But no matter what you do, edits degrade
the data in an image file in three different ways.

Clipping. The black and white input sliders in Photoshop's Levels command and the Exposure and Shadows sliders in Camera Raw are clipping controls. They let you force pixels to pure white (level 255) or solid black (level 0).

Depending on how you use the sliders, you may clip some levels—in fact, it's often desirable to do so. On the highlight end, you normally want to make sure that specular highlights are represented by level 255, so if the image is underexposed, you usually want to take pixels that are darker than level 255 and force them to pure white. But if you go further than that, you may clip some levels—for example, if you have pixels at levels 252, 253, and 254, and you set the white input slider in Levels to level 252, then all the pixels at levels 252, 253, and 254 are forced to 255. Once you make this edit permanent, the differences between those pixels are gone, permanently.

On the shadow end, you often want to clip some levels because typically there's a good deal of noise in the shadows. If everything below level 10 is noise, for example, it makes perfect sense to set the black input slider in Levels to 10, to force everything at level 10 and below to solid black. Again, you lose the distinction between the unedited levels 0 through 10 permanently, but it's not necessarily a bad thing. Figure 2-5 shows how clipping works.

However, if you're used to adjusting clipping in Photoshop's Levels, you'll find that the Exposure and Shadow controls in Camera Raw behave a bit differently from Levels' black and white input sliders, partly because the latter works on linear-gamma data rather than the gamma-corrected data that appears in Photoshop, partly because Camera Raw's Exposure slider can make negative as well as positive moves.

If the camera can capture the entire scene luminance range, as is the case with the image in Figure 2-5, it's usually best to adjust the Exposure and Shadows sliders to near-clipping, leaving a little headroom (unless you actually want to clip to white or black for creative reasons). If the camera can't handle the entire scene luminance range, you'll have to decide whether to hold the highlights or the shadows, and your choice may be dictated by the captured data—if highlights are completely blown, or shadows are completely plugged, there isn't much you can do about it in the raw conversion. See the sidebar "How Much Highlight Detail Can I Recover?" later in this chapter.

Figure 2-5
Black, white, and
saturation clipping

This raw image is under-exposed, but it captures the full luminance range of the scene, with no clipping of highlights or shadows.

highlight clipping

When you increase the Exposure slider value too far, you clip highlight pixels to solid white.

Ideally, you want to adjust the Exposure slider to push the data as far toward the right end of the histogram as possible without actually forcing clipping.

shadow clipping

When you increase the Shadows slider value too far, you clip shadow pixels to solid black.

saturation clipping

In addition to clipping highlights with Exposure or shadows with the Shadows slider, you can force individual channels to clip by adding too much saturation. In this case, increasing the saturation has clipped the blue channel.

Tonal range compression. When you compress a tonal range, you also lose levels, in a somewhat less obvious way than you do with clipping moves. For example, when you lighten the midtones without moving the white clipping point, the levels between the midtone and the highlight get compressed. As a result, some pixels that were formerly at different levels end up being at the same level, and once you make the edit permanent, you've lost these differences, which may potentially represent detail. See Figure 2-6.

Tonal range expansion. A different type of image degradation occurs when you expand a tonal range. You don't lose any data, but you stretch the data that's there over a broader tonal range, and hence run the danger of losing the illusion of a continuous gradation. Almost everyone who has used Photoshop for more than a week has encountered the experience of pushing edits just a little too far and ending up with banding in the sky or posterization in the shadows. It's simply caused by stretching the data over too broad a range, so that the gaps between the available levels become visibly obvious. See Figure 2-6.

Figure 2-6
Tonal range compression
and expansion

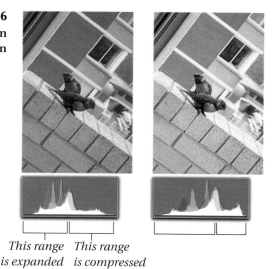

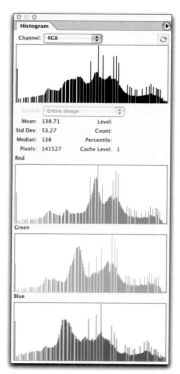

This range   This range
is expanded   is compressed

When you use the Brightness slider in Camera Raw or the gray slider in Levels to brighten the midtones, you compress the highlights and expand the shadows. The images and histograms above show Camera Raw's Brightness control, and the histogram at right shows the results of using the gray input slider in Levels on an 8-bit/channel image. The gaps are from expansion, the spikes from compression.

If all this makes you think that editing images is a recipe for disaster, you've missed the point. You need to edit images to make them look good. Sometimes you *want* to throw away some data—shadow noise being a good example—and the inherent data loss is simply something that comes with the territory. It isn't something to fear, just something of which you should be aware. The importance of the preceding information is that some editing methods allow you more flexibility than others.

Color Space Conversions

One other operation that usually entails all three of the aforementioned types of image degradation is color space conversions. When you convert from a larger gamut to a smaller one, colors present in the source space that are outside the gamut of the destination space get clipped (see Figure 1-7 in the previous chapter for an illustration of gamut clipping).

A significant number of levels also get lost in conversions between spaces with different gammas or tone curves. The bigger the difference between the gammas, the more levels get lost. Figure 2-7 shows what happens when you convert a linear-gamma gradient to a gamma 1.8 working space in both 8-bit/channel and 16-bit/channel modes. Even in 16-bit/channel mode, you see some spikes and holes, and in 8-bit/channel mode, about 25 percent of the levels have disappeared.

Figure 2-7
Gamma conversions

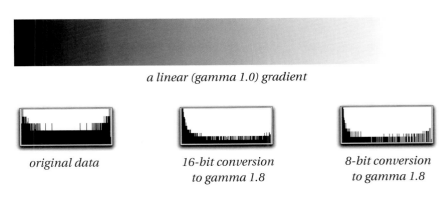

a linear (gamma 1.0) gradient

original data　　　　*16-bit conversion*　　　　*8-bit conversion*
　　　　　　　　　　to gamma 1.8　　　　　　*to gamma 1.8*

The Camera Raw Advantage

The reason all this stuff about data loss and image degradation is relevant is that one of the main tasks Camera Raw performs is to tone-map images from native, linear-gamma camera RGB to a gamma-corrected working space. When you use the controls in Camera Raw, you aren't just editing the pixels you captured, you're also tailoring the conversion. As you saw back in Figures 2-3 and 2-4, it's possible to arrive at the same image appearance with a robust file that contains plenty of data and hence offers plenty of editing headroom, or a very fragile file containing relatively little data that will fall apart under any further editing.

Since the raw conversion is at the beginning of the image-processing pipeline, and the converted images may be subjected to many different color space conversions and many different edits to optimize them for different output processes, you'll save yourself a world of grief if you use Camera Raw's controls to deliver as robust a file as you can muster. The new defaults in Camera Raw 3.0, unlike their predecessors, adapt to the image content—Camera Raw actually attempts to autocorrect each image—but even though the defaults often work well, it's rare that they can't be improved, and sometimes Camera Raw simply makes the wrong decision as to what's important in the image. It's eminently worthwhile learning to use Camera Raw effectively. If you do, you'll get better images, with much less work in Photoshop.

From Raw to Color

At long last, we come to the nitty-gritty of the conversion from Camera Raw to gamma-corrected RGB. In Chapter 5, *Hands-On Camera Raw*, we'll look at the various ways it makes sense to use the controls Camera Raw offers. Here, though, we'll look at how they actually apply to the raw conversion.

Demosaicing and Colorimetric Interpretation

The first stage of the process, demosaicing, introduces the color information, turning the grayscale image into an RGB one. This stage is also where the initial colorimetric interpretation occurs—the grayscale is converted to a "native camera space" image, with linear gamma and primaries (usually, but not always, R, G, and B—some cameras add a fourth color filter) defined by the built-in profiles that define each supported camera's color space. (See the sidebar "Camera Raw and Color" for more details on how Camera Raw handles the tricky task of defining camera color.) The demosaicing and colorimetric interpretation happen automatically to produce the default rendering you see in Bridge and the larger one you see when you open the image in Camera Raw.

Operationally, the first step is the colorimetric interpretation. The demosaicing is then performed in linear-gamma camera space. A little noise reduction, and any chromatic aberration corrections, are also done in the native camera space. (Chromatic aberration corrections could cause unwanted color shifts if they were done later in a non-native space.)

White Balance and Calibrate Adjustments

White Balance (Color Temperature and Tint), in addition to any adjustments made in Camera Raw's Calibrate tab, actually tweak the conversion from native camera space to an intermediate, large-gamut processing space. (This intermediate space uses ProPhoto RGB primaries and white point, but with linear gamma rather than the native ProPhoto RGB gamma 1.8.)

These operations work by redefining the colorimetric definition of the camera RGB primaries and white rather than by redistributing the pixel values. It's simply impossible to replicate these corrections in Photoshop,

Camera Raw and Color

One of the more controversial aspects of Camera Raw is its color-handling, specifically the fact that Camera Raw has no facility for applying custom camera profiles. Having tried most camera profiling software, and having experienced varying degrees of disappointment, I've concluded that unless you're shooting in the studio with controlled lighting and a custom white balance for that lighting, camera profiling is an exercise in frustration if not futility, and I've come to view Camera Raw's incompatibility with custom camera profiles as a feature rather than a limitation.

The way Camera Raw handles color is ingenious and, thus far, unique. For each supported camera, Thomas Knoll, Camera Raw's creator, has created not one but two profiles: one built from a target shot under a D65 (daylight) light source, the other built from the same target shot under an Illuminant A (tungsten) light source. The correct profiles for each camera are applied automatically in producing the colorimetric interpretation of the raw image. Camera Raw's White Balance (Color Temperature and Tint) sliders let you interpolate between, or even extrapolate beyond, the two built-in profiles.

For cameras that write a readable white balance tag, that white balance is used as the "As Shot" setting for the image; for those that don't, Camera Raw makes highly educated guesses. Either way, you can override the initial settings to produce the white balance you desire.

It's true that the built-in profiles are "generic" profiles for the camera model. Some cameras exhibit more unit-to-unit variation than others, and if your camera differs substantially from the unit used to create the profiles for the camera model, the default color in Camera Raw may be a little off. So the Calibrate controls let you tweak the conversion from the built-in profiles to optimize the color for your specific camera. This is a much simpler, and arguably more effective, process in most situations than custom camera profile creation (see "The Calibrate Tab" in Chapter 4, *Camera Raw Controls*, for a detailed description of the process.

so it's vital that you take advantage of Camera Raw to set the white balance and, if necessary, to tweak the calibration for a specific camera. (I'll save the detailed description of how to use these controls for Chapter 4, *Camera Raw Controls.*)

Most remaining operations are carried out in the intermediate linear-gamma version of ProPhoto RGB. You may be able to achieve a similar appearance by editing in Photoshop, but the Camera Raw controls still offer some significant advantages. The tone-mapping controls—Exposure, Shadows, Brightness, Contrast, and the Curve—present the most obvious case. The Exposure control is paramount—if you don't use it, you simply aren't making the best use of your bits—but the others are important too.

Tone-Mapping Controls

The tone-mapping controls work together to let you tailor Camera Raw's conversion from linear capture to gamma-encoded output. Collectively, they have a huge influence of the overall tonality of the image. Even if you plan to do significant post-conversion editing in Photoshop, it's well worth using Camera Raw's tone-mapping features to get the image as close to the desired end result as possible.

Why? Because doing so produces a gamma-encoded image in Photoshop with the bits distributed optimally. That means that the image will better withstand subsequent editing (see "Losing Data and Limiting Options," earlier in this chapter) *and* you have less work to do after the conversion in Photoshop.

The adjustments made by Exposure, Shadows, Brightness, Contrast, and the Curve tab are applied as a single operation on the raw conversion, so the order in which you make the adjustments doesn't matter from a quality standpoint. We'll discuss the workflow reasons for making adjustments in a specific order in Chapter 5, *Hands-On Camera Raw.*

Exposure. The Exposure slider is really a white-clipping control, even though it affects the whole tonal range. You can achieve superficially similar results using Exposure or using Brightness, but even though Brightness values greater than 100 can produce white clipping, Brightness is at heart a midtone adjustment.

At positive values, the Exposure slider behaves very much like the white input slider in Photoshop's Levels command, or the Exposure slider in Photoshop's new Exposure command, clipping levels to white. But since it's operating on linear data, it's gentler on the midtones and shadows than white clipping in Photoshop on a gamma-corrected image, and it offers finer control over the white clipping than do Photoshop's controls.

When you set the Exposure slider to negative values, the story is very different, because one of Camera Raw's most remarkable features comes into play. Unlike most raw converters (or Photoshop's Exposure command), Camera Raw offers "highlight recovery." Most raw converters treat all pixels where one channel has clipped highlights as white, since they lack complete color information, but Camera Raw can recover a surprising amount of highlight detail from even a single channel. It does, however, maintain pure white (that is, clipped in all channels) pixels as white (unlike most converters that turn clipped pixels gray), and darkens the rest of the image using special algorithms to maintain the nonwhite pixels' color. See the sidebar "How Much Highlight Detail Can I Recover?" for more technical details, and see Figure 2-8 for a real-world example.

It's simply impossible to match Camera Raw's highlight detail recovery in Photoshop on a gamma-corrected image. In linear space, half of the captured data describes the brightest f-stop, so you have a large number of bits describing the highlights. Once the image is converted to a gamma-corrected space, you have far fewer highlight bits to play with.

Shadows. The Shadows slider is the black clipping control. It behaves very much like the black input slider in Photoshop's Levels command, but its effect tends to be a little more dramatic, simply because it's operating on linear-gamma data, which devotes very few bits to the deepest shadows. In the first edition of this book, I characterized the Shadows control as "a bit of a blunt instrument," but changes to the logic in Camera Raw 2.3 and later have made it a much more sensitive tool. I now use it fearlessly to set the black point.

Tip: Check clipping at 100% view. At zoomed-out views, you may wind up clipping pixels you didn't intend to. Always check the 100% view before doing the conversion to make sure that you aren't clipping pixels you wanted to preserve.

Brightness and Contrast. The Brightness and Contrast controls let you tweak the conversion of the intermediate tones from the linear capture

Figure 2-8
Highlight recovery

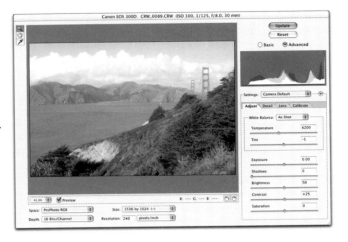

This image is overexposed, as indicated by the white spike at the right end of the histogram.

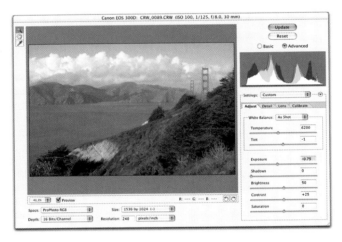

Reducing the value of the Exposure slider to -0.75 stops brings the highlights back into range. The amount of headroom varies from camera to camera, but this camera easily allows a three-quarter-stop recovery on this image.

Increasing the Brightness slider value to 60 and the Contrast slider value to 64 counteracts some of the darkening effect of the Exposure adjustment. Raising the Shadow slider to 6 puts some punch back in the shadows.

How Much Highlight Detail Can I Recover?

The answer, of course, is "it depends." If the captured pixel is completely blown out—clipped to white in all three channels—there is no highlight detail to recover. If a single channel, (or, better, two channels) still contain some information, Camera Raw will do its best to recover the detail and attribute natural-looking color to it.

The first stage of highlight recovery is to use any headroom the camera leaves by default, which varies considerably from vendor to vendor, with some leaving no headroom at all. The next stage uses Camera Raw's highlight recovery logic to build color information from the data in one or two unclipped channels. Next, the amount of highlight compression introduced by the Brightness slider is reduced, stretching the available highlight data over a wider tonal range. The final stage is application of a curve to map the midtones and shadows.

Several factors limit the amount of highlight data you can recover, and these vary from camera model to camera model. The first is the sensor clipping itself—the point at which all three channels clip. You can recover a lot of highlight data when only one channel contains data, but if you stretch the highlights too far, the transition between the totally blown-out highlights and the recovered ones looks unnatural. Also, some cameras run the sensor chip slightly past its linear range, producing hue shifts near the clipping point, and these hue shifts get magnified by the extended highlight recovery process—if you try to stretch the highlight data too far, you'll get strange colors—so in either case the practical limit may be lower than the theoretical one.

Most cameras use analog gain to provide different ISO speeds, but some use digital gain instead—a high-ISO image from these cameras is essentially just an underexposed image with built-in positive exposure compensation applied—so a lot of highlight data can be recovered by undoing the positive exposure compensation.

The white balance also has an effect on highlight recovery, since it scales the clipped channels to match the unclipped one. When you're attempting extreme highlight recovery it's often a good idea to adjust the Exposure slider before setting white balance, because the white balance is likely to change as you stretch the highlights anyway.

In practice, most cameras will let you recover at least a quarter stop of highlight data if you're willing to compromise a little on the white balance. Many cameras will let you recover at least one stop, possibly more, but the full four-stop range offered by the Exposure slider is beyond the useful range for most cameras. I don't advocate deliberate overexposure, but if you're shooting in changing lighting conditions, the linear nature of digital captures makes it preferable to err on the side of *slight* overexposure rather than underexposure, because underexposing to hold the highlights will make your shadows noisier than they need be. In these situations, Camera Raw's highlight recovery provides a very useful safety net.

to the gamma-corrected output space. They work completely differently from the similarly named Photoshop Contrast and Brightness controls. Instead, they behave similarly to Photoshop's Levels and Curves, respectively (Brightness is a midtone adjustment, Contrast is an S-curve) but with one important difference. The Camera Raw controls use an algorithm that preserves the original hue, whereas hard curve adjustments to the composite RGB curve in Photoshop can cause slight hue shifts.

If you make little or no adjustment with the Exposure slider, it's mildly advantageous to use Camera Raw's Brightness and Contrast sliders rather than using Photoshop's tools. But the bigger your Exposure adjustments, the more essential making matching Brightness and Contrast moves becomes (see Figure 2-8, earlier in this chapter).

Saturation

The Saturation slider operates similarly to the master saturation slider in Photoshop's Hue/Saturation command, but does a slightly better job of avoiding hue shifts. As with the Exposure and Shadows controls, the Saturation slider can introduce clipping, so exercise caution. I'll discuss how to spot saturation clipping in detail in Chapter 4, *Camera Raw Controls*.

Size

Camera Raw allows you to convert images at the camera's native resolution, or at larger or smaller sizes—the specific sizes vary from camera model to camera model, but they generally correspond to 50 percent, 66 percent, 100 percent, 133 percent, 166 percent, and 200 percent of the native size.

For cameras that capture square pixels, there's usually very little difference between resizing in Camera Raw and upsizing in Photoshop using Bicubic Smoother or downsizing in Photoshop using Bicubic Sharper. However, if you need a small file, it's usually more convenient to convert to a smaller size in Camera Raw than to downsample in Photoshop after the conversion.

For cameras that capture nonsquare pixels, the native size is the one that most closely preserves the original pixel count, meaning that one dimension is upsampled while the other is downsampled. The next size up preserves the pixel count along the higher-resolution dimension, upsampling the lower-resolution dimension to match and create square pixels in the converted image. This size preserves the maximum amount of detail for non-square-pixel cameras, and it typically produces better results than converting to the smaller size and upsampling in Photoshop.

The one size up is also useful for Fuji SuperCCD cameras, which use a 45-degree rotated Bayer pattern. The one size up keeps all the original pixels and fills in the holes caused by the 45-degree rotation. The native pixel count size actually uses the rotation and filling in from the one-size-up processing, and then downsamples to the native pixel count.

Sharpening

Camera Raw's sharpening is relatively unsophisticated, with only one parameter: strength. It's handy for doing quick-and-dirty sharpening for preliminary versions of images, but it's not as flexible as Photoshop's sharpening features because it's applied to the entire image, and it lacks a radius control to let you tailor the sharpening to the image content.

Camera Raw offers the option to apply sharpening to the preview image only, leaving the converted image unsharpened. This option is useful in helping you set the overall image contrast, because a completely unsharpened image generally looks flatter than one that has had some sharpening applied. Some pundits claim that sharpening should always be applied in linear-gamma space (as is Camera Raw's sharpening). Frankly, I've yet to see any major benefit in doing so, and the relative lack of control over sharpening in Camera Raw always leads me to sharpen post-conversion in Photoshop unless speed outweighs quality.

Luminance and Color Noise Reduction

While the Sharpening control is mildly convenient, the Luminance Smoothing and Color Noise Reduction controls in Camera Raw are simply indispensable. Luminance noise manifests itself as random variations in tone, usually in the shadows, though if you shoot at high ISO speeds it can spread all the way up into the midtones. Color noise shows up as random variations in color.

Before the advent of Camera Raw, I relied on rather desperate Photoshop techniques that involved converting the image to Lab so that I could address color noise and luminance noise separately, usually by blurring the a and b channels to get rid of color noise, and blurring or despeckling the Lightness channel to get rid of Luminance noise. Compared to the controls offered by Camera Raw, these techniques were very blunt instruments indeed—the round trip from RGB to Lab and back is fairly destructive due to rounding errors, and working on the individual channels is time-consuming.

Thanks to some nifty algorithms, Camera Raw lets you address color noise and luminance noise separately without putting the data through a conversion to Lab—the processing is done in the intermediate large-gamut linear RGB. Camera Raw's noise reduction controls are faster, less destructive, and more effective than anything you can do in Photoshop. So use them!

Watch the Histogram!

The histogram display is one of Camera Raw's most useful but often most-overlooked features. Throughout this chapter, I've emphasized the usefulness of the histogram as a tool for analyzing the image, and especially for judging clipping. But the histogram in Camera Raw differs from the histograms you see on-camera in an important way.

Camera Raw's histogram is more trustworthy than the histograms that cameras display—they show the histogram of the JPEG you'd get if you shot JPEG at the current camera settings rather than raw. As a result, they're useful as a rough guide to exposure, but not much more. The same applies to the overexposure warnings offered by most cameras—they're usually quite conservative. Camera vendors tend to apply a fairly strong default tone curve to the default, in-camera raw-to-JPEG conversion, perhaps in an effort to produce a default result that more closely resembles transparency film, so the histogram and exposure warning derived from the JPEG very often are not an accurate reflection of the raw capture.

Camera Raw's histogram is a great deal more reliable. It shows you, dynamically, the histogram of the converted image, displaying clipping in its various forms—clipping highlights to white, clipping shadows to black, or clipping one or more channels to totally saturated color. It also lets you see the effect of the various controls on the converted image data. Watching what happens to both the histogram and the preview image as you operate the controls will give you a much better understanding of what's happening to the image than simply looking at the preview alone. In later chapters, we'll look in detail at the many ways you can use the Camera Raw controls to get the best out of your raw captures. But if you're new to digital imaging, or even if you're just new to digital capture, it's well worth spending some time mulling over the contents of this chapter, because digital capture really is significantly different from film. Understanding how numbers are used to represent images is key to grasping and, eventually, exploiting that difference.

3 Raw System Overview

Camera Raw, Bridge, and Photoshop

This chapter provides a 30,000-foot overview of the whole digital raw system. I'll discuss the individual components in much more detail in subsequent chapters, but before delving into the minutiae (and there are a *lot* of details), it's helpful to have some idea of what the components do, and how they interrelate.

Camera Raw is an amazing piece of technology, but it's only one component of a powerful system that helps you do everything from making your initial selects from a shoot, to adding copyright and keywording metadata, to producing final files for delivery. One of the components of this system is, of course, Photoshop itself.

Photoshop is truly one of the deepest applications available on any platform, and has probably had more words written about it than just about any other application in existence. It's also seductive. One of my goals in writing this book is to wean photographers from doing everything in Photoshop—if you just treat Camera Raw as a quick way to get raw images into Photoshop for correction, you're making extra work for yourself, and probably not getting everything you can from your raw captures.

For the purposes of this book, Photoshop is simply a tool for making localized corrections, hosting automated processes, and writing images out to different file formats. My friend and colleague Jeff Schewe remarked jokingly during the beta period of Photoshop CS2 that Photoshop had become a plug-in for Camera Raw rather than vice versa, to which I can only add that rarely was a truer word spoken in jest.

One of the biggest challenges the digital raw shooter faces is to avoid drowning in data. Raw captures typically create smaller files than film scans, but we have to deal with so many more raw captures than we did film scans that spending hours correcting an individual image in Photoshop has to become the exception rather than the rule if we want to make a living, or even have a life. So in this short chapter, I'll lay out the basics of the raw workflow.

Adobe Bridge

Adobe Bridge is a brand-new application that comes bundled with every copy of Photoshop CS2. It replaces the File Browser that was introduced in Photoshop 7. Bridge lies at the center of the entire Adobe Creative Suite—it can manage all sorts of file types besides Camera Raw files and images created by Photoshop, including InDesign and Illustrator files and the ever-ubiquitous PDF format, but since this is a book about digital raw capture, I'll focus on its use with digital raw files.

The Virtual Light Table

One of the key roles that Bridge plays is as a virtual light table. As soon as you point Bridge at a new folder of raw images, Camera Raw goes to work behind the scenes, generating thumbnails and large-size previews using its default settings. As a virtual light table, Bridge lets you view, sort, rank, and make selects from your raw images.

Bridge is highly configurable for different purposes. The thumbnails and previews are resizable, so you can see anything from tiny thumbnails to previews that are large enough to let you decide whether or not an image is a keeper. As with a physical light table, you can sequence and sort images by dragging them into position, but unlike the physical light table, Bridge can find and sort images based on all sorts of *metadata* criteria, such as the time shot, focal length, shutter speed, aperture setting, or any combination of the aforementioned. You can apply ratings or labels to images to further facilitate sorting and selecting, and you can use Bridge as the source for automated processing into Photoshop by selecting the thumbnails of the images you want to process. Figure 3-1 shows some of the many ways you can configure Bridge for different tasks. I'll discuss Bridge in much greater detail in Chapter 6, *Adobe Bridge*.

Figure 3-1
Bridge configurations

A general-purpose configuration gives access to all of Bridge's tabs—the Folder and Favorites tabs for navigation, the thumbnails and previews for viewing images, and the Metadata and Keywords tabs for working with metadata.

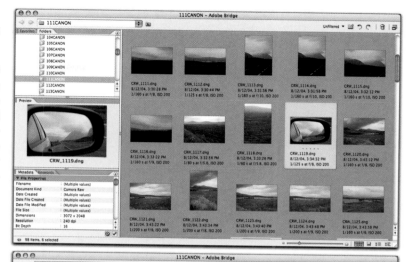

You can enlarge the preview for detailed examination of each image.

You can enlarge the thumbnails to compare images.

Managing Metadata

Metadata literally means "data about data." One of the useful aspects of shooting digital rather than film is that your images contain a wealth of metadata right out of the camera—the shutter speed, aperture, ISO speed, focal length, and other technical metadata are embedded right in the image. But you can and should supplement the camera-generated metadata with custom metadata of your own—copyright and rights-management notices, keywords, and anything else that will make your life easier and add value to your images.

Moreover, the time and place to add custom metadata is as soon after loading your raw captures into Bridge as possible, for two reasons:

▶ Metadata added to raw files gets carried through to any image produced from that raw file, so if you enter key metadata such as copyright notices on your raw files, all your converted PSDs, TIFFs, and JPEGs will already have that metadata entered.

▶ Whereas Photoshop's File Info command lets you edit metadata on one image at a time, Bridge lets you edit metadata for multiple images in a single operation.

If you're new to metadata, consider that as your collection of digital imagery grows, the role of metadata becomes ever-more vital in letting you and your clients find your images. I faked Figure 3-2 to make a point—don't try to cache a folder containing 6,798,348 images on today's hardware! But if it seems fanciful, consider the plight of an editorial shooter who shoots 1,000 images a day, three days a week, 48 weeks a year, over a 40-year career....

Figure 3-2
The need for metadata

If you fail to take advantage of metadata, you'll eventually end up drowning in image data!

If you shoot even a tenth of this number of images, you will at some future date have a major challenge on your hands if you don't start planning for that future date now, and taking advantage of the power of metadata to help you manage your image collection. I'll discuss metadata in much greater detail in Chapter 8, *Mastering Metadata*.

Hosting Camera Raw

As a standalone application, Bridge can do things that the old File Browser could not, and one of those things is to act as a host for the Camera Raw plug-in. Hence, when you open raw images in Camera Raw, you have the choice of opening them in Camera Raw hosted by Bridge, or Camera Raw hosted by Photoshop.

Camera Raw edits are saved as metadata—the raw files themselves are read-only so editing in Camera Raw never changes the raw file itself. What you're doing when you edit in Camera Raw is to set the parameters for the conversion from the raw file to an RGB image. So you can use Camera Raw hosted by Bridge to edit raw images—to set conversion parameters—without actually performing the conversions. Then when you open the images in Photoshop, Camera Raw creates an RGB version of the image using the conversion parameters you set in Camera Raw hosted by Bridge.

Of course, if your immediate goal is to open the file in Photoshop, you can host Camera Raw in Photoshop instead, and either open raw images directly into Photoshop, bypassing the Camera Raw dialog box (but not Camera Raw itself, which still carries out the conversion), or you can host the Camera Raw dialog box in Photoshop when it makes more sense to do so. I'll discuss these workflow decisions in detail in Chapter 7, *It's All About the Workflow*.

Camera Raw

Camera Raw is both the engine that translates your raw captures into color images, and the user interface that lets you control that translation. The role that Camera Raw plays when the user interface is exposed is fairly obvious: its role behind the scenes is less so.

One of the key roles that Camera Raw plays is to generate the thumbnails and previews you see in Bridge. When you first point Bridge at a folder full of new raw images, you may see, typically for a few seconds, the camera-generated thumbnails. But Camera Raw immediately goes to work behind the scenes, generating the large, high-quality previews and downsampling them to produce new thumbnails.

Camera Raw also has the interesting property of being shared by Bridge and Photoshop, which opens up some new workflow possibilities. You can, for example, edit images in Camera Raw hosted by Bridge, and hand off the processing of the raw image out to a saved RGB image file to Camera Raw running in Photoshop while you continue to edit more images in Camera Raw hosted by Bridge.

Camera Raw Defaults

The role of Camera Raw's default settings in generating Bridge's thumbnails and previews is pretty straightforward. Unless and until you tell it to do otherwise, Camera Raw uses its default settings to build thumbnails and previews for images that Bridge hasn't seen before.

The defaults aren't sacred, or "objectively correct," or "as shot"—they're simply one arbitrary interpretation of the raw image. There's no such thing as an "as shot" interpretation any more than there's a single correct way of printing a negative. One of the most common complaints I hear about Camera Raw is that the images don't look like the in-camera JPEGs or the default conversions from the camera vendors' raw converters. Invariably, those making the complaints haven't bothered to actually *use* Camera Raw's controls—they just use the defaults.

Part of the problem is likely that Camera Raw gives you access to all the data the camera captured. Many proprietary raw converters bury shadow noise by applying a strong contrast curve that maps most of the shadow data to black. A good many also boost the saturation. Camera Raw's default interpretations tend to be conservative by comparison, with flatter contrast and more open shadows. I prefer this approach because it makes it easier to see just what usable data the image contains, but that's only my personal preference. More importantly, Camera Raw offers sufficient control over the interpretation of the image that, with a very little practice, you can get just about any "look" you want.

So if you consistently find that Camera Raw's default settings produce images that are too dark, too light, too flat, or too contrasty for your taste, *change them!* It only takes a very few minutes. I'll discuss Camera Raw's controls, and how to use them—including changing the defaults—in the next chapter, *Camera Raw Controls.*

Adobe DNG Converter

Adobe DNG Converter is a handy standalone application that converts camera vendors' proprietary raw images to Adobe's new DNG format. It's entirely up to you whether or not you choose to use it—Camera Raw, Bridge, and Photoshop are equally happy with proprietary raw files or DNGs—but the following discussion may help you decide. My personal bias is that the advantages of DNG outweigh any disadvantages, and using DNG sends camera vendors an important message about the future of digital photography, but it *is* a bias. The choice is really up to you.

To DNG or Not to DNG

Adobe developed the DNG format in response to a very real concern over the longevity of digital raw captures. One of the major problems with camera vendors' proprietary raw formats is that they're undocumented—only the camera vendor knows for sure what they contain. I bear no ill will to any camera vendor, and I hope that they'll all be around for decades to come, stimulating competition and innovation, but it's not beyond the bounds of possibility that one of today's vendors may not be around five, ten, or fifty years hence. The question then becomes, what happens to all the images locked up in a defunct vendor's proprietary raw format?

Archival format. A kindly third-party vendor *may* decide to take on the work of reverse-engineering the format to continue support (and let's all give a huge vote of thanks to Thomas Knoll for the enormous amount of work he's already done in decoding all those proprietary raw formats), but absent that, you'll be stuck with old, non-upgradable software at best, and gigabytes of unreadable data at worst.

The DNG format provides insurance against obsolescence because unlike proprietary raw formats, it's an open, documented format whose file spec is readily available, so any reasonably talented programmer can build a converter that reads DNG files without any reverse engineering, even if Adobe should, perish the thought, no longer be in business. So unlike the proprietary raw formats, DNG can fairly lay claim to being an archival format.

The first release of Adobe DNG Converter had one potential flaw—it stripped any private metadata that it couldn't understand. While the only things that could possibly use this metadata were the vendors' proprietary raw converters, few of us like the idea of losing something in the translation. Subsequent releases of Adobe DNG Converter address this problem by letting you embed a bit-for-bit copy of the proprietary raw file that can be extracted at any time, at the cost of a somewhat larger file size.

Metadata-friendly. A related issue is that, because proprietary raw files are undocumented, Adobe treats them as read-only files, since writing to them runs the risk of overwriting potentially useful data. So when you add metadata to an image, it gets stored in either a sidecar .xmp file or in one or another application's database.

In contrast, since DNG is a documented file format that's designed to hold metadata, it's safe to write metadata directly into the DNG file, eliminating the need for sidecar files and thus simplifying the workflow. As with proprietary raw formats, the actual image data in the DNG never gets changed. If you work for a client who demands that you submit raw files (as does National Geographic, for example), it's safer to hand off a DNG file with all metadata embedded than it is to submit a proprietary raw along with a sidecar file that may get discarded.

Third-party support. As an open format, DNG is much easier for third parties to support than are the proprietary raw formats. Asset managers and cataloging applications that support DNG automatically gain support for every camera supported by Camera Raw. Thumbnails and previews can be stored directly in the image file so applications don't have to spend time building their own, and there's no possibility of the image losing its metadata because the metadata is right in the image file.

More specialized applications are also beginning to support DNG. For example, DxO Labs' DxO Optics Pro, which provides sophisticated corrections for distortions introduced by many common lenses, now offers the ability to write the corrected images as DNG files, so you can apply lens corrections, write them to DNG files, then process the images in Camera Raw.

Ultimately, the proliferation of proprietary raw formats serves no one's interest, not even that of the camera vendors (although at the time of writing, many of them still seem to need convincing on this point). The

DNG spec is flexible enough to let those vendors who insist on doing so put private, secret metadata tags into their images, while ensuring that those images will still be readable by any DNG-compliant converter.

Downsides. The major disadvantage to using DNG is that DNG files will likely not be readable by your camera vendor's proprietary converter. If you typically use Camera Raw on some images and a proprietary converter on others, it's fairly inconvenient to extract the proprietary raws from the DNG file, so you'll want to either keep versions of the images in both formats, or forego the advantages of DNG. If you don't use the camera vendor's software, this disadvantage doesn't apply.

The second disadvantage is that when you choose the "bulletproof" option that embeds the entire proprietary raw file in the DNG, your files will be somewhat larger than the original proprietary raws.

My own solution has been to archive one copy of each image as DNG-with-raw-embedded to long-term storage, while using the smaller, losslessly compressed DNG option for my working files. An equally viable option is to archive a copy of the original raws (bearing in mind that they'll only be readable as long as the camera vendor chooses to support them) while using DNG for working files.

Using Adobe DNG Converter

Adobe DNG Converter is a very simple application. It's not the only way to convert proprietary raws to DNG—you can save DNGs right out of Camera Raw—but it's a very convenient way to process large numbers of images into DNG format. See Figure 3-3.

Figure 3-3
Adobe DNG Converter

Select source. ——

Select destination. ——

Set filenames. ——

Choose conversion options. ——

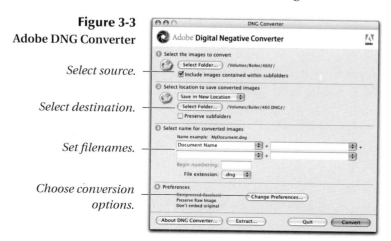

The main screen lets you set the following options:

► You can choose a source folder full of raw images for conversion, and optionally include subfolders.

► You can choose a destination, either in the same location as the source raw files or in a new folder, with the option to preserve the subfolder organization.

► You can rename the converted images with the same options as the Batch Rename command in Photoshop and Bridge.

► If you have previously saved DNG files with the original raw file embedded, you can extract the original raw file.

To change the conversion options, click the Preferences button to open the Preferences screen—see Figure 3-4.

Figure 3-4
Adobe DNG Converter
Preferences

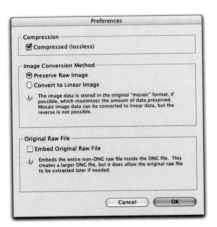

The conversion options are likewise very straightforward.

► **Compression (lossless)** applies lossless conversion. Unless you own stock in a hard drive vendor, I can't think of a reason to turn this off.

► **Preserve Raw Image** preserves the raw pixel data in its original mosaic format. Use this option if you want to be able to take advantage of all Camera Raw's features. You can convert a DNG saved this way to a linear DNG, but not vice versa.

▶ **Convert to Linear Image** saves a demosaiced version of the image. This option is mostly useful if you want to use a DNG-compliant raw converter other than Camera Raw on images from a camera with a mosaic pattern that isn't supported by the raw converter. Linear DNGs are much larger than mosaic-format ones, so if you're thinking you can save processing time by converting to linear DNG, think again—any savings in processing time are offset by the extra time needed to read the data.

▶ **Embed Original Raw File** embeds a bit-for-bit copy of the original raw file in the DNG, from which it can be extracted at any time. I use this option for my archived images just in case I need to retrieve the original raw files at some future date, but I turn it off for my working files to save space, because embedding the original raw file increases the file size considerably.

When you click Convert, Adobe DNG Converter goes to work converting the selected raw files to DNG format using the options specified in Preferences, and displays a status window that shows the progress of the conversions—see Figure 3-5.

Figure 3-5
Adobe DNG Converter
status window

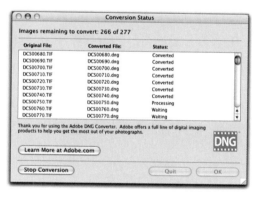

To extract the original raw files from DNGs with the original raw embedded, click Extract, which opens the Extract Originals dialog box. Here you can specify source and destination folders for the extraction. When you click Extract, Adobe DNG Converter extracts the original raw files from the DNGs. See Figure 3-6.

Figure 3-6
Extract Originals

At the time of writing, the main benefit offered by DNG is the elimination of sidecar files, and it's entirely up to you whether or not you want to use it, though it's very easy to do so. There's no particular urgency to adopting DNG, but if you care about the longevity of your images, I do recommend archiving at least one copy of each image in DNG format, and if you want to be able to retrieve the original raw files, embed the original raw in the DNG. That way, you've preserved the raw image in a format that's documented and hence is likely to readable as long as humans can still read.

Photoshop

Photoshop is an extremely powerful and very deep application that has grown in power and, it must be said, complexity for over a decade (which is something close to a century in software years). Legions of scribes, myself included, have penned millions of words on its capabilities and quirks. This isn't, however, a book about Photoshop. Instead, it's a book about how to get raw images into Photoshop as quickly, as efficiently, and in as close to an optimal state as possible.

In short, it's mostly about all the things you do *before* the image lands in Photoshop.

Automation and Actions

The one key area of Photoshop that this book covers in some depth is automation, and especially Photoshop Actions. As a digital photographer, you will routinely be called upon to push amounts of data through your system that only a few years ago would have given NASA nightmares. The hardware you use to do so will doubtless get faster, but one key component in the system, the wetware, the part that occupies the space between the keyboard and the chair, will almost certainly continue to operate at the same speed it has done for the past 20,000 years or so.

Exploiting the power of Photoshop Actions to automate repetitive tasks isn't just good sense—it's a key survival strategy. Writing Actions isn't without its quirks and challenges, but if you're saying to yourself "but I'm not a programmer," rest assured that writing Actions is like programming the way driving to the grocery store is like competing in the Dakar Rally.

Any repetitive Photoshop task is a candidate for automation. My copy of Photoshop spends a lot of time doing its own thing, and my hope is that by the time you've finished this book, yours will too. It's rare for me to open an image directly from Camera Raw into Photoshop—I almost invariably apply my raw edits in Bridge, then use batch processes to open the already-edited images into Photoshop.

The batch processes may also include things like sharpening routines, adding adjustment layers, and renaming and saving the files so that when I do get them into Photoshop, the layers are there ready for me to go to work on localized corrections, and the files are already named and saved in the format I need so that when I've done my work, I can simply press Command-S. Automating simple things like file renaming, or saving in a specific format with the necessary format options, only saves a small amount of time on any one image. But doing so brings at least three benefits:

▶ Small savings on one image add up to significant savings on dozens or hundreds of images.

▶ My brain likes being liberated from repetitive drudgery.

▶ Automated processes don't make mistakes!

I'll talk about the ways we can make the computer do our work for us in detail in Chapter 9, *Exploiting Automation*.

Putting It All Together

Collectively, Bridge, Camera Raw, Photoshop and, optionally, Adobe DNG Converter provide a powerful system for managing and converting raw images. As you go through the following chapters, which examine each component in detail, keep this bigger picture in mind, because it provides the context that makes the details relevant.

► Raw images don't change. Instead, they're like negatives. You can interpret them many different ways during the conversion to an RGB image just as you can make many different prints from the same negative.

► Bridge is the tool for sorting and selecting images, and for adding and editing metadata. The thumbnails and previews you see in Bridge are generated by Camera Raw using the last settings you applied to the image, or (if you haven't edited the image) the Camera Raw default settings for the camera model from which the image came.

► If you don't like Camera Raw's default settings for a particular camera model, you can and should change them to ones that are closer to your taste.

► Editing raw images and converting raw images are logically separate operations, though you can combine them.

► If you have 100 raw images from which you need to produce, for example, a high-res TIFF and a low-res JPEG, the most efficient way to do so is to first edit the images in Camera Raw hosted by Bridge, then run batch operations hosted by Photoshop to open the raw images, using the Camera Raw settings you've applied, and save them in the appropriate formats.

With the bigger picture this chapter presents in mind, it's time to drill down in detail on the Camera Raw plug-in, which is the topic of the next chapter.

4 Camera Raw Controls

Digital Darkroom Tools

In this chapter, we'll look at the Camera Raw controls in detail. Camera Raw starts working as soon as you point Adobe Bridge at a folder full of raw images, creating thumbnails and previews, but its real power is in the degree of control and flexibility it offers in converting raw images to RGB.

Bear in mind as you go through this chapter that, while Camera Raw lets you make painstaking edits on every image, it doesn't force you to do so! Unless you're being paid by the hour, you'll want to take advantage of Camera Raw's ability to synchronize edits between multiple images, and to save settings and subsets of settings that you can apply to multiple images in Bridge without actually launching Photoshop, or even opening them in Camera Raw.

But before you can run, you have to learn to walk, and before you can batch-process images with Camera Raw, you need to learn to deal with them one at a time. If raw files are digital negatives, Camera Raw is the digital darkroom that offers all the tools you need to put your own unique interpretation on those digital negatives.

Like negatives, raw files are simply a starting point. The tools in Camera Raw offer much more control over the interpretation of the raw file than any wet darkroom. Camera Raw is a plug-in the way *War and Peace* is a story and The Beatles were a pop group—at first, the sheer number of options may seem overwhelming, but they're presented in a logical order, and you can master them in a fraction of the time it takes to learn traditional darkroom skills.

Camera Raw, Photoshop and Bridge

If you're used to the old Camera Raw/File Browser combination in Photoshop CS, you'll notice that things have changed in several ways, all for the better. If you're new to Camera Raw, this section explains why the screen shots in this chapter may look different from your copy of Camera Raw when you launch it.

As I mentioned in the previous chapter, unlike the old Photoshop File Browser, Adobe Bridge is a standalone application. One of the many advantages that its standalone status confers is that it's capable of hosting Camera Raw when Photoshop is either not running, or more likely, is busy doing something else. You can open Camera Raw in Bridge *or* Photoshop, whichever is the more efficient for the task at hand.

If you want to edit the Camera Raw settings for one or more images, but don't plan on opening them in Photoshop, you can open Camera Raw in Bridge while Photoshop is, for example, busy running a batch process. Or you can edit images in Camera Raw in Photoshop while Bridge is busy caching a new folder. You can even open one Camera Raw window in Bridge and another in Photoshop, though doing so has the potential to make you a very confused puppy! The subtle clue as to which application is currently hosting Camera Raw is the default button—see Figure 4-1.

A second important workflow enhancement is the "filmstrip" mode of Camera Raw. Now you can open and edit multiple images in Camera Raw, and transfer settings from one image to another right inside the Camera Raw interface (see Figure 4-2).

These new enhancements offer much more flexibility in the workflow. However, in this chapter, I'll first concentrate on the tools Camera Raw offers for editing a single image, because as previously noted, you must learn to walk before you can run. So most of the screen captures of Camera Raw in this chapter will use a single image.

The image controls are the same no matter which application is hosting Camera Raw and no matter how many images you've chosen to edit. I'll discuss workflow and ways to handle multiple images efficiently in Chapter 7, *It's All About the Workflow*, but for the bulk of this chapter, let's take our images one at a time, and focus on the tools themselves.

Figure 4-1
Camera Raw in Bridge
and in Photoshop

*When Camera Raw is
hosted by Bridge, the
default button is Done.
Clicking it closes
Camera Raw, applies the
settings to the raw file,
and returns you
to Bridge.*

*When Camera Raw is
hosted by Photoshop, the
default button is Open.
Clicking it closes
Camera Raw, applies the
settings to the raw file,
and opens the
converted image
in Photoshop.*

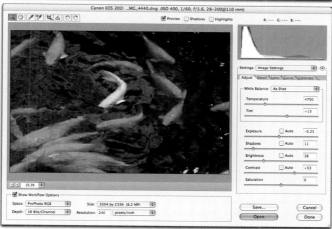

Figure 4-2
Camera Raw in
filmstrip mode

*When you open multiple
raw images in Camera
Raw, they appear in the
filmstrip at the left of the
Camera Raw window,
allowing you to work
with multiple images in
several useful ways.*

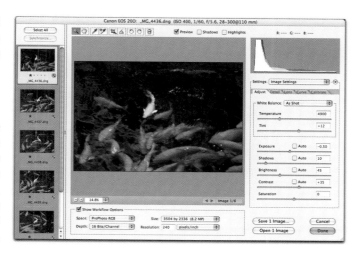

Camera Raw Anatomy

Camera Raw opens automatically whenever you open a raw image. In addition to the static elements—the Tool palette, the histogram, the RGB readout, the rotate controls—it offers two sets of controls; one static workflow set that is "sticky" (the settings remain unchanged unless and until you change them) and another dynamic image-specific set that changes depending on which tab is currently selected (see Figure 4-3).

Figure 4-3
Camera Raw controls

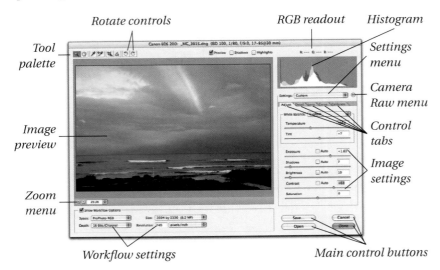

Rotate controls · RGB readout · Histogram · Tool palette · Settings menu · Camera Raw menu · Control tabs · Image preview · Image settings · Zoom menu · Workflow settings · Main control buttons

The static elements include the Tool palette; the Rotate controls; the Zoom menu; the Preview, Highlight and Shadow clipping toggles; the main Save, Open, Done, and Cancel buttons; the RGB readout; a live histogram that shows the conversion that the current settings will produce; and a Settings menu that lets you load and save settings. See Figure 4-4.

The workflow controls govern the kind of output Camera Raw will produce—they let you choose the color space, bit depth, size, and resolution of converted images. You can choose whether to show or hide the Workflow setting by checking or unchecking the Show Workflow Options toggle. See Figure 4-5.

The image controls, which apply to individual images, appear immediately below the Settings menu. Camera Raw offers five separate panels, Adjust, Detail, Lens, Curve, and Calibrate, each with its own set of controls. See Figure 4-6.

Figure 4-4
Camera Raw
static elements

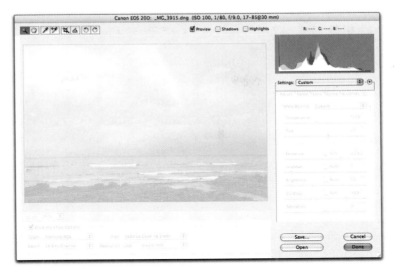

Figure 4-5
Camera Raw workflow
controls

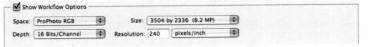

Figure 4-6
Camera Raw
image controls

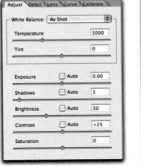

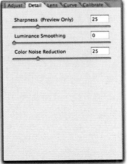
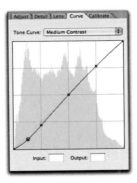

Camera Raw Static Controls

The static controls, which appear all the time in Camera Raw, fall into several groups: the Tool palette; the rotate buttons; the Preview controls; the main control buttons; the histogram; the RGB readout; the Settings menu; and the Camera Raw menu. Let's look at each of these in turn.

The Tool Palette

Camera Raw's Tool palette contains six tools, three from the previous version, plus three new ones. See Figure 4-7.

Figure 4-7
Camera Raw Tool palette

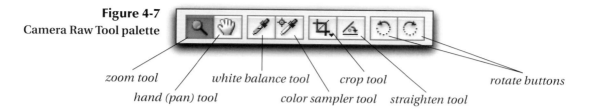

zoom tool   white balance tool   crop tool   rotate buttons

hand (pan) tool   color sampler tool   straighten tool

Zoom and pan. The zoom (magnifying glass) and pan (grabber hand) tools work just like their Photoshop counterparts.

Tip: Use Keyboard Shortcuts for Fast Navigation. Choose the zoom and pan tools from the Tool palette if you get paid by the hour! If you want to work quickly, there are much faster ways to navigate. First, you can always get the zoom tool by holding down the Command key (Mac) or Ctrl key (Windows). To zoom out, add Option/Alt. For the pan tool, hold down the spacebar. Or, press Z for the zoom tool and H for the hand tool.

But all the other zoom shortcuts for Photoshop also work in Camera Raw. Command -+ zooms in, Command -- (minus) zooms out. Command-0 (zero) fits the entire image in the preview, as does double-clicking the hand tool, and Command-Option-0 (zero) or double-clicking the zoom tool zooms to Actual Pixels view, where one image pixel equals one screen pixel. So use them!

White balance. The white balance tool (press I), however, works differently from the white eyedroppers that appear elsewhere in Photoshop.

The white balance tool lets you set the white balance by clicking on the image. Unlike the white eyedropper in Levels or Curves, it doesn't allow you to choose a source color, and it doesn't affect the luminance of the image. Instead, it lets you set the white balance—the color temperature and tint—for the capture by clicking on pixels you think should be neutral.

Don't confuse the white balance tool with the gray eyedropper tool offered by Photoshop's Levels command, which is designed to balance a midtone gray. Camera Raw's white balance tool works best on light grays close to diffuse highlight values.

Tip: Click-Balance on Diffuse Highlights. The white balance tool is best used on a diffuse highlight white that still contains detail, rather than on a specular highlight that's pure white—the second-to-lightest gray patch on the old 24-patch Macbeth ColorChecker works well, as do bright (but not blown-out) clouds.

Click-balancing with the white balance tool provides a very quick way to set color temperature and tint simultaneously. You can always fine-tune the results using the individual Temperature and Tint controls in the Adjust tab, which we'll cover in due course.

Color samplers. The new color sampler tool (press S) lets you place up to nine individual color samplers, each of which gets its own readout, in the image. See Figure 4-8.

Figure 4-8
The color sampler tool

color sampler readout

color sampler

Combined with the static RGB readout, the color sampler tool lets you monitor the values of up to 10 different locations in the image, which should be enough for any reasonable use!

Crop. The new crop tool (press C) lets you drag a freeform crop, choose one of several common predefined aspect ratios, or define your own custom aspect ratio from the tool's pull-down menu. The same menu allows you to clear the crop. See Figure 4-9.

Figure 4-9
The crop tool and menu

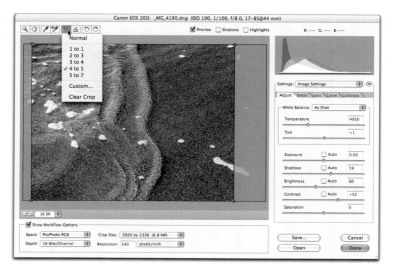

The Camera Raw preview always shows the crop in the context of the whole image, but the crop is applied to filmstrip previews, to Bridge previews and thumbnails, and of course to the image itself when you open it in Photoshop.

Straighten. The new straighten tool (press A) is an enormous time-saver for those of us who occasionally fail to keep their horizons horizontal. The reason that it's an enormous time-saver is that it should really be called the straighten *and crop* tool—it not only straightens the image, it also automatically applies the crop that maintains the maximum rectangular image when the crop tool is set to Normal, or a straightened crop of the specified aspect ratio when the crop tool is set to something else. If there's an existing crop, it's preserved and rotated. Clearing the crop using the crop tool's menu also clears the rotation.

If you've ever futzed with the tedious process of straightening and cropping an image in Photoshop using the measure tool, Arbitrary Rotate, and the crop tool, you'll be delighted by the speed and simplicity of the straighten tool. Camera Raw's preview always shows the crop rectangle on the uncropped, unstraightened image, but the thumbnails and previews in Bridge show the straightened cropped version you get when you open the image in Photoshop. Straighten and crop the raw image *once*, and the image is straightened and cropped each time it's opened. See Figure 4-10.

Figure 4-10
Straighten and crop

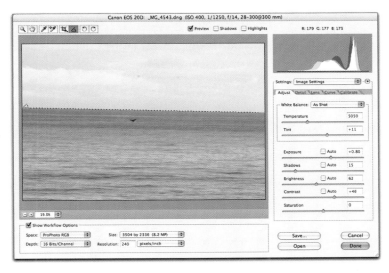

Drag the straighten tool to define a horizontal or vertical.

A rotated crop appears in Camera Raw. The cropping and rotation are applied to the Bridge thumbnail and preview (below) and to the image when it's opened in Photoshop.

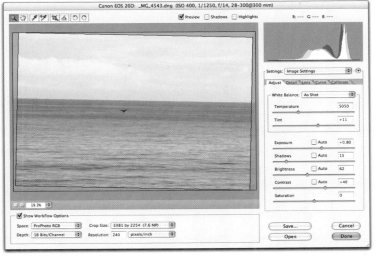

Rotate buttons. The Rotate 90 Degrees Left and Right buttons (press L and R, respectively) aren't strictly speaking tools, in that you don't have to do anything inside the image preview, but since they're placed in such close proximity to the tool palette, we may as well deal with them here. Clicking on them, or pressing their keyboard shortcut, immediately applies a rotation to Camera Raw's preview. When you finish editing the image in Camera Raw, the rotation is applied to Bridge's thumbnails and previews, and is honored whenever you open the raw image in Photoshop.

The Preview Controls

Two sets of controls affect the preview image. The Zoom buttons and the Zoom level menu control the size of the preview image, while the Preview, Shadows, and Highlights checkboxes affect its content.

Zoom Level menu. The Zoom Level menu lets you choose a zoom level for the image preview—zoom in to check fine details, zoom out to see the global effects of your adjustments on the image (but go back and reread the earlier tip, "Use Keyboard Shortcuts for Fast Navigation"—they really are much faster). See Figure 4-11.

Figure 4-11
Zoom controls

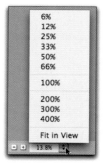

Preview, Shadows, and Highlights checkboxes. The functionality of the Preview checkbox (press P) has changed in Camera Raw 3.0—it applies only to the current editing tab, toggling between its current settings and those that were in effect when you opened the image. It has no effect on changes you've made in other tabs. The old functionality is still available—to see the settings that applied before you opened the image, toggle between Image Settings and Custom on the Settings menu—see Figure 4-12.

Figure 4-12
Toggling previews

The Preview checkbox toggles the settings in the current editing tab, in this case, Curve.

For a before-and-after of all the edits you've made since opening the image in Camera Raw, choose Image Settings from the Settings menu to see the settings that were in effect when you opened the image, and Custom to see the current settings from all the editing tabs.

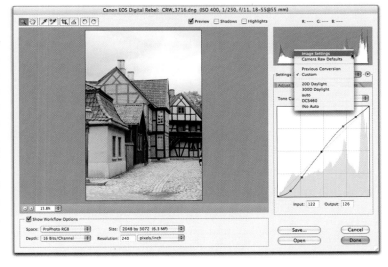

The Shadows and Highlights checkboxes (press U—for underexposed—and O—for overexposed, respectively) provide a quick way to check for shadow and highlight clipping. These are most useful for a quick check on the state of the image—see Figure 4-13. For a more nuanced clipping display that's more useful when you're actually making adjustments, you can hold down the Option/Alt key while dragging the Exposure or Shadows slider. See "The Adjust Tab," later in this chapter for more detail on clipping and clipping displays.

Figure 4-13
Shadows and Highlights
clipping display

*The Shadows and
Highlights checkboxes
show highlight clipping
in red, and shadow
clipping in blue.*

Figure 4-13
Shadows and Highlights
clipping display

*The Shadows and
Highlights checkboxes
show highlight clipping
in red, and shadow
clipping in blue.*

Tip: Use Keyboard Shortcut for Shadow Clipping. While the highlight clip is visually obvious, the dark blue overlay of the shadow clip is often less so. Pressing U to toggle the Shadows clipping on and off makes it much easier to see.

The Histogram and RGB Readout

The histogram and the RGB readout provide information about the current state of the image. The histogram displays the histograms of the red, green, and blue channels that will be created by the current conversion settings, *not* the histogram of the raw image (which would look strange since digital cameras capture at linear gamma—all the image data would be scrunched over to the left).

The histogram lets you check exposure—a white spike at both ends indicates clipping of shadows and highlights because the scene dynamic range was more than the camera could capture, space at both ends of the histogram indicates that you've captured the entire scene dynamic range, and a white spike at one end shows that you may need to adjust the Exposure or Shadows slider to avoid clipping. A colored spike at either end may indicate gamut clipping, or tonal clipping in one or two channels—see Figure 1-7 in Chapter 1, *Digital Camera Raw*. If the clipping disappears when you set the Space in the Workflow Settings to ProPhoto RGB, you can be certain that it's showing gamut clipping from a smaller output space.

A red, green, or blue spike indicates color clipping in that channel. A cyan spike indicates clipping in both green and blue, a magenta spike indicates clipping in both red and blue, and a yellow spike indicates clipping in both red and green, so with a very little practice, the histogram can show you at a glance exactly what's happening to your endpoints at the current image settings. See Figure 4-14.

Clipping isn't always bad, and if the scene dynamic range exceeds that of the camera, it's inevitable. If you see one- or two-channel clipping at the shadow end when the Space is set to ProPhoto RGB, you're probably driving the color into science-fiction territory, so check the setting of the Saturation slider. If an image contains no white objects, though, you may see single-color clipping at the highlight end, even in ProPhoto RGB.

The RGB readout shows the RGB values that will result from the conversion at the current settings—it shows the RGB value for the pixel under the cursor. The RGB readout always reads 5-by-5 screen pixels at zoom levels of 100% or less, so it may give different values at different zoom levels. When you fit the entire image into Camera Raw's preview, you're sampling an average of a fairly large number of pixels—the exact number depends on both the camera's native resolution and the size you've chosen from the Size menu in the workflow controls (see "Camera Raw Workflow Controls," later in this chapter). At zoom levels greater than 100%, the sample size is always 5 x 5 actual image pixels.

Figure 4-14
The histogram and the RGB readout

The RGB readout shows the values of the pixels under the cursor.

The histogram is a bar chart that displays the relative pixel count at different levels. It's mostly useful for checking exposure and clipping.

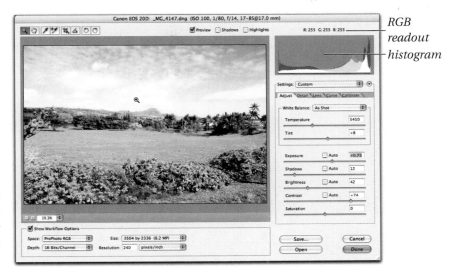

RGB readout
histogram

The Settings Menu

The Settings menu lets you apply any saved Camera Raw settings (see Figure 4-15). The items that always appear are Image Settings, Camera Raw Default, Previous Conversion, and Custom.

Figure 4-15
The Settings menu

Image Settings. Image Settings indicates that you've previously applied edits to the image. If you're working on an image, choosing Image Settings will show you the settings that were in effect before you started editing. If the image is brand-new and has never been edited, Image Settings is the same as the next item, Camera Raw Default.

Camera Raw Defaults. Camera Raw Defaults is what it says—it's the default setting that applies to all images unless and until you override them. If you find that the shipping default settings aren't to your liking, you can set your own Camera Raw Defaults for each supported camera model, or if you get yourself in a mess by doing so, you can return Camera Raw to the shipping default settings using the appropriate commands from the Camera Raw menu—see the next section, "The Camera Raw Menu."

Previous Conversion. Choosing Previous Conversion applies the settings from the last image you opened in Camera Raw to the current image. This is somewhat useful for editing a series of similar images, but there are better ways to do so—see "Filmstrip Mode" in Chapter 5, *Hands-On Camera Raw*, and "Apply Camera Raw Settings" in Chapter 6, *Adobe Bridge*.

Custom. Custom denotes the current settings you're applying in Camera Raw. As previously mentioned in "The Preview Controls," earlier in this chapter, you can toggle between Image Settings and Custom to compare your current edits with the ones that were in effect when you opened the image in Camera Raw.

You can also save your own custom settings as presets, which then become available from this menu. It's easy to overlook the mechanism for doing so, though, because it lives on the Camera Raw menu, which besides being one of the most important of the static controls, is also (for reasons unknown) unlabeled.

The Camera Raw Menu

Cleverly hidden under the small unlabeled right-facing triangle is the Camera Raw menu, which allows you to load, save, and delete settings or subsets of settings, turn Camera Raw's Auto corrections on or off, set default settings for an individual camera model, restore Camera Raw's default settings for a camera model, and set Preferences. See Figure 4-16.

Figure 4-16
The Camera Raw menu

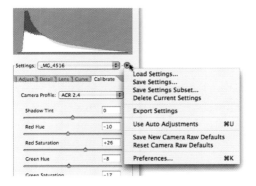

We'll start with Preferences, because until you understand the various behaviors controlled by Preferences, the other commands may not make a whole lot of sense. Camera Raw's Preferences are fairly simple, but they have far-reaching implications for your workflow. See Figure 4-17.

Figure 4-17
Camera Raw Preferences

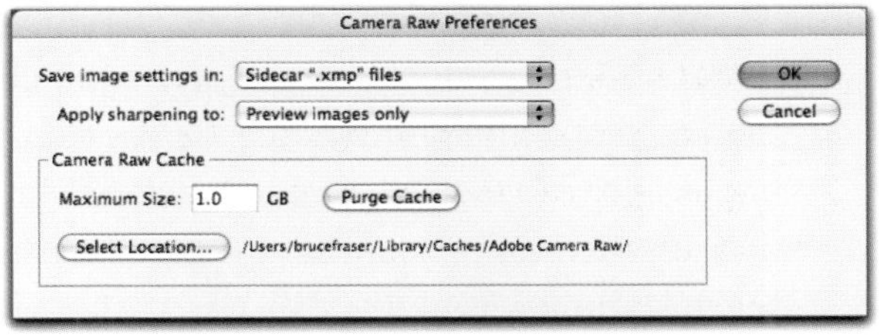

Preferences

Camera Raw's Preferences let you decide whether your raw edits are saved in the Camera Raw database or in "sidecar" .xmp files, and whether to apply sharpening to the converted image or to the preview only. It also allows you to choose the location and size of the Camera Raw cache, and lets you purge the Camera Raw cache.

Save image settings in. The "Save image settings in" option lets you save settings in the Camera Raw database, or in individual sidecar .xmp files. Camera Raw treats the raw images as read-only (which is a Good Thing since your raw images never get overwritten), so your Camera Raw edits for the image get saved either in a sidecar .xmp file—a small file designed to travel with the image—or in the Camera Raw database. Each approach has strengths and weaknesses.

Saving your edits in the Camera Raw database means that you don't have to keep track of sidecar files or worry about making sure that they get renamed along with the image—the Camera Raw database indexes the images by file content rather than name, so if you rename the raw file, the Camera Raw database will still find the correct settings. The major disadvantage of this approach is that if you move the images onto a different computer, or burn them to a CD or DVD, the edits won't travel with the images.

Saving your edits in sidecar files allows the edits to travel with the images. You have more files to deal with, but Adobe gives you a lot of help in doing so. By default, Bridge hides .xmp sidecar files, and automatically keeps them with their respective images when you use Bridge to move or rename them. The only danger is that if you move or rename the images *outside* Bridge, you need to keep track of the sidecars yourself.

A solution to this potentially confusing issue is to convert your raw images to DNG format. Camera Raw treats raw files as read-only because all the vendors' proprietary formats—Canon's .CRW and .CR2, Nikon's .NEF, Olympus' .ORF, and so on—are undocumented. Rather than taking the risk of overwriting potentially useful information by writing metadata such as Camera Raw settings into the file, Camera Raw uses sidecar files or its own database. But DNG is a completely documented, open format, so when you use DNG, Camera Raw settings and other metadata get written drectly into the DNG file itself. See "Working With DNG" in Chapter 7, *It's All About the Workflow.*

Apply sharpening to. The "Apply sharpening to" option lets you choose whether to apply sharpening to the previews *and* to the converted image, or to the previews only. I prefer to apply selective sharpening to the converted images, so I set this option to "Preview images only"—that way I can enjoy reasonably sharp previews, but apply more nuanced sharpening to the converted images. Note that this preference only affects the Sharpness setting, not either of the noise reduction settings, which are found on the same Detail tab as the Sharpness control (see "The Detail Tab," later in this chapter).

Camera Raw cache. The Camera Raw cache holds pre-parsed raw data for the most recently used raw files, which is used to speed up the following operations:

► Opening the Camera Raw dialog

► Switching between images in the Camera Raw filmstrip

► Updating the thumbnails in the Camera Raw filmstrip in response to settings changes

► Rebuilding the thumbnails/previews in Bridge in response to settings changes

The cache file sizes average about 5MB, so at the default size limit of 1GB, the Camera Raw cache will hold the pre-parsed data for about the 200 most recently accessed images. If you commonly edit folders with more than 200 raw files, you probably want to increase the Camera Raw cache's size limit. Nothing is stored exclusively in the Camera Raw cache, so purging it never loses data.

Loading and Saving Settings

The Load Settings, Save Settings, and Save Settings Subset commands let you load and save settings or settings subsets you make with any of the image-specific (Adjust, Detail, Lens, Curve, and Calibrate) controls. The Save Settings Subset command lets you save subsets of image settings—for example, you can create settings that only adjust the exposure value up or down in 1/4-stop increments such as +0.25, +0.50, -0.25, -0.5, and so on. See Figure 4-18.

Figure 4-18
Loading and saving
settings subsets

To make saved settings or subsets appear on the Settings menu automatically, save them in User/Library/Application Support/Adobe/Camera Raw/Settings (Mac), or Documents and Settings\User\Application Data\ Adobe\Camera Raw\Settings (Windows). These saved settings also appear in the Apply Camera Raw Settings submenu on Bridge's Edit menu. If you save settings anywhere else, you can load them using Camera Raw's Load Settings command.

Export Settings

The Export Settings command offers a way to write a sidecar .xmp file when you have the Camera Raw Preferences set to save edits in the Camera Raw cache—it offers a way to produce sidecar files when you want to copy the images to removable media for use on another computer while preserving the edits. If the preference is set to use sidecar files, Export Settings will export a sidecar file only if no sidecar file already exists. If there's an existing sidecar file, or if the raw file is in DNG format, Export Settings does nothing.

Use Auto Adjustments

One of the interesting new features in Camera Raw is the ability to have it perform autocorrections on images. This feature isn't as simple as it might appear at first glance! When it's turned on, which it is by default, Camera Raw tries to come up with optimum settings for each image, essentially autocorrecting tone and exposure. In my experience, it does something close to what I want slightly more than half the time, so it's quite useful.

But keeping Use Auto Adjustments as part of the default settings makes it difficult to learn the behavior of a camera, because each image has been adjusted individually, so you don't get to see a consistent baseline interpretation. That's not a problem for everyone, and if it isn't a problem for you, then by all means leave the default settings alone. However, much better photographers than I am have confided to me that they usually want to see a consistent interpretation of their images. Beginners will likely find that Use Auto Adjustments provides a quick way to get decent results, but it also makes it much more difficult for them to learn the relationship between shutter speed, aperture setting, and the photographic result.

Fortunately, Use Auto Adjustments isn't an all-or-nothing proposition, but the alternate methods of using it aren't terribly obvious. First, you can toggle Use Auto Adjustments on and off by pressing Command/Ctrl-U, but if you do so on an already-edited image, you may get some surprises. The autocorrection algorithms ignore any adjustments made in the Curve tab, and also ignore any Vignetting adjustments made in the Lens tab: they're really designed to work on top of Camera Raw default settings. If you toggle Use Auto Adjustments on when the values for Curve or Vignetting are significantly different from defaults, you won't get good results!

Auto adjustments for initial previews. The Command/Ctrl-U toggle is useful for comparing auto adjustments with a static baseline interpretation, either the old Camera Raw 2.4 defaults (which are what you get if you just turn Use Auto Adjustments off without doing anything else), or with your own customized camera defaults that don't use auto adjustments—see the next section, Setting Camera Raw defaults. If you want to take advantage of the auto adjustments to generate the initial previews and thumbnails in Bridge, just keep the Camera Raw defaults at their factory settings. Then you can either use the auto adjustments as a starting point for edits, or press Command/Ctrl-U to turn them off before you start editing.

Applying auto adjustments over baseline defaults. If you need to see a baseline interpretation of your images, but want to apply autocorrections quickly as a reality check or starting point, you'll need to create a new camera default setting without auto adjustments—see the next section. Then you can simply use the Command/Ctrl-U toggle to switch the autocorrections on and off.

Comparing auto adjustments with your own edits. This is a little trickier, because, as previously noted, if you simply toggle Use Auto Adjustments on top of edits that include Curve or Vignetting adjustments, you may get very nasty results.

If you've kept Use Auto Adjustments as part of your camera default settings, you can simply toggle between Camera Default and Image Settings (for a newly opened but already-edited image) or Custom (for edits in progress) by choosing them from the Settings menu.

If you prefer a baseline default that treats all images identically, create that default setting (which I'll tell you how to do in the next section) then open an unedited image and press Command/Ctrl-U to turn on the auto adjustments. Once you've done so, choose Save Settings from the Camera Raw menu, make sure that you're saving them in the appropriate folder for your platform, and name the setting Auto. It will then appear on the Settings menu, so you can toggle between Auto and Image Settings or Auto and Custom to compare the auto adjustments with your own edits. See "Loading and Saving Settings," earlier in this chapter.

Setting Camera Defaults

Camera Raw contains factory default settings for each supported camera model, which are used as the defaults for images originated by that model of camera. But you can create your own defaults—the image metadata tells Camera Raw which default to use for each camera model. The Reset Camera Raw Defaults command resets the default setting for the camera that shot the current image to Camera Raw's factory default, so you can always get back to the factory default behavior.

If you don't want auto adjustments on by default, you'll need to create new default settings for each camera model you use. If you want the old Adobe Camera Raw 2.x behavior, open an unedited image, turn off Use Auto Adjustments, then choose Save New Camera Raw Defaults from the Camera Raw menu. If you want different default behavior—for example, you may find the default Shadows setting of 5 a little too high—set the controls the way you want, then choose Save New Camera Raw Defaults from the Camera Raw menu. Likewise, if you notice that you consistently find yourself lowering the Color Noise Reduction slider, or consistently raising the Contrast slider, you may as well incorporate those settings in your camera default.

Getting good default settings ("good default settings" means different things to different shooters) is generally an iterative process. Don't be afraid to experiment. It won't harm your raw files in any way, and if you get hopelessly messed up, you can easily set everything back to the shipping defaults and start over.

No set of defaults will do equal justice to every image, so just try to find default settings that reduce the amount of work you need to do on each image. Default settings are only one arbitrary interpretation of your raw images, and there's nothing special about that arbitrary interpretation. The goal is to come up with settings that provide a good starting point for your images, and hence save you time.

The Main Control Buttons

The main control buttons let you specify the action that Camera Raw will perform on your raw image. They also provide a subtle yet visually obvious clue as to whether Camera Raw is being hosted by Bridge or by Photoshop—see Figure 4-19.

Figure 4-19
The main control buttons in Camera Raw hosted by Bridge and by Photoshop

When Camera Raw is hosted by Bridge, the default button is Done. When hosted by Photoshop, it's Open.

No matter which application is hosting Camera Raw, the functionality of the buttons is the same.

The Save... button (Command-S) lets you save an image as a DNG, TIFF, JPEG, or Photoshop file directly from the Camera Raw dialog box without actually opening it in Photoshop. Clicking Save opens the Save Options dialog box shown in Figure 4-20. It lets you specify the destination, the file format, any format-specific save options such as compression, and the name for the saved file or files. When you click Save in the Save Options dialog box, you're returned to Camera Raw, and the file gets saved in the background.

In single-image mode, this feature is only mildly useful. Its real power becomes apparent when you open multiple images in Camera Raw's "film-strip" mode, because the conversion from the raw to a saved RGB image

Figure 4-20
Save Options dialog box

Save Options for DNG

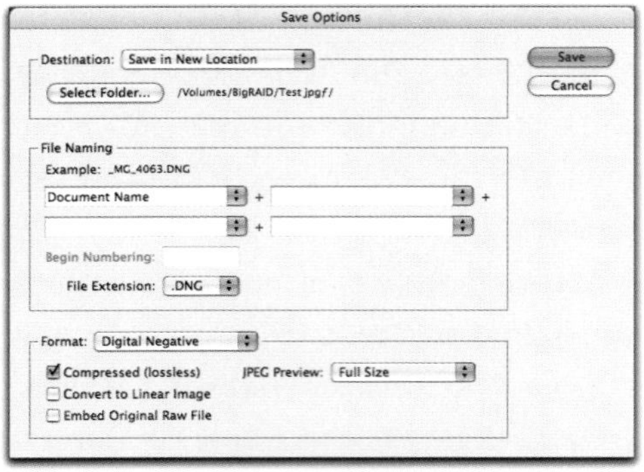

Save Options for JPEG

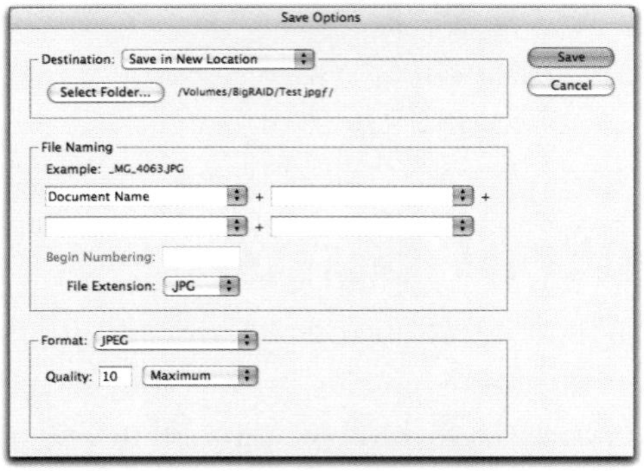

Save Options for TIFF

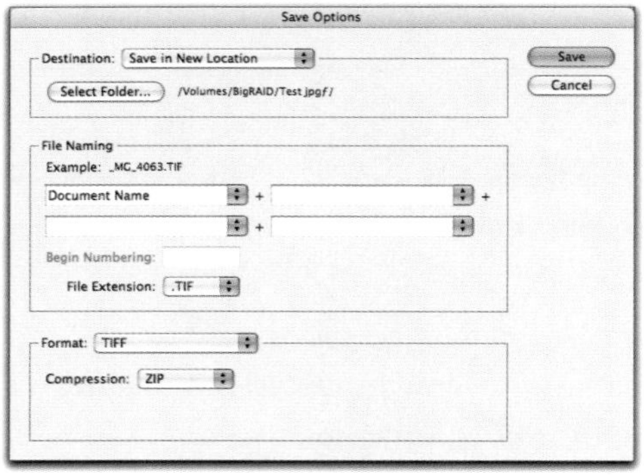

happens in the background. That means that you can continue to edit other images while Camera Raw processes the ones you're saving, a workflow that wasn't possible with previous versions of Camera Raw. See "Saving Images in the Background," in Chapter 5, *Hands-On Camera Raw*, and "Background Processing" in Chapter 7, *It's All About the Workflow*, for deeper discussion of the workflow implications of this feature.

It's also worth noting that Camera Raw is in itself a DNG converter. If you've decided that you want to stay with proprietary raws as your working files, but would prefer to hand off DNG files when you need to submit raw images (to make sure that your metadata gets preserved), it's much easier to save out DNG files as you need them from Camera Raw than it is to run them through Adobe DNG Converter.

The Cancel button (Escape) does exactly what it says. It ignores any adjustments you've made since opening Camera Raw, dismisses the Camera Raw dialog box, and returns you to the host application, leaving the raw file settings unchanged.

The Open button (Command-O) dismisses the Camera Raw dialog box and opens the image in Photoshop, using the settings you applied in Camera Raw. These settings are written to the raw file's metadata, and Bridge's previews and thumbnails are updated to reflect the new settings. When Camera Raw is hosted by Photoshop, Open is the default button.

The Done button (Return or Enter) dismisses the Camera Raw dialog box, writes the settings you applied in Camera Raw to the raw file's metadata, and returns you to the host application. Bridge's previews and thumbnails are updated to reflect the new settings. When Camera Raw is hosted by Bridge, Done is the default button.

When you press Option/Alt, the buttons change, as shown in Figure 4-21. Note the different behavior depending on which application is hosting Camera Raw.

Figure 4-21
The main control buttons
with Option/Alt pressed

Bridge

Photoshop

Save (Command-Option-S) saves the image, bypassing the Save Options dialog box, using the settings that were in effect the last time you opened the Save Options dialog box, and keeps Camera Raw open.

Reset returns all Camera Raw settings to the state they were in when you launched Camera Raw (either Image Settings, if the image had previously had its own Camera Raw settings applied, or Camera Raw Defaults if it hadn't), and keeps Camera Raw open.

Open a Copy (Photoshop only—press Command-Option-O) dismisses the Camera Raw dialog box and opens a copy of the raw file *without writing the settings to the file's metadata.* This feature is especially useful when you want to blend different renderings of the same raw image in Photoshop, but it's also handy when you have a rendering of an image that you like but suspect is capable of improvement. You can quickly try different tweaks without losing the settings that gave you the rendering you liked, and without having to go to the trouble of saving those settings.

Camera Raw Workflow Controls

At the bottom of the dialog box, four controls let you set output parameters for the converted image. See Figure 4-22.

Figure 4-22
Camera Raw
workflow settings

The settings made using these controls apply to the current image, or to all the images being converted in a batch process. Unlike the settings made with the image-specific controls, these settings aren't saved with images. This is useful, because you can set the workflow controls to produce large files in a large-gamut color space for print or final delivery, or change them to produce small files in sRGB for review on the Web or e-mail.

Space lets you choose the destination color space for the conversion from one of four preset working spaces: Adobe RGB (1998), Colormatch RGB, ProPhoto RGB, or sRGB IEC61966-1 (the last being the "standard" flavor of the sRGB standard). See the sidebar "Camera Raw and Color" in Chapter 2, *How Camera Raw Works,* for details on how Camera Raw handles the color management aspect of the conversion.

Depth lets you choose whether to produce an 8-bit/channel image or a 16-bit/channel one. A 16-bit/channel file needs twice as much storage space as an 8-bit/channel one, but it provides *128 times* as many tonal steps between black and white, so it offers much more editing headroom. See the sidebar "The High-Bit Advantage," in Chapter 5, *Hands-On Camera Raw,* for the pros and cons of 8-bit/channel and 16-bit/channel modes.

Size lets you resample the image on the fly, or convert it at the native camera resolution. The actual sizes offered depend on the camera from which the image came, but they generally correspond to the native resolution; downsampling to 66 percent or to 50 percent; and upsampling to 133 percent, 166 percent, and 200 percent. For a discussion on the pros and cons of resampling in Camera Raw versus resampling in Photoshop, see the sidebar "When to Resample," in Chapter 5, *Hands-On Camera Raw.*

Resolution lets you specify a resolution for the converted image, in pixels per inch or pixels per centimeter, giving you the option to save yourself a trip to the Image Size dialog box once the image is converted. Unlike the Size control, it has no effect on the number of pixels in the converted image—it just specifies a default resolution for the image. You can always override it later using Photoshop's Image Size command.

Camera Raw Image Controls

The image controls—the ones you're likely to change with each image—occupy the rest of the Camera Raw dialog box. The five control tabs are:

▶ Adjust, which deals with color balance and basic tone mapping

▶ Detail, which deals with sharpening and noise reduction

▶ Lens, which deals with chromatic aberration and vignetting

▶ Curve, which lets you fine-tune the tone-mapping

▶ Calibrate, which lets you fine-tune Camera Raw's built-in color profiles to better match the behavior of your specific camera body

You can switch quickly between tabs by pressing Command-Option-1 through Command-Option-5. The image controls are really the meat and potatoes of Camera Raw, offering very precise control over your raw conversions. Some of the controls may seem to offer functionality that also exists in Photoshop, but there's a significant difference between editing the tone mapping in Camera Raw, which tailors the conversion from linear to gamma-corrected space, and editing the tone mapping by stretching and squeezing the bits in a gamma-corrected space in Photoshop—see "Image Editing and Image Degradation" in Chapter 2, *How Camera Raw Works.*

The more work you do in Camera Raw, the less work you'll need to do afterwards in Photoshop. At the same time, if you get your images close to the way you want them in Camera Raw, they'll be able to withstand much more editing in Photoshop—which you may need to do to optimize for a specific output process, or to harmonize the appearance of different images you want to combine into a single image.

The Adjust Tab

The controls in the Adjust tab let you tweak the white balance, exposure, tonal behavior, and saturation. It's the default tab in Camera Raw but you can always get to it by pressing Command-Option-1. Three controls in this tab are key: the Temperature, Tint, and Exposure controls let you do things to the image that simply cannot be replicated using Photoshop's tools on the converted image.

The Contrast, Brightness, and Shadows controls provide similar functionality to Photoshop's Levels and Curves, with the important difference that they operate on the high-bit linear data in the raw capture, rather than on gamma-encoded data post-conversion. If you make major corrections ("major" meaning more than half a stop) with the Exposure slider, you'll certainly want to use the Brightness, Contrast, and Shadows controls to shape the raw data the way you want it before converting the raw image. With smaller Exposure corrections, you may still need to shape the tone in Camera Raw rather than in Photoshop, especially if you want to avoid shadow noise in underexposed images.

The Saturation control in Camera Raw offers slightly finer global adjustments than Photoshop's Hue/Saturation command, though unlike the Photoshop command, it doesn't allow you to address different color ranges selectively. See Figure 4-23.

White Balance. The two controls that set the white balance, Temperature and Tint, are the main tools for adjusting color in the image. Setting the white balance correctly should make the rest of the color more or less fall into place in terms of hue. Note that "correct white balance" includes, but isn't limited to, "accurate white balance"—you can use white balance as a creative tool.

If you find yourself consistently making the exact same selective color corrections in Photoshop on your processed raws, you may want to visit the Calibrate tab to tweak the color for your specific camera—see "The Calibrate Tab," later in this chapter.

Figure 4-23
The Adjust tab

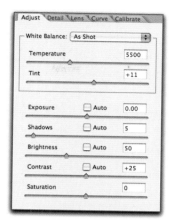

The Temperature and Tint sliders set the overall color balance.

The Exposure, Shadows, Brightness, and Contrast sliders shape the tone mapping.

The Saturation slider sets global saturation.

▶ **Temperature.** The Temperature control lets you specify the color temperature of the lighting in Kelvins, thereby setting the blue-yellow color balance. Lowering the color temperature makes the image more blue to compensate for the yellower light; raising the color temperature makes the image more yellow, to compensate for the bluer light. (If this seems counterintuitive—we think of higher color temperatures as bluer and lower ones as yellower—the trick is to remember that the Temperature control *compensates* for the color temperature of the light, so if you tell Camera Raw that the light is bluer, it makes the image yellower.)

When the Temperature field is selected, the up and down arrow keys adjust the color temperature in increments of 50 Kelvins. Adding Shift adjusts the temperature in increments of 500 Kelvins.

▶ **Tint.** The Tint control lets you fine-tune the color balance along the axis that's perpendicular to the one controlled by the Temperature slider—in practice, it's closer to a green-magenta control than anything else. Negative values add green; positive ones add magenta. The up and down arrow keys change the tint in increments of 1. Adding Shift changes the tint in increments of 10.

Figure 4-24 shows an image as shot, and the same image with some fairly gentle white balance adjustments that nevertheless greatly alter the character of the image. Notice that the adjustments involve the use of both the Temperature and Tint sliders. In Chapter 5, *Hands-On Camera Raw,* I'll look at some more extreme uses of white balance adjustments.

Figure 4-24
White Balance
adjustments

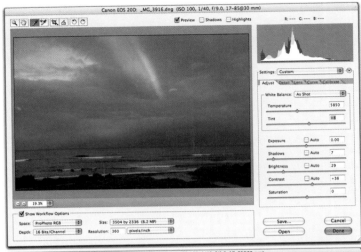

White Balance as shot

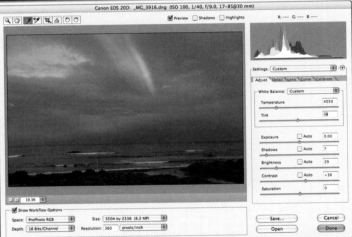

*White Balance adjusted
to cool the image*

*White Balance adjusted
to warm the image*

Tip: Use the White Balance Tool for Rough White Balance, Then Fine-Tune with the Sliders. To get the approximate settings for Temperature and Tint, click the white balance tool on an area of detail white. This automatically sets the Temperature and Tint controls to produce as close to a neutral as possible. Then make small moves with the Temperature (and, if necessary, the Tint) control to fine-tune the results.

The white balance controls let you alter the color balance dramatically with virtually no image degradation, which you simply can't do on the converted image in Photoshop. Camera Raw's controls alter the colorimetric interpretation of the image in the conversion to RGB, while Photoshop's Color Balance and Photo Filter features stretch or squeeze the levels in individual channels. Compared to changing color balance in Photoshop, doing so in Camera Raw is almost lossless.

Tone mapping controls. Learning how the four tone mapping controls—Exposure, Shadows, Contrast, and Brightness—interact is essential if you want to exercise control over the image's tonal values. It may not be obvious, but the controls work together to produce a five-point curve adjustment.

Exposure and Shadows set the white and black endpoints, respectively. Brightness adjusts the midpoint. Contrast applies an S-curve around the midpoint set by Brightness, darkening values below the midpoint and brightening those above. Figure 4-25 shows Brightness and Contrast adjustments translated approximately into Photoshop Curves.

Figure 4-25
Tonal adjustments

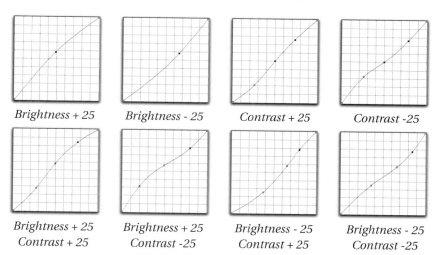

Brightness + 25	*Brightness - 25*	*Contrast + 25*	*Contrast -25*
Brightness + 25 *Contrast + 25*	*Brightness + 25* *Contrast -25*	*Brightness - 25* *Contrast + 25*	*Brightness - 25* *Contrast -25*

When you use significant negative Exposure adjustments, the logic of the tonal controls changes somewhat, because extended highlight recovery tries to undo some of the highlight compression applied by the Brightness slider, but the same general principles still apply.

▶ **Exposure.** The Exposure slider controls the mapping of the tonal values in the image to those in your designated working space, but it's first and foremost a white-clipping adjustment. Remember—half of the captured data is in the brightest stop, so Exposure is a highly critical adjustment!

   Large increases in exposure value (more than about 0.75 of a stop) will increase shadow noise and may even make some posterization visible in the shadows, simply because large positive exposure values stretch the relatively few bits devoted to describing the shadows further up the tone scale. If you deliberately underexpose to hold highlight detail, your shadows won't be as good as they could be.

   When set to negative values, the Exposure control offers the amazing ability to let you recover highlight information from overexposed images. For the technical details behind highlight recovery, see the sidebar "How Much Highlight Detail Can I Recover?" in Chapter 2, *How Camera Raw Works*; I'll show practical hands-on examples of highlight recovery in Chapter 5, *Hands-On Camera Raw*.

   When the Exposure field is selected, the up and down arrows change the exposure in increments of 0.05 of a stop. Adding Shift changes the exposure in increments of 0.5 of a stop.

▶ **Shadows.** The Shadows slider is the black clipping control. It works very like the black input slider in Photoshop's Levels, letting you darken the shadows to set the black level. But since the Shadows control operates on the linear-gamma data, small moves tend to make bigger changes than the black input slider in Levels. In early (prior to 2.3) versions of Camera Raw, the Shadows slider was something of a blunt instrument, but in more recent versions it has a much gentler effect. That said, you may find the default value of 5 (when Use Auto Adjustments is off) a little too aggressive. See the tip on the following page for checking black clipping.

When the Shadows field is selected, the up and down arrow keys change the shadows in increments of 1. Adding Shift changes the shadows in increments of 10.

Tip: Use the Clipping Display in Exposure and Shadows. For years, I've relied on the threshold clipping display in Levels to show me exactly what's being clipped in each channel as I adjust the black and white input sliders. Camera Raw offers the same feature for the Exposure and Shadows sliders (I wish it offered it for Saturation, too). Hold down the Option key as you move the Exposure or Shadows slider and you'll see the clipping display. White pixels indicate highlight clipping, black pixels indicate shadow clipping, and colored pixels indicate clipping in one or two channels. See Figure 4-26.

Figure 4-26
Exposure and Shadows clipping display

The image

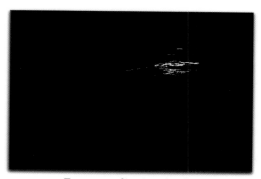

Exposure clipping display

Shadows clipping display

▶ **Brightness.** Unlike its image-destroying counterpart in Photoshop, Camera Raw's Brightness control is a non-linear adjustment that works very much like the gray input slider in Levels. It lets you redistribute the midtone values without clipping the highlights or shadows. Note, however, that when you raise Brightness to values greater than 100, you can drive 8-bit highlight values to 255, which looks a lot like highlight clipping, but if you check the 16-bit values after conversion, you'll probably find that they aren't clipped. See the tip on the previous page for an easy way to check highlight clipping.

The up and down arrow keys change the brightness in increments of 1. Adding Shift changes the brightness in increments of 10.

▶ **Contrast.** The Contrast slider also differs from the Photoshop adjustment of the same name. While Photoshop's Contrast is a linear shift, Camera Raw's Contrast applies an S-curve to the data, leaving the extreme shadows and highlights alone. Increasing the Contrast value from the default setting of +25 lightens values above the midtones and darkens values below the midtones, while reducing the Contrast value from the default does the reverse. Note that the midpoint around which Contrast adds the S-Curve is determined by the Brightness value (see Figure 4-25, a few pages back).

The up and down arrow keys change the contrast in increments of 1. Adding Shift changes the contrast in increments of 10.

Saturation. The Saturation slider acts like a gentler version of the Saturation slider in Photoshop's Hue/Saturation command. It offers somewhat finer adjustments than Hue/Saturation; but a Hue/Saturation Adjustment Layer allows you to fine-tune by varying the layer opacity, so as with Shadows, Brightness, and Contrast, it's pretty much a wash whether you make the adjustments in Camera Raw or in Photoshop. The up and down arrow keys change the saturation in increments of 1. Adding Shift changes the saturation in increments of 10.

Figure 4-27 shows a normally exposed image as shot, and a typical set of adjustments that we might make in Camera Raw's Adjust tab. I'll look at the fairly complex interaction of the Exposure, Shadows, Brightness, and Contrast controls on more difficult exposures in Chapter 5, *Hands-On Camera Raw*.

Figure 4-27
Typical Adjust tab adjustments

The image as shot, with my Camera Raw Default settings (they differ from the shipping defaults in that Use Auto Adjustments is disabled, and the Shadows slider value is set to 2).

The image at Camera Raw 3.0 shipping default settings, with Use Auto Adjustments enabled—in this case, auto did the opposite of what I wanted!

The adjusted image. I warmed the image by increasing the color temperature and tint; brightened it by raising the Brightness value, which in turn required reducing the Exposure value to hold detail in the sky; and added contrast with the Contrast and Shadows sliders. I'll fine-tune the contrast using the Curve tab.

The Detail Tab

The sliders in the Detail tab (press Command-Option-2) let you apply global sharpening and reduce noise in both luminance and color (see Figure 4-28). To see the effect of these controls, you need to zoom the preview to at least 100%—often 200% or higher is more useful—because while the Camera Raw preview tries to show their effect at 50% or higher zoom, they're hard to see until you zoom in. The up and down arrow keys move the sliders in increments of 1. Adding Shift moves the sliders in increments of 10.

Figure 4-28
The Detail tab

Most cameras need some amount of color noise reduction regardless of ISO speed. Each camera vendor makes its own compromise between image softness and color artifacting—if an image detail falls on only a red, only a green, or only a blue pixel, the demosaicing algorithm has to make some guesses to figure out what color the resulting image pixel should really be, and sometimes single-pixel color artifacts result. Color noise reduction can also eliminate rainbow artifacts in highlights and green-magenta splotches in neutral grays. The need for luminance noise reduction, though, is more dependent on ISO speed and image content.

Sharpness. The Sharpness slider lets you apply a variant of Unsharp Mask to the preview image or to both the preview and the converted image, depending on how you set Camera Raw Preferences (see "The Camera Raw Menu," earlier in this chapter). Unlike Unsharp Mask, Camera Raw's Sharpness only offers a single control—the Threshold value is calculated automatically based on the camera model, ISO, and exposure compensation values reported in the image's metadata.

I find the Sharpness control a bit of a blunt instrument. I usually set the preference so that Sharpness only applies to the preview, and apply more controlled sharpening post-conversion in Photoshop. But if I'm simply trying to get a bunch of images processed for approval, trying to make them good rather than great, I may apply a quick sharpen here, knowing that I can reprocess the "hero" shots from the raw file with no sharpening once I know which ones they are.

Luminance Smoothing. The Luminance Smoothing slider lets you control grayscale noise that makes the image appear grainy—it's typically a problem when shooting at high ISO speeds. The default setting is zero, which provides no smoothing; but many cameras benefit from a small amount—say 2 to 4—of luminance smoothing even at slow speeds, so you may want to experiment to find a good default for your camera. At high ISO speeds—800 and up— you'll almost certainly need to apply luminance smoothing at much higher settings.

At very high settings, the Luminance Smoothing slider produces images that look like they've been hit with the Median filter, so always check the entire image at 100% view or above before committing to a setting.

Bear in mind that the controls in the Adjust tab can have a huge impact on the visibility of noise. Unlike many raw converters, Camera Raw gives you access to everything the camera has captured, including, sometimes, extremely noisy shadows that other converters may simply map to black. Attempting to pull shadow detail out of an underexposed image will almost certainly result in noisy shadows.

Color Noise Reduction. Color noise manifests itself as random speckles of color rather than gray, and in my experience, all cameras need some amount of color noise reduction. While the visibility of color noise varies with ISO speed, the required correction seems to vary much less than that that required for luminance noise, so you can generally find a good default value for your camera and deviate from it only when you see an obvious problem.

It's difficult to show typical noise scenarios in print (bear in mind that noise that looks objectionable on the displayed RGB file is often quite invisible by the time the image has been converted to CMYK and printed), so Figure 4-29 shows something close to a worst-case scenario—ISO 1600 with sodium-vapor lighting!

Figure 4-29
Noise reduction

The image at 200% view (right), and the entire image (below)

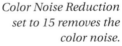

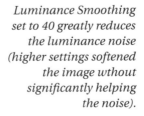

Color Noise Reduction set to 15 removes the color noise.

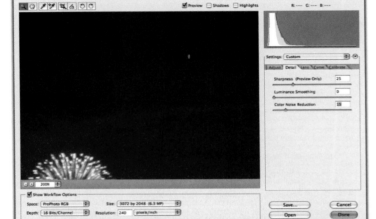

Luminance Smoothing set to 40 greatly reduces the luminance noise (higher settings softened the image wthout significantly helping the noise).

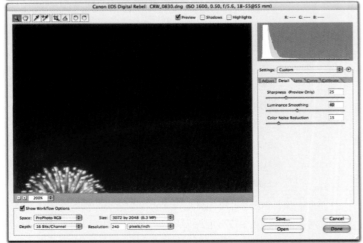

The Lens Tab

The controls in the Lens tab (press Command-Option 3) let you address two problems that occasionally show up in digital captures, one much more common than the other (see Figure 4-30). The up and down arrow keys move the sliders in increments of 1. Adding Shift moves the sliders in increments of 10.

Figure 4-30
The Lens tab

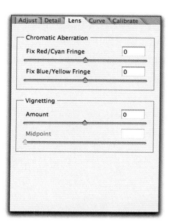

Chromatic aberration. Chromatic aberration is a phenomenon where the lens fails to focus the red, green, and blue wavelengths of the light to exactly the same spot, causing red and cyan color fringes along high-contrast edges. In severe cases, you may also see some blue and yellow fringing. It typically happens with wide-angle shots, especially with the wide end of zoom lenses. Vignetting happens when the lens fails to illuminate the entire area of the sensor evenly, and shows up as darkening in the corners of the image. It's common when shooting at wide apertures.

Some pundits claim that chromatic aberration in digital captures is caused by the microlenses some camera vendors place in front of each element in the array, but I'm skeptical—I've seen it happen on cameras without microlenses, using wide-angle lenses that don't display chromatic aberration when shooting film. I believe it's simply because digital capture is more demanding on lenses—film scatters the incoming light due to grain and to the presence of the multiple layers in the emulsion, so it's somewhat more forgiving than digital sensors. Whatever the reason, it's entirely likely that you'll encounter chromatic aberration in some wide-angle shots.

▶ **Chromatic Aberration R/C.** This slider lets you reduce or eliminate red/cyan fringes by adjusting the size of the red channel relative to the green channel. While the red/cyan fringes are usually the most visually obvious, chromatic aberration usually has a blue/yellow component too.

▶ **Chromatic Aberration B/Y.** This slider lets you reduce or eliminate blue/yellow fringes by adjusting the size of the blue channel relative to the green channel.

Figure 4-31 shows before-and-after versions of a chromatic aberration correction. As with the controls in the Detail tab, zoom the preview to 100% or more when making corrections with the chromatic aberration sliders.

Figure 4-31
Chromatic aberration correction

Detail from the image (below left) shown before chromatic aberration correction (right) and after chromatic aberration correction (below right). Note that before applying the correction, I set Sharpness in the Detail tab to zero to make it easier to see where the fringing starts and ends.

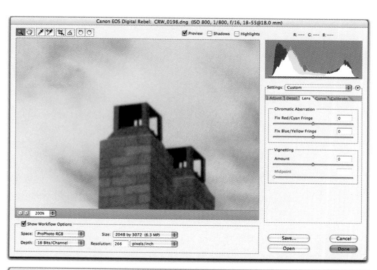

Vignetting. Vignetting, where the lens fails to illuminate the entire sensor area, darkening the corners, is usually a less-obvious problem, but you may encounter it when shooting wide open. See Figure 4-32.

▶ **Vignetting Amount.** This slider controls the amount of lightening or darkening (negative amounts darken, positive amounts lighten) applied to the corners of the image.

▶ **Vignetting Midpoint.** This slider controls the area to which the Vignetting Amount adjustment gets applied. Smaller values reduce the area; larger ones increase it.

Figure 4-32
Vignetting correction

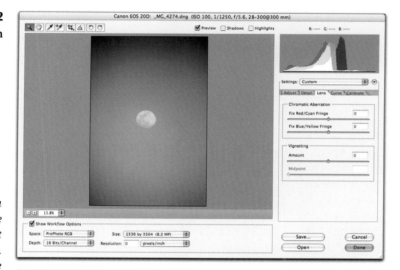

Vignetting often becomes objectionable when shooting a bright sky at wide apertures. The image before vignetting correction is shown above right; the corrected image is shown below right.

The Curve Tab

New to Camera Raw 3.0, the Curve tab (press Command-Option-4) offers a luminosity-based curve control that lets you fine-tune the image's tonality. If you're used to thinking of Photoshop's Curves command as the best way to edit images, you may be tempted to skip the slider controls in the Adjust tab and use the Curve tab for all your tone-mapping adjustments, but that's not a good idea! To understand *why* it isn't a good idea, you need to know a little about how the Curve tab actually works.

Like the sliders on the Adjust tab, the Curve tab operates on the linear capture—in fact, the slider adjustments and the curve adjustments get concatenated into a single operation during the raw conversion. But the user interface for the Curve tab makes it appear that the curve is operating on gamma-2.2-encoded data. If the curve interface corresponded directly to the linear data, the midtone value would be around level 50, and the three-quarter tone would be all the way down at level 10 or so, which would make it pretty hard to edit! (If this paragraph went straight over your head, go back and take another look at "Exposure and Linear Capture" in Chapter 1, *Digital Camera Raw,* and "Gamma and Tone Mapping" in Chapter 2, *How Camera Raw Works!*)

The upshot of this is that, from a user interface standpoint, the Curve tab works on top of the slider adjustments in the Adjust tab. You'll find that it's much easier to use the sliders for rough tonal shaping and the Curve tab for fine-tuning than it is to try to do all the heavy lifting in the Curve tab. See Figure 4-33.

Figure 4-33
The Curve tab

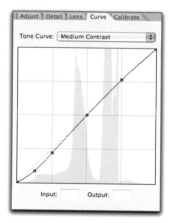

Navigation. Camera Raw's Curve tab shares many convenience features with Photoshop's Curves dialog box, along with a few subtle differences. When you press Command and mouse over the image, a small white circle appears on the curve showing where on the curve the pixels under the cursor lie. Command-clicking places a point on the curve at that location. To delete a curve point, Command-click it, select it and press the Delete key, or drag it over one of the adjacent curve points.

Control-Tab selects the next curve point, Control-Shift tab the previous point. To select multiple curve points, Shift-click on each one. The up, down, left, and right arrow keys move the selected curve point by one level: add Shift to move in increments of 10 levels. You can also enter numeric values for the selected curve point in the Input and Output entry fields.

Tone Curve menu. The Tone Curve menu contains three preset curves—Linear, Medium Contrast, and Strong Contrast—and Custom, which indicates a custom-edited tone curve. The default tone curve is Medium Contrast, but if you prefer a different default, you can change it, then save a new Camera Raw Default. In addition, you can save tone curves just like you can save any other custom subset of settings.

To make saved tone curves appear automatically on the Tone Curve menu, save them in User/Library/Application Support/Adobe/Camera Raw/Curves (Mac), or Documents and Settings\User\Application Data\Adobe\Camera Raw\Curves (Windows)—this is a different folder from the one for all other Camera Raw settings and subsets, but if you save a subset containing only a tone curve, it gets saved in this folder automatically. If you save tone curves anywhere else, you can load them using Camera Raw's Load Settings command. See "Loading and Saving Settings," earlier in this chapter.

Adjustments and Previewing. One key difference between Photoshop's Curves and Camera Raw's Curve tab is that the latter doesn't offer a real-time preview. Photoshop's Curves simply adjusts pixel values directly, but Camera Raw's Curve tab controls have to do a lot more work in mapping the edits you've specified in the gamma 2.2 interface of the tone curve onto the linear data as modified by the sliders in the Adjust tab. Today's machines simply don't have enough horsepower to update the preview in real time.

I find that the most practical way to adjust the curve is to place points by Command-clicking, then use the arrow keys to make an adjustment, wait for the preview to update, and continue to fine-tune using the arrow keys. Figure 4-34 shows a typical Curve tab adjustment.

Figure 4-34
Curve tab adjustments

The image from Figure 4-27 with the default Medium Contrast tone curve

The image after a curve adjustment. The points at the top of the curve put some detail back in the sky, while the point at the bottom of the curve punches the shadows.

The curve is particularly effective for fine-tuning highlight detail, simply because in a linear capture, that's where most of the data lies. Notice that in the above example, I bent the curve in the highlight region about the same amount as I did in the shadows, but the difference it made to the highlights is much more visually obvious than the change to the shadows. To shape the shadows, things go much more easily when you get as close as possible with the slider controls in the Adjust tab, and reserve the curve for small tweaks to the slider results.

The Calibrate Tab

The controls in the Calibrate tab (press Command-Option-5) let you fine-tune the behavior of the built-in camera profiles to tweak for any variations between *your* camera and the one that was used to build Camera Raw's built-in profiles for the camera model (see Figure 4-35). The up and down arrow keys move the sliders in increments of 1. Adding Shift moves the sliders in increments of 10.

Figure 4-35
The Calibrate tab

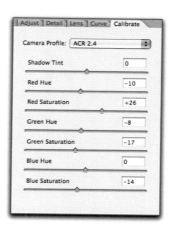

Camera Profile. For most cameras, the only choice on the Camera Profile menu is ACR 2.4, indicating that the built-in profiles used in Camera Raw 3.0 are the same as the ones in Camera Raw 2.4. For a few cameras, Camera Raw 3.0 offers new, improved profiles. If you have legacy images adjusted for the Camera Raw 2.4 profiles you can choose the ACR 2.4 profiles from this menu, while taking advantage of the new profiles for new images.

Calibration targets. I find that the most effective way to use the Calibrate controls is to shoot a 24-patch Macbeth ColorChecker, and then compare it with an accurate version of the target converted to the ProPhoto RGB working space. You can download a ProPhoto RGB image of the Color-Checker, made from averaged measurements of several physical targets, from www.colorremedies.com/realworldcolor/downloads.html.

Make sure that the target you're shooting is evenly lit, and if you're relying on the camera's built-in metering, avoid having anything significantly brighter than the target's white patch in the scene—using shiny metal clips to hold the target in place is a Bad Idea! Ideally, with no Exposure correction, the white patch should be around level 237–245.

The process. The object of the exercise is to edit the raw image of the captured target to match as closely as possible the values in the reference ProPhoto RGB image of the ColorChecker. By far the easiest way to do this is to employ the free Colorbrator script written by my friend and colleague Thomas Fors. You can download the script, along with the instructions for using it, from www.Chromoholics.com/Colorbrator.html.

But for those of you who like to do things the hard way, or simply want to understand what the script is doing, I'll describe the manual process that the script automates. It's a two-step process (though you may find that you need to do each of the two steps more than once).

Start by adjusting the tonal controls in the Adjust tab to first get approximately the same luminance values for the black and white patches as are in the ProPhoto RGB file, and then to get an approximate visual match to the gray patches in the ProPhoto RGB image. It's better to concentrate on getting a good visual match rather than trying obsessively to match the numbers *exactly*, but the numbers can be very helpful in guiding you towards the visual match. You'll find that the ProPhoto RGB file from www.colorremedies.com displays the numerical values for each patch, so you can easily compare the RGB numbers in the ColorChecker image with those supplied by Camera Raw's RGB readout and color samplers—see Figure 4-36.

Once you've matched the tonality of the gray patches to the reference ProPhoto RGB file, you can proceed to the Calibrate tab, where you can adjust red, green, and blue hue and saturation as well as shadow tint. Don't try to achieve an exact numeric match for every patch—that's a fast route to the funny farm! Instead, try to nail the relative overall hue and saturation relationships, using the numbers as a guide. Now let's look at the adjustments in detail.

Tonal adjustments. Before touching the Calibrate controls, use the tonal controls in the Adjust tab to create a reasonable contrast match to the ColorChecker image. I suggest the following step-by-step procedure, always comparing the patches in the raw image to those in the Color-Checker image.

▶ Use the Exposure control to match the white patch.

▶ Click the White Balance tool on the second-lightest gray patch (Row 4, Column 2 of the target).

Figure 4-36
Calibration setup

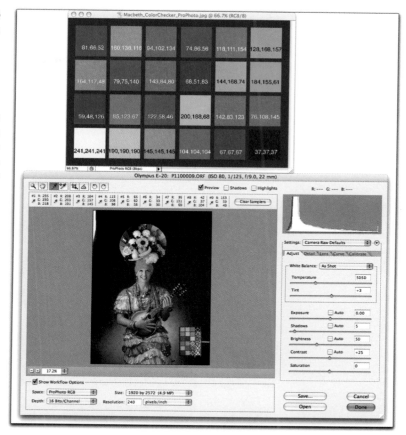

Your capture of the ColorChecker may look quite different from this one, but the same principles apply! Arrange your windows so that you can see both the ProPhoto RGB reference file and the target capture, then place color samplers on all six gray patches and on the red, green, and blue patches.

▶ Use the Brightness control to match the mid-gray patches (R4C3 and R4C4).

▶ Use the Contrast control to fine-tune the darkest patches (R4C5 and R4C6) and the second-to-lightest patch (R4C2). In some cases, you may need to use the Shadows slider to get the darkest patches where you want them.

You'll usually need to bring the Brightness and Contrast values down to the point where the image looks extremely flat. Don't worry—this is normal, and the goal is simply to get the overall contrast to match the relatively low contrast of the ColorChecker. Once you've tweaked the color response in the Calibrate tab, you're free to tweak the tonality without affecting hue and saturation. But if you don't match the overall contrast of the target, your color tweaks will be wildly off, and will produce unpredictable color shifts as you tweak the tonal values. See Figure 4-37.

Figure 4-37
Tonal adjustments

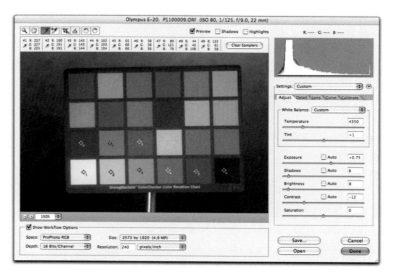

Use the Exposure,
Shadows, Brightness,
and Contrast sliders
to get the values in the
gray patches as close as
possible to those in the
ProPhoto RGB file.

Once you've adjusted the sliders to get as close as possible, you can fine-tune the result with the Curve tab—place a point for each gray patch, and tweak the curve to get the closest possible match. See Figure 4-38.

Figure 4-38
Fine-tuning with the
Curve tab

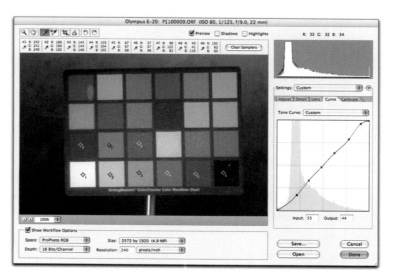

In the Curve tab,
Command-click on each
gray patch to make a
curve point, then adjust
the curve to fine-tune
the gray patch values.

Calibrate adjustments. Now you're ready to proceed with the Calibrate tab adjustments. The Calibrate tab offers a Shadow Tint control, and separate Hue and Saturation controls for Red, Green, and Blue.

▶ **Shadow Tint.** This slider controls the green-magenta balance in the shadows. Negative values add green; positive values add magenta. Check the darkest patch on the target. If it's significantly non-neutral, use the Shadow Tint control to get the R, G, and B values to match as closely as possible—normally, there shouldn't be more than one level of difference between them.

▶ **Red, Green, and Blue Hue.** These sliders work like the Hue sliders in Photoshop's Hue/Saturation command. Negative values move the hue angle counterclockwise; positive values move it clockwise.

▶ **Red, Green, and Blue Saturation.** These sliders work like gentler versions of the Saturation slider in Photoshop's Hue/Saturation command. Negative values reduce the saturation; positive values increase it.

The key point to wrap your head around in using the Hue and Saturation adjustments is this: The Red Hue and Red Saturation sliders don't adjust the red value, rather they adjust the blue and green; the Green Hue and Saturation sliders adjust red and blue; and the Blue Hue and Saturation sliders adjust red and green.

Concentrate on the red (R3C1), green (R3C2), and blue (R3C3) patches in the target. Positive adjustments to the Red Hue slider increase green and decrease blue; negative ones decrease green and increase blue. Positive adjustments to the Red Saturation slider decrease green and blue equally; negative ones increase green and blue equally. Adjust the Red Hue and Saturation while checking the red patch, the Green Hue and Saturation while adjusting the green patch, and the Blue Hue and Saturation while adjusting the blue patch. I suggest adjusting green, then blue, then red.

You'll quickly notice that everything you do here affects everything else! You may have to go through two or three rounds of tweaking the sliders, and possibly revisit the tweaks you made in the Curve tab. But if you persevere, five to ten minutes' work can get you a very close visual match.

An exact numeric match is unlikely, but you can get close. The important things to nail are the relative proportions of red, green, and blue in the red, green, and blue patches—when you get these right, the rest of the color pretty much falls into place—see Figure 4-39. You may want to create separate calibrations for tungsten and for strobe or daylight—many cameras respond significantly differently to tungsten and to daylight (or daylight-like) sources.

Figure 4-39
Calibrate tab edits

Use the Calibrate controls to adjust the proportions of red, green, and blue in each of the red, green, and blue patches.

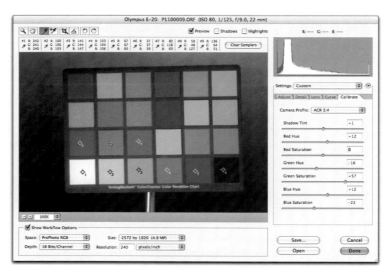

The key is to match the proportions of red, green, and blue in each patch rather than the absolute values. For example, the red patch in the physical ColorChecker measures R122, G58, B46 when the Lab measurements are converted to ProPhoto RGB, but the red value of the patch in the capture is around 136, so you need to adjust the aim points accordingly. If you divide 136 (the actual red value) by 122 (the reference red value), you get 1.1. Calculate the aim points for the red patch's blue and green values by multiplying the values in the reference image by 1.1 to get the aim points of 64 for green and 51 for blue.

Once you've dialed in your camera's response, you can incorporate the Calibrate settings into a new Camera Default for that camera, using the Save New Camera Raw Defaults command on the Camera Raw menu. But don't forget to zero out the Adjust and Curve tabs to your desired default rather than the very low-contrast settings required by this exercise!

It may be tempting to use the Calibrate controls as color-correction tools, and within limits you can do so; but if you often need to do so, it's a sign that the calibration for your camera leaves something to be desired. That said, the Calibrate controls offer some interesting creative possibilities that I'll demonstrate in Chapter 5, *Hands-On Camera Raw.*

Figure 4-40 shows images from several cameras before and after applying custom calibration settings. They demonstrate the effectiveness of the feature in dialing in the performance of very different cameras.

Figure 4-40
Before and after
calibration

The top row shows images at camera default settings; the bottom row shows the same images after applying Calibrate adjustments.

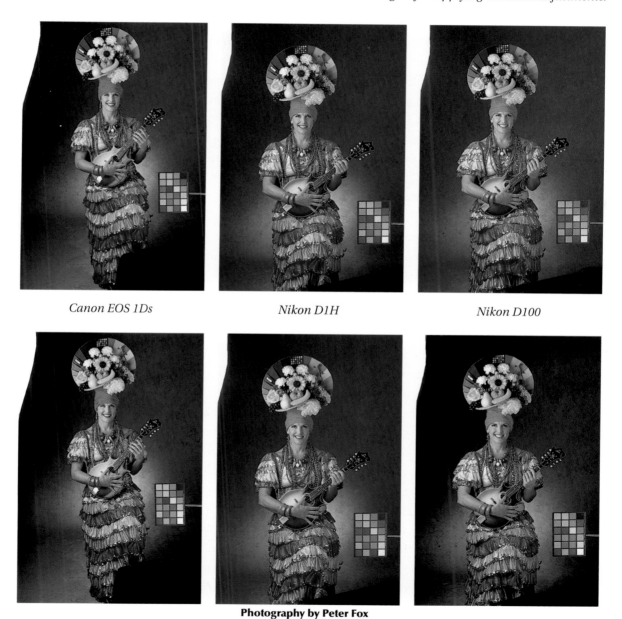

Canon EOS 1Ds   Nikon D1H   Nikon D100

Photography by Peter Fox

The Darkroom Toolkit

In this chapter, I've concentrated on describing each of the tools individually, with simple examples of their effects on images. But it's a mistake to fall in love with a single tool and ignore the others—when all you have is a hammer, everything tends to look like a nail! The way the tools interact is as important as their individual functions.

Many different combinations of Camera Raw settings can produce superficially similar results, but when you look closely, or when you start to push the converted images further in Photoshop, you'll invariably find that one combination works better than the others, so in the next chapter, I'll show you how the tools all work together to let you evaluate and optimize your images.

5 Hands-On Camera Raw

Evaluating and Editing Images

Knowing what each control does in Camera Raw is only half the battle. The other half is in knowing how the various controls interact, and when (and in what order) to use them. So with these goals in mind, let's first look at a simple scenario, processing individual images, one at a time, in Camera Raw. Later in this chapter we'll look at the ways Camera Raw lets you apply edits to multiple images at the same time, and to transfer edits from one image to another, but unless you've mastered the art of editing one image at a time, these features are as likely to help you destroy multiple images as to enhance them!

It's useful to split the work into three phases, even though the third phase is where most of the work gets done, because if you mess up the first phase, you won't get the results you wanted, and if you skip the second phase you may miss critical issues in the image when you execute phase three. The three phases are:

▶ Setting up Camera Raw—Preferences and workflow settings

▶ Evaluating the image

▶ Editing the image

Let's look at these in turn.

Camera Raw Setup

The first order of business is to set up Camera Raw to make it work the way you want it to. To do that, you must open a raw image, because until you actually launch Camera Raw you can't do anything with it. Size the Camera Raw window by dragging the handle at the lower-right corner so that you can see a decent-sized image preview, with the controls conveniently placed. If most of your images are verticals, you may prefer a narrower Camera Raw window than if you mostly shoot horizontals. While the screen shots in this book show Camera Raw at its minimum size, I like to size the Camera Raw window to fill the entire screen.

Preferences. Next, make sure that Camera Raw's Preferences are set to behave the way you want them to. There's no right or wrong answer to how the Preferences should be set other than that they should produce the behavior you want. You can open Camera Raw's Preferences either by choosing Preferences from the Camera Raw menu or by choosing Camera Raw Preferences in Bridge from the Bridge menu (Mac) or the Edit menu (Windows).

Camera Raw's Preferences are pretty straightforward. You only have two settings to worry about—where to save settings and how to apply sharpening.

▶ **Save image settings in:** Controls where your image settings get saved, with two choices: "Camera Raw database" or "Sidecar .xmp files." Each has its advantages and disadvantages.

When you save settings in the Camera Raw database, they're indexed by file content rather than name, so even if you rename the raw file, Camera Raw will associate the correct settings with the image. But if you move the image to a different computer, the settings won't be available because they're stored in the Camera Raw database on the first computer.

When you save settings as sidecar .xmp files, they're saved as separate files, in the same folder as the image, and with the same name as the image except that they take a .xmp extension instead of the raw file extension (.crw, .nef, and so on). Bridge automatically keeps the sidecar files with the images as long as you use Bridge to move or copy them. You can run Batch Rename, and the sidecar files will get renamed along with the images; but if you move or copy the images outside Bridge, it's up to you to make sure that the sidecar files go with them.

If you only use a single computer and never send your raw files to anyone else, it may make sense to store all the Camera Raw settings in the Camera Raw database, but I find that sidecar files offer more flexibility at the cost of slightly more complex file management. If you want to archive your settings along with the images when you burn them to CD or DVD, sidecar files are the only way to go. If you use the DNG format, the issue is moot because the settings get written directly into the DNG file.

▶ **Apply sharpening to:** controls whether sharpening applied by the Sharpness slider in the Detail tab is applied to the image preview only or to the converted image. (When you choose Preview Images Only, a label reminding you that you've done so appears beside the Sharpness slider.)

I usually prefer to sharpen the image post-conversion in Photoshop, but it's often useful to apply some sharpening to the preview to aid in making decisions about contrast. So I normally leave Camera Raw's preference set to Preview Images Only. (Note that this setting has no effect on the previews and thumbnails displayed by Bridge.)

However, if I need to process a lot of images quickly, I'll use Camera Raw's sharpening and change the preference to apply sharpening to All Images—that way, the sharpening I set with the Sharpness slider is applied to the converted image as well as to the preview.

If either preference is set incorrectly, you'll need to redo all of your work once you've set them the way you want, so always make sure that they're set the way you think they are—it will save time in the long run.

Workflow settings. The workflow settings govern the color space, bit depth, size, and resolution of the converted image. They're called "work-flow settings" because you'll typically change them to produce different types of output. For example, when you want to create JPEGs for online viewing or review, it would make sense to choose sRGB as the color space, 8-bit for bit depth, the smallest size for your camera for size, and 72 ppi for resolution. But to produce images for large prints, you'd probably switch to a wider color space, use 16-bit for bit depth to accommodate further editing in Photoshop, the largest size supported for your camera, and 240 ppi for resolution.

The workflow settings are recordable in actions, so once you've learned your way around, you can easily incorporate the workflow settings you want in batch processes—I'll discuss building actions for batch processes in Chapter 9, *Exploiting Automation.*

Four different menus make up the workflow settings (see Figure 5-1).

Figure 5-1
Camera Raw
workflow settings

▶ **Space** dictates the color space of the converted image. The choices are Adobe RGB, Colormatch RGB, ProPhoto RGB, and sRGB. If you use one of these spaces as your Photoshop RGB working space, choose that space here, unless you're producing imagery for the Web, in which case you should choose sRGB.

A huge number of words have already been expended on the subject of RGB working spaces, and I don't want to add to them here—if you want to read some of mine, www.creativepro.com:80/story/feature/8582.html is a good place to start. The one practical recommendation I'll make regarding choice of working space is to use Camera Raw's his-togram to detect colors being clipped by the chosen output space. If a space clips colors, look to see if they're important to you. If they are, choose a wider space. See "Evaluating Images," later in this chapter.

Tip: When You Need a Different Output Space... If none of the four spaces supported by Camera Raw suits your workflow, use ProPhoto RGB as the space in Camera Raw, set the bit depth to 16-bit, then use Photoshop's Convert to Profile command to convert the images into your working space of choice, using Relative Colorimetric rendering. ProPhoto RGB is large enough that it makes any color clipping extremely unlikely, so the intermediate conversion won't introduce any significant loss.

▶ **Depth** lets you choose whether to produce an 8-bit/channel image or a 16-bit/channel one. Unless I'm creating JPEGs for Web or e-mail use, I always convert to 16-bit/channel images, because they allow a great deal more editing headroom than 8-bit/channel ones. The inevitable trade-off is that the files are twice as large.

If you plan on doing minimal editing in Photoshop, converting to 8-bit/channel may save you time, particularly if you run Photoshop on older, slower machines. Everyone has their own pain point! See the sidebar "The High-Bit Advantage" for more on 16-bit/channel images.

▶ **Size** lets you choose one of several output sizes. The specific sizes vary from camera to camera, but they always include the camera's native resolution as well as higher and lower ones.

The High-Bit Advantage

Any camera that shoots raw captures at least 10 bits per pixel, offering a possible 1,024 tonal values, while most capture 12 bits for 4,096 levels, and a few capture 14 bits, for 16,384 possible tonal values. An 8-bit/channel image allows only 256 possible tonal values in each channel, so when you convert a raw image to an 8-bit/channel file, you're throwing away a great deal of potentially useful data.

The downsides of 16-bit/channel images are that they take up twice as much storage space (on disk and in RAM) as 8-bit/channel ones, and an ever-shrinking list of Photoshop features don't work in 16-bit/channel mode. The advantage is that they offer massively more editing headroom.

If you're preparing images for the Web or you need to use a Photoshop feature such as Liquify that only works in 8-bit/channel mode, by all means go ahead and process the raw images to 8-bit channel files. In just about every other scenario, I recommend processing to a 16-bit/channel file. Even if you think the image will require little or no editing in Photoshop, it's likely that at some point the image will have to undergo a color space conversion for output, and making that conversion on a 16-bit/channel image can often avoid problems such as banding in skies or posterization in shadows that suddenly appear after an 8-bit/channel conversion.

On cameras that produce non-square pixels, there's a clear advantage to using Camera Raw to go one size up from native, in which case an asterisk appears beside that choice in the menu—see "Size" in Chapter 2, *How Camera Raw Works*—but for the majority of cameras, the difference is less clear-cut and is equally about workflow convenience as image quality. See the sidebar "When to Resample" for further discussion.

▶ **Resolution** lets you set a default resolution for the image. This is purely a workflow convenience—you can always change it later using Photoshop's Image Size command. If you need 240-ppi images for inkjet printing or 72-ppi images for Web use, set that resolution here to save yourself a trip to the Image Size dialog box later.

You can't load and save workflow settings as you can image settings, but you *can* record workflow settings in actions that you can then use for batch processing. The Size and Resolution settings are sticky per camera model, so always check to make sure that they're set the way you need them.

Evaluating Images

Before starting to edit a raw image, it's always a good idea to do a quick evaluation. Is the image over- or underexposed? Does the subject matter fall within the camera's dynamic range, or do you have to sacrifice highlights or shadows? Camera Raw offers three features that help you evaluate the raw image and answer these questions.

▶ **The histogram** lets you judge overall exposure and detect any clipping to black, white, or a fully saturated primary.

▶ **The image preview** shows you exactly how the converted image will appear in Photoshop, and the clipping display, available when you adjust the Exposure and Shadows sliders, lets you see exactly which pixels, if any, are being clipped.

▶ **The RGB readout and color samplers** let you sample the RGB values from specific spots in the image.

If an image is too dark or too light, you need to decide whether to fix it by adjusting Exposure or Brightness. If it's too flat, you need to decide whether to increase the Contrast or add snap to the shadows with the Shadows control. Camera Raw's histogram aids these decisions by showing at a glance what's happening at the extreme ends of the tone scale.

When to Resample

A good deal of controversy surrounds the question of whether to upsample in Camera Raw or post-conversion in Photoshop. Be very wary of absolute answers—in most cases, the differences are quite subtle and likely camera-dependent. (And it's also quite likely they're photographer-dependent, too!) That said, I'll give half an absolute answer: if you need a smaller-than-native file, it's a no-brainer to choose the size closest to your needs in Camera Raw. The controversy really revolves around upsizing.

With the exception of images captured on non-square-pixel cameras, the differences between upsampling in Camera Raw and upsampling in Photoshop using Bicubic Sharper are quite subtle (though I prefer to use Bicubic Smoother for upsampling). If you factor in the other variables, and in particular the huge variable of how and when you sharpen the image, the question of when to resample becomes even more complex. I personally prefer to convert raw images at the camera's native resolution and do as much work as

possible before upsampling, because the work goes faster on a smaller file than on a larger one. But others whose judgment I respect prefer to upsample in Camera Raw.

Ultimately, it's a question you'll have to answer for yourself. You may even find that some types of imagery respond better to one method, while others respond better to another. If you're disinclined to devote a lot of time to testing, another entirely rational strategy is to punt on the whole question and simply do whatever is most convenient in your workflow.

The histogram. Camera Raw's histogram is simply a bar chart that shows the relative populations of pixels at different levels. The colors in the histogram show what's going on in each channel.

White in the histogram means that this level has pixels from all three channels. Red, green, and blue mean that this level has pixels from these individual channels. Cyan means that this level has pixels from the green and blue channels, magenta means this level has pixels from the red and blue channels, while yellow means that this level has pixels from the red and green channels. (If it's easier, you can think of cyan as "no red," magenta as "no green," and yellow as "no blue.")

Spikes at either end of the histogram indicate clipping—white pixels mean that all three channels are being clipped, and colored ones indicate clipping in one or two channels—see Figure 5-2.

**Figure 5-2
Clipping and
the histogram**

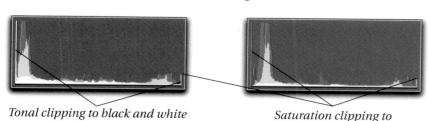

Tonal clipping to black and white

*Saturation clipping to
yellow and red*

The histogram can help you determine whether or not the captured scene fits within the camera's dynamic range. If there's no clipping at either the highlight or the shadow end, it clearly does. If there's clipping at both ends, it probably doesn't. If there's clipping at only one end, you may be able to rescue highlight or shadow detail (if you want to) by adjusting the Exposure slider.

The histogram also shows clipping in individual channels. Typically, clipping in one or two channels indicates one of two conditions.

▶ The RGB space selected in the Space menu is too small to hold the captured color. In that case, try switching to a larger space if the color is important.

▶ You've pushed the saturation so far that you've driven one or more channels into clipping. Again, this isn't necessarily a problem. To see exactly what's being clipped, you can use the Exposure or Shadows slider's clipping display, which I'll discuss next.

Image preview. The main function of the image preview is, of course, to show you how the converted image will appear. But it also offers a couple of indispensable tricks in the form of the highlight clipping display and shadow clipping display offered by using the Option key in conjunction with the Exposure and Shadows sliders, respectively. Hold down the Option key, and then hold down the mouse button on either slider to see the clipping display. The display updates dynamically as you move the slider, so it's useful for editing as well as evaluation.

▶ **Exposure clipping display.** Holding down the Option key as you move the Exposure slider turns the image Preview into a highlight clipping display—see Figure 5-3.

Unclipped pixels display as black. The other colors show you which channels are being clipped to level 255. Red pixels indicate red channel clipping, green pixels indicate green channel clipping, and blue pixels indicate blue channel clipping. Yellow pixels indicate clipping in both red and green channels, magenta pixels indicate clipping in the red and blue channels, and cyan pixels indicate clipping in the green and blue channels. White pixels indicate that all three channels are clipped.

Figure 5-3
Exposure clipping display

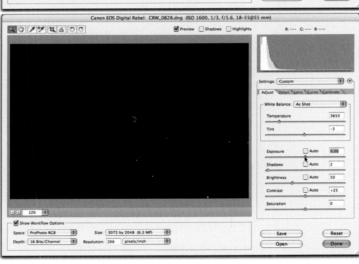

*Holding down the
Option key while
pressing or moving the
Exposure slider produces
the Exposure clipping
display, below right.*

*In this image, we can
see that a few bright
highlights are being
clipped when the
Exposure slider is
set to zero.*

Of all the controls in the Adjust tab, the Exposure slider is the most
critical due to the nature of linear captures, which devote many more
bits to describing the highlights than to describing the shadows. On
the vast majority of images, my first edit is to set the Exposure slider
so that the highlights are as close as possible to clipping. If the image
exceeds the camera's dynamic range, I may choose to sacrifice highlight
detail when the nature of the image dictates that the shadow detail is
more important, but even then, careful setting of the Exposure slider
is vital, and the clipping display is invaluable in making that setting.

▶ **Shadows clipping display.** Holding down the Option key as you move the Shadows slider turns the image preview into a shadow clipping display—see Figure 5-4.

Figure 5-4
Shadows clipping display

Holding down the Option key while pressing or moving the Shadows slider produces the Shadows clipping display for the image shown in Figure 5-3. Both Exposure and Shadows clipping are present, so something will have to give.

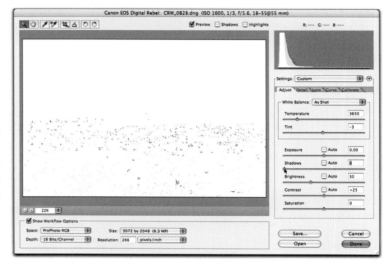

Unclipped pixels display as white. The other colors show you which channels are being clipped to level 0. Cyan pixels indicate red channel clipping, magenta pixels indicate green channel clipping, and yellow pixels indicate blue channel clipping. Red pixels indicate clipping in both green and blue channels, green pixels indicate clipping in the red and blue channels, and blue pixels indicate clipping in the red and green channels. Black pixels indicate that all three channels are clipped.

While the histogram shows you whether or not clipping is taking place, the clipping displays show you *which* pixels are being clipped. If you want to evaluate clipping on single pixels, you'll need to zoom in to 100% view. Camera Raw does its best to show you clipping at lower zoom percentages, but it's only completely accurate at 100% or higher zoom levels.

RGB readout. The RGB readout lets you sample the RGB values of the pixel under the cursor. At 100% or lower zoom percentages, the readout always reports the average of a five-by-five sample of screen pixels. At higher zoom levels, the readout is an average of five by five actual image pixels, which is the minimum sample size.

The RGB readout helps you distinguish between, for example, a yellow cast and a green one, or a magenta cast and a red one. Sample an area that should be close to neutral. If the blue value is lower than red and green, it's a yellow cast; if the green value is higher than red and blue, it's a green cast.

If you need to keep track of important colors in the image, you can use the color sampler tool to place up to nine color samplers, so including the RGB cursor readout you can track 10 sets of color values should you need to.

The evaluation process. The first thing I do is simply to look at the image. I set my Camera Raw defaults with Use Auto Adjustments turned off—I need to be able to see the effects of bracketing rather than having Camera Raw normalize all my exposures, and I'm neither good enough nor bad enough to benefit from the auto adjustments. At default settings, images usually look flat, and are often too bright or too dark.

▶ The first thing I do is to check for clipping. An image that's too dark may be underexposed, requiring an Exposure adjustment, or it may be holding some bright highlights and need a Brightness adjustment to remap the midtones instead. By the same token, an image that's too bright may be overexposed, requiring highlight recovery with the Exposure slider, or it may need darkening of the midtones by reducing the Brightness value. The histogram and clipping displays help me determine which is the case.

▶ It's much easier to add contrast than to reduce it. Depending on the tonal range involved, it may be best to use the Shadows slider, the Contrast slider, the Curve tab, or any combination thereof, but I only do so after I've set the endpoints.

▶ If I need to make big Exposure moves, I'll do so before setting white balance, because changes in the Exposure value can have a big effect on the white balance. Other than that, it doesn't really matter when you set the white balance.

▶ After editing for tone and color, I zoom in to 100% or higher, and check for color and luminance noise and for chromatic aberration.

Figure 5-5 shows the evaluation process for several different images, with a variety of exposures. In the next section, I'll edit these images.

Figure 5-5
Evaluating images

This image is
overexposed, as
evidenced by the
preview and
histogram.

The Exposure clipping
display confirms the
overexposure.

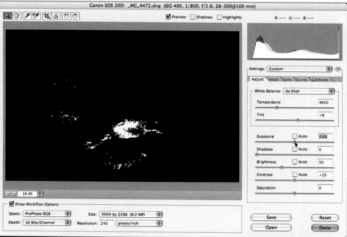

The Shadows clipping
display shows that no
important shadow
detail is being clipped.
This image is a good
candidate for highlight
recovery with the
Exposure slider.

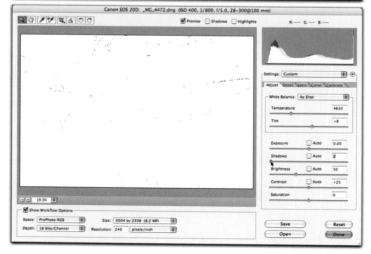

Figure 5-5
Evaluating images,
continued

This image is considerably underexposed, as shown by the preview and the histogram.

The Shadows clipping display shows no significant clipping, so I'll brighten the image by increasing the Exposure value, and keep a careful watch on the shadow noise.

This image is flat and a little washed-out, but it's actually a decent exposure that lies comfortably inside the camera's dynamic range. I'll add contrast by reducing the Brightness, raising the Shadows, and increasing the Contrast slider.

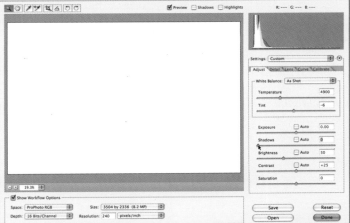

Figure 5-5
Evaluating images,
continued

This image appears flat and washed-out, but the histogram and clipping displays show that the entire dynamic range was captured without clipping. I'll fix it using the Shadows, Brightness, and Contrast sliders, and fine-tune with the Curve tab.

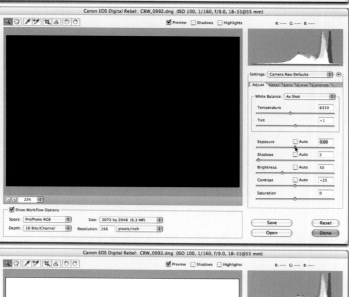

Figure 5-5
Evaluating images,
continued

This image may appear underexposed, but it's doing a reasonable job holding the window highlights, and the Shadows clipping display reveals no important clipping. I'll start my edits by redistributing the midtones using the Brightness slider.

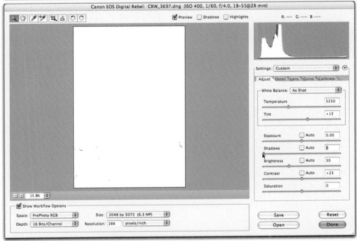

This image is a bit underexposed, but the main problems are that it's too cold, and the midtones need brightening.

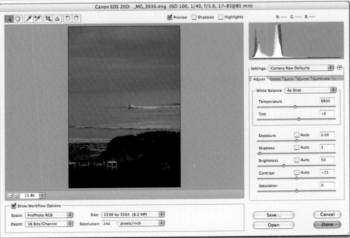

Editing Images

At last, we come to the heart of the matter—editing raw images! I always start with the controls in the Adjust tab, followed by those in the Curve tab. Then I zoom in and check for noise that needs adjusting with the Detail tab, and for chromatic aberration that needs adjusting in the Lens tab. Normally, I don't make adjustments to individual images in the Calibrate tab, reserving it for fine-tuning the response of specific cameras; but on occasion, it can be a handy creative tool, too.

The Adjust tab contains the controls that let you set the overall contrast and color balance for the image, and it's always where I start. A simple rule of thumb that has served me well over the years is to fix the biggest problem first. In the case of raw images, this almost always boils down to adjusting tone or adjusting white balance.

If the image needs a major (more than 0.25-stop up or down) exposure adjustment, it's better to do that before setting the white balance, because the exposure adjustment will probably affect the white balance. If the image needs little or no exposure adjustment, I usually set white balance first.

Highlight recovery. The biggest problem in the first image from Figure 5-5 was overexposure, so I'll start by trying to recover the highlights with the Exposure slider—see Figure 5-6.

Figure 5-6
Highlight recovery with the Exposure slider

The Exposure clipping display shows that a -1.15-stop Exposure correction gets rid of all the highlight clipping except for a handful of specular highlights. A larger correction doesn't improve anything, so I commit to Exposure -1.15.

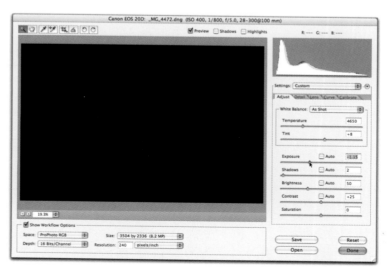

The Exposure correction produces the result shown in Figure 5-7.

Figure 5-7
The recovered highlights

The Exposure tweak recovers a great deal of highlight data, but it inevitably darkens the image.

Next, I need to adjust the Brightness and Contrast sliders to counteract the darkening effect of the Exposure adjustment, as shown in Figure 5-8.

Figure 5-8
Brightness and Contrast adjustments

Raising the Brightness value counteracts the darkening effect of the Exposure adjustment. Reducing the Contrast slider preserves the recovered highlight detail.

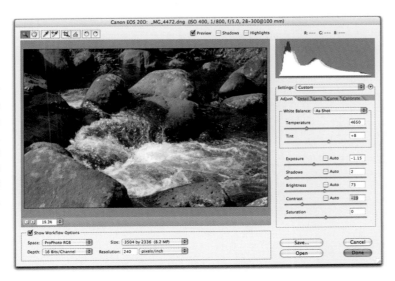

Tip: Don't Be Afraid to Reduce Contrast. Many photographers are hesitant to reduce the value of a slider labeled "Contrast," but if you're looking to brighten the dark three-quarter tones without affecting the midtones, reducing the Contrast value will do a better job than increasing the Brightness value. If you're worried about the image going flat, rest assured that you can put plenty of punch back into the shadows using either the Shadows slider or the Curve tab. In the case of this image, leaving the Contrast slider at default, or increasing the Contrast value, would have a much greater effect on the highlights (due to the high Brightness value) than on the darker tones, and would actually undo some of the highlight recovery!

At this point, I'm happy with the white balance, so I'll leave it "As Shot." I want to fine-tune the highlight detail with the Curve tab, so rather than adjusting the Shadows slider to punch the blacks, I'll leave it as is and handle the shadows, as well as the highlights, in the Curve tab, as shown in Figure 5-9.

Figure 5-9
Fine-tuning with the Curve tab

Most of the points on this curve are anchor points to prevent the other curve points from bending the curve in undesirable ways. This curve adds detail to the highlights, makes a slight tweak to the midtone contrast, and darkens the shadows.

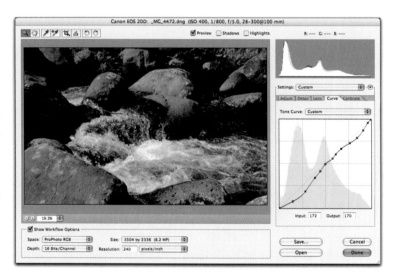

Zooming in to 200% view, I check for noise and lens problems, but find none. I'm done, so I click the Done button to make Camera Raw write the settings into the DNG file, and update Bridge's thumbnail and preview. (If I'd used a proprietary raw file—in this case, a Canon .CR2—the settings would be written to the Camera Raw database or to a sidecar .xmp file, depending on Camera Raw's Preferences setting.) All I'll have to do to this image in Photoshop is sharpening, which I do with my sharpening tool of choice, PhotoKit Sharpener—it offers finer control than Camera Raw's Sharpness slider, as do virtually all Photoshop sharpening techniques.

Underexposure. Moving on to the second image from Figure 5-5, we'll look next at handling a significantly underexposed image. Underexposed images often present bigger problems than do overexposed ones, because they contain much less data—remember, half of the captured data lies in the brightest f-stop—so you need to stretch the data that *is* there to cover the entire tonal range. That means you need to watch out for posterization and shadow noise. As with the previous example, I start with the Exposure slider—see Figure 5-10.

Figure 5-10
Checking Exposure clipping

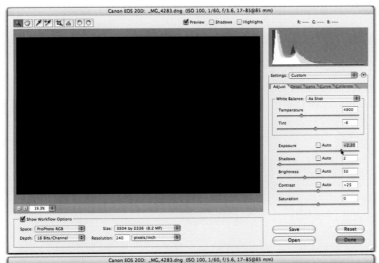

The Exposure clipping display shows a tiny clipped highlight at +2.35, so I set the Exposure to that value, producing the result shown below right.

Next, I check for Shadow clipping, and adjust the Shadows, Brightness, and Contrast sliders—see Figure 5-11.

Figure 5-11
Shadows, Brightness, and
Contrast adjustments

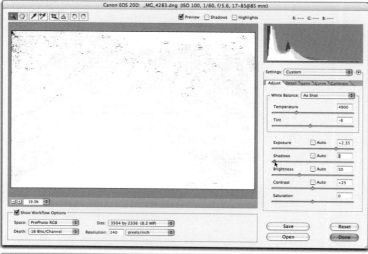

At my customized default setting of 2, the Shadows clipping display shows a fair bit of clipping, so I back it off to zero. Then I increase Brightness to 60, and Contrast to 91, to produce the result shown below right.

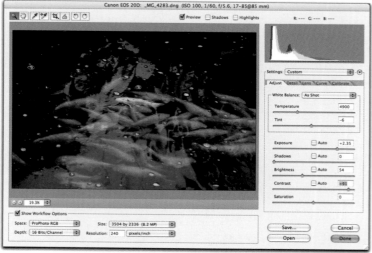

The reason for backing off the Shadows slider isn't to preserve any important shadow detail—there really isn't any—but to avoid any posterization that may end up biting me where I'd rather not be bitten! The relatively large Contrast move darkens the shadows and compresses the highlights. I kept the Brightness move quite small, because the further Brightness is set from its default, the more asymmetrical the effect of Contrast on shadows versus highlights. I'll tweak contrast with the Curve tab next—see Figure 5-12.

Figure 5-12
Curve tab adjustments

The curve adjustment adds a little extra contrast, with more control than the Contrast slider can provide.

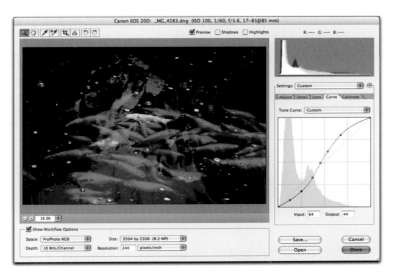

The Curve tab tweaks complete the tonal adjustments, but I'll revisit the Adjust tab to tweak the white balance—the image is a little yellow-green. In many cases, I'll adjust an image's white balance before making tonal adjustments, but on an image like this, the huge tonal moves may alter the white balance, which is why I left it until now. See Figure 5-13.

Figure 5-13
White balance adjustments

Bringing down the Temperature slider from 4900 to 4000 Kelvins and raising the Tint slider value from -6 to -2 eliminates the yellow cast from the reflections, and makes the yellow fish pop.

With tone and white balance adjustments complete, it's time to zoom in and inspect the image for noise and chromatic aberration. I don't expect to find the latter—the image was shot at the longest focal length of the lens—but I'll be surprised if I don't find some noise extending well up into the tonal range since the image was more than two stops underexposed. So I'll switch to the Detail tab, and zoom in to 200% view—see Figure 5-14.

Figure 5-14
Noise reduction with the Detail tab

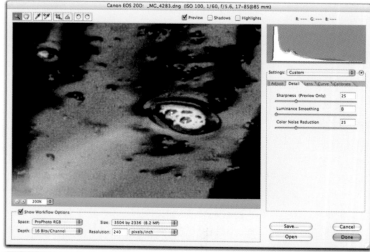

The default Color Noise Reduction value of 25 does a good job of eliminating color noise, but there's a good deal of luminosity noise in the midtones, requiring an unusually high Luminance Smoothing value of 30.

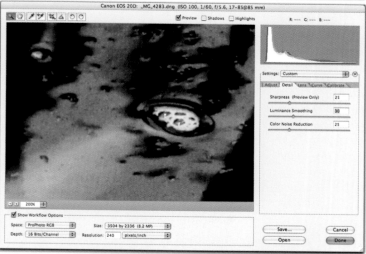

On any given camera, while color noise may extend higher into the tonal range at higher ISO speeds, the required correction tends to remain constant, so it makes sense to incorporate that correction in your Camera

Raw Default Settings for that camera. Luminance noise, however, is a different story. With optimal exposures, Luminance noise tracks fairly well with ISO speed—faster speeds need more correction. But as this image demonstrates, it's also very much related to exposure—underexposed images are always noisier than optimally exposed ones—so the setting for Luminance Smoothing is image-dependent.

Tone mapping. You may never have to deal with exposure errors as large as the ones in the two previous examples, but even if your exposures are always spot-on, you'll almost certainly need to tweak the tone mapping in a good many images. Figure 5-15 shows a case in point.

Figure 5-15
Initial evaluation

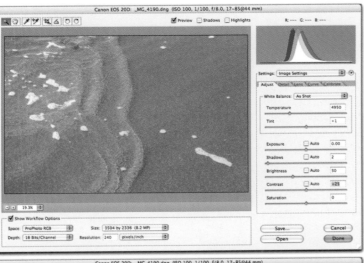

The Exposure clipping display shows slight highlight clipping when Exposure is set to zero. This image has plenty of headroom at the shadow end, so it's quite safe to reduce the Exposure and eliminate the clipping.

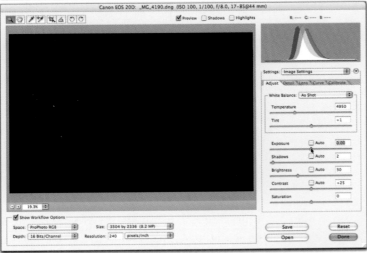

If the image exceeded the dynamic range of the sensor, I'd accept the minor highlight clipping, but in this case there's plenty of room at the shadow end, so I reduce the Exposure value to -0.30 to eliminate the clipping, producing the result shown in Figure 5-16.

Figure 5-16
The Exposure adjustment

The -0.30 Exposure adjustment ensures that I'll hold the highlights, but does little to improve the image's appearance.

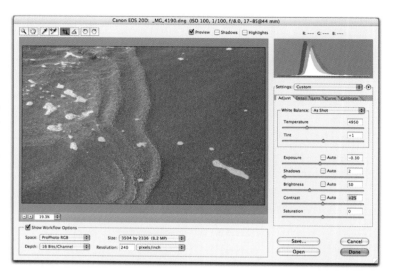

The next step is to care of the shadow end—currently, there's nothing even close to a true black in the image. So I'll check the Shadows clipping display and set a more useful Shadows value—see Figure 5-17.

Figure 5-17
Shadows clipping display

The Shadows clipping display shows that I can run the Shadows slider up to around 38 before any clipping occurs.

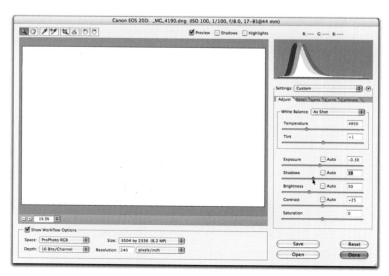

Adjusting the Shadows slider produces the image shown in Figure 5-18. Now the image covers the full dynamic range, so I can concentrate on distributing the tonal information.

Figure 5-18
The Shadows adjustment

The Shadows tweak helps considerably, but the image is now dark, and it's still flat.

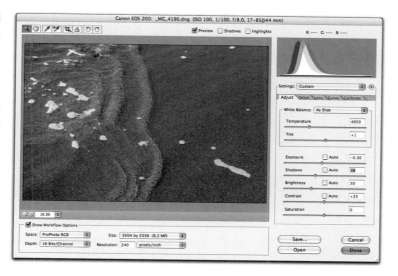

Two quick moves with the Brightness and Contrast sliders produce the much-improved result shown in Figure 5-19.

Figure 5-19
Brightness and Contrast adjustments

Raising Brightness to 65 and Contrast to 96 produces this much-improved result.

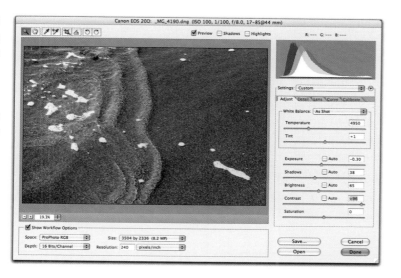

I'll use the Curve tab to add snap to the highlights—see Figure 5-20.

Figure 5-20
Highlight adjustment
with the Curve tab

Zooming in far enough
to see detail, I tweak
the highlight end of
the curve to add a
little contrast in the
highlights.

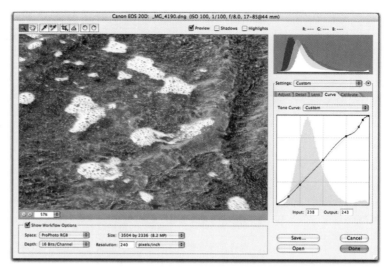

The image is very close to being done. It shows no noise or lens problems, but I decide that a small white balance tweak would help, and that the image would really work better with a 4x5 aspect ratio, so I tweak the white balance and apply the preset 4 to 5 crop (by choosing it from the crop tool's drop-down menu and dragging) to produce the result shown in Figure 5-21.

Figure 5-21
The final image

Raising the Temperature
value from 4950 to
5250 warms the image
slightly. I apply a 4 by 5
crop to tighten up the
composition.

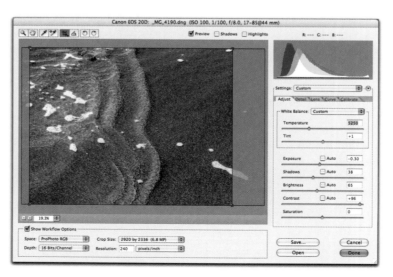

A glance back to Figure 5-15 shows that this image has come a long way, but it may seem that it took a lot of work to get there. In fact, the entire editing process took less than two minutes to accomplish. (I wasn't explaining my reasoning process as I went along.) So I'll offer a similar example, this time concentrating on the physical rather than the mental process. Figure 5-22 shows a well-exposed image that's nevertheless washed-out and flat.

Figure 5-22
A flat image

The image at my default settings for the camera

Option-clicking the Exposure slider shows a scant handful of pixels on the prow of the boat that are clipped in only the red channel. The Exposure value is fine, so I proceed with the quick moves shown in Figure 5-23.

Figure 5-23
A series of quick moves

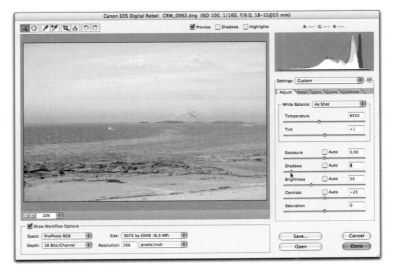

I Option-drag the Shadows slider until I see a hint of clipping.

Figure 5-23
A series of quick moves,
continued

I press Tab until the Brightness field is active, then press Shift-down arrow twice to set Brightness at 30. I press Tab once more to highlight the Contrast field, then press Shift-up arrow to set Contrast to 65.

I press Command-Option-4 to go to the Curve tab. I Command-click on the top of the distant rock to set a curve point, and nudge it with the up arrow key. I press Control-Shift-Tab twice to activate the midtone curve point, and press left arrow three times.

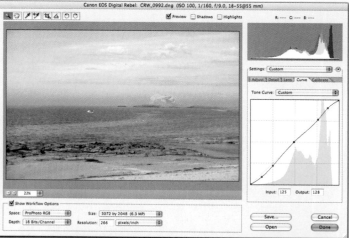

I press Command-Option-1 to return to the Adjust tab, press Tab until the Saturation field is highlighted, then press Shift-up arrow twice to set Saturation to +20.

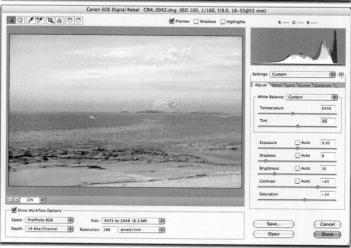

Figure 5-23
A series of quick moves,
continued

*The image is a little
green, so I press Tab
until the Tint field is
highlighted, then I
press the up arrow
key four times to set
the Tint to +5.*

I check for any noise or lens problems at 200% view, but find none, so I press Return to click the Done button. Camera Raw writes the settings into the DNG file and updates Bridge's thumbnail and preview.

Camera Raw navigation. No one, myself included, knows all the keyboard shortcuts built into Photoshop! But I strongly recommend absorbing the following small set of shortcuts for Camera Raw.

▶ Tab advances to the next edit field; Shift-Tab goes to the previous one.

▶ The up and down arrow keys adjust the value in the selected field by the smallest increment (50 Kelvins for Temperature, 1 for everything else). Add Shift to adjust by 10 (or 500 Kelvins for Temperature). The same shortcuts work on curve points in the Curve tab, but you can also use the left and right arrow keys, with or without Shift.

▶ Command-click in the image to set curve points in the Curve tab. Setting points by eyeball and dragging them with the mouse is a very inefficient way to make curve adjustments!

▶ Command-O fits the image in the window. Command-Option-O zooms to 100% (actual pixels) view.

If you master these shortcuts, you'll find that you can power your way through images very quickly indeed. I'll attempt to demonstrate that in the next example.

Fast Camera Raw. Figure 5-24 shows a series of adjustments done in the Adjust tab and the Curve tab. The top image shows the Camera Raw Default settings, the middle one shows the adjustments made in the Adjust tab, and the bottom one shows the adjustments made in the Curve tab. Let's look at these in detail.

The first adjustment, as usual, was to the Exposure slider—I set it to -0.30 to avoid the windows being featureless white blobs by Option-dragging the slider until the clipping went away. Then I pressed Tab to highlight the Brightness field, and Shift-up arrow five times to set the Brightness to 100. I pressed Tab again to highlight the Contrast field, then Shift-up arrow twice to set the Contrast to 55. This proved a little too harsh in the highlights, so I pressed the down arrow key three times, examining the image after each keystroke, until I got a Contrast value of 52, which I accepted.

Next, I adjusted the Temperature slider, pressing Shift-Tab six times to move the focus from the Contrast field to the Temperature field. Shift-up arrow changed the Temperature value from 5250 ot 5750. This left the floor looking distinctly magenta, so I pressed Tab once to get to the Tint field, then pressed Shift-down arrow to reduce the Tint to 5. This looked very slightly green, so I pressed the up arrow key once to increase the Tint value to 6. This completed the Adjust tab work, so I pressed Command-Option-4 to move to the Curve tab.

I started out by brightening the midtones. I pressed Control-Tab four times to highlight the midtone curve point, then Shift-left arrow followed by left arrow five times until I arrived at the adjustment I wanted. To improve the contrast in the dark areas on the bottom of the longship, I pressed Control-Shift-Tab to move to the next lower point on the curve, and nudged it to the left with the left arrow. Then I pressed Control-Shift-Tab again to get to the next lower point on the curve, and nudged it down with the down arrow. This bent the curve too sharply, flattening the contrast, so I added a point by clicking in-between the two points I'd just adjusted. Then I dragged it with the mouse until the curve segment between the two adjacent points was almost straight. (My hand was on the mouse rather than the keyboard, so dragging the curve point made sense.)

The complete set of adjustments took less than a minute, and probably 10 seconds of that time was spent looking at the results of the tweaks and evaluating them before proceeding to the next adjustment.

Figure 5-24
Fast adjustments

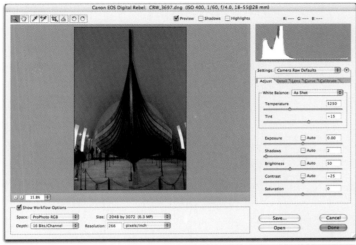

The image at Camera Raw defaults is dark and muddy, but the windows are actually blown out, so the image needs a reduction in Exposure and a big increase in Brightness.

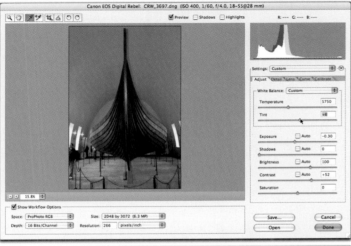

I reduced the Exposure slightly to put detail back in the edges of the windows, increased Brightness to brighten the midtones, then I added Contrast. Finally, I adjusted the Temperature and Tint values.

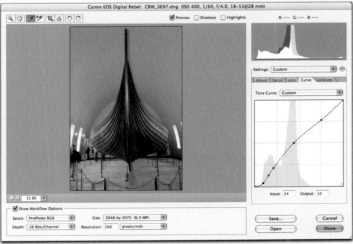

The curve adjustments brightened the midtones a little further, and improved the shadow contrast.

Checking details. Next, I checked for lens and noise problems, and found both. Zooming in to 200% view (by pressing Command-+), I noticed some slight chromatic aberration along the high-contrast edges of the window, along with the luminosity noise I expected from an ISO 400 capture. Figure 5-25 shows the required adjustments.

Camera Raw's Lens tab offers extraordinarily effective corrections for chromatic aberration. They work by resizing the red and blue channels in relation to the green in an intelligent manner. Photoshop's new Lens Correction filter does a reasonably good job on converted images, but it's a little slower, and it's harder to use because it lacks the convenience features mentioned in the two tips that follow this paragraph. Mainly, though, the best place to fix the chromatic aberration is in the raw file, because then every image you derive from the raw has already had the correction applied. I switched to the lens tab by pressing Command-Option-3, and made the chromatic aberration adjustments by Option-dragging the sliders—see the second tip, below.

Tip: Turn Off Sharpening. To see the color fringes clearly and to judge the optimum settings for the sliders, turn off any sharpening you've applied with the Sharpness slider in the Detail tab. The color fringes are usually most prominent along high-contrast edges, and sharpening applies a halo to such edges that makes it harder to see exactly where the color fringes start and end.

Tip: Option-Drag the Sliders to Hide the Other Channel. Red/cyan fringing is usually much easier to see than blue/yellow fringing, but chromatic aberration is almost always a combination of both. Holding down the Option key as you drag either of the Chromatic Aberration sliders hides the channel that isn't being affected by the adjustment, making it much easier to apply exactly the right amount of correction to both channels.

Switching to the Detail tab, I raised the Luminance Smoothing value until the luminance noise had all but disappeared. All noise-reduction technologies present a trade-off between noise reduction and sharpness, and Camera Raw's is no exception. In this case, setting Luminance Smoothing to 25 reduced the noise to the point where it won't appear in prints. To eliminate it completely would have required a considerably higher setting that would likely have done as much harm as good.

Figure 5-25
Checking details

At 200% view, both chromatic aberration and luminosity noise are clearly visible.

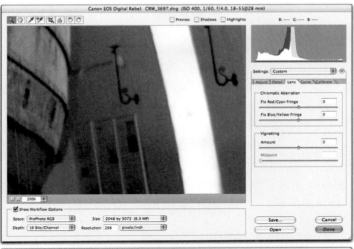

Using the tips on the previous page, I adjusted the chromatic aberration sliders to remove the color fringing.

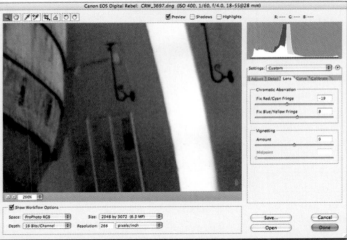

I raised the Luminance Smoothing value to eliminate the noise.

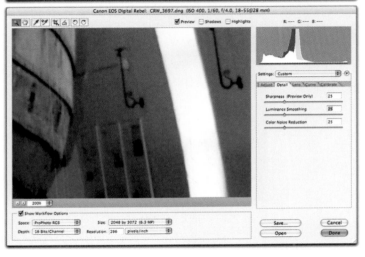

Camera Raw limitations. You can accomplish a great deal in Camera Raw, but one thing you cannot do is selective correction, which this image needs—the mixed-lighting situation leaves the ceiling with an unappetizing yellow-green cast, and there's simply no way to fix that in Camera Raw without breaking something else in the image.

I also prefer to sharpen images in Photoshop rather than using Camera Raw's relatively unsophisticated Sharpness adjustment. Figure 5-26 shows the final image, selectively corrected and sharpened in Photoshop.

Figure 5-26
Checking details

The final image after selective color correction and sharpening in Photoshop. I created a rough selection of the vaulted ceiling using Color Range, refined it by painting in Quick-Mask mode, then I used Hue/Saturation to desaturate the selected area. I used the history brush to put back some color around the light fixtures—masking them would have taken much longer—then I used PhotoKit Sharpener to sharpen the image.

Exposure or Brightness? With the extended range of correction offered by the Brightness control, it may seem that Exposure and Brightness can produce similar results. It's true that either one can produce a superficially similar appearance, but they differ in the way they affect the highlight data, and in the way they influence the behavior of the Contrast slider and the Curve tab. Figure 5-27 shows a dark image that needs some brightening.

Figure5-27
A dark image

This image is dark and muddy, so it needs some brightening.

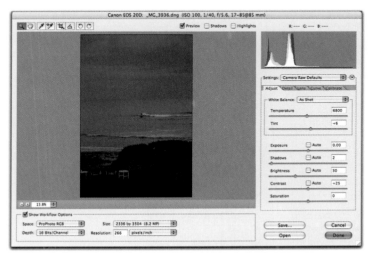

But I shot the image a few minutes after sunset. I want to preserve the subdued light, and convey the impression of the fading day. Camera Raw's Use Auto Adjustment doesn't help—see Figure 5-28.

Figure 5-28
Auto Adjustment

Figure 5-29 shows two superficially similar renderings of the image, but when you look closely you'll see that the slight contrast adjustment (raising Contrast from its default value of 25 to 30) has a very different effect on the two different renderings.

Figure 5-29
Exposure or Brightness?

These two renderings may appear superficially similar, but they differ in an important way.

The upper image has the Exposure set to +1.95 and the Brightness set to zero, so the data-rich highlight region gets stretched, while the midtone is darkened, forcing more bits into the shadows.

The lower image has Exposure set to 0.00 and Brightness set to 110, so the highlight region gets compressed, while the relatively data-poor shadow region gets stretched up into the midtones.

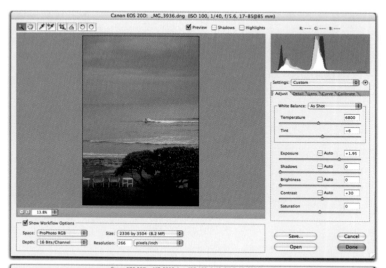

The big difference between the two renderings is the way they distribute the captured bits. In the image adjusted by increasing Exposure and reducing Brightness, the Exposure adjustment stretches all the captured bits to cover a wider tonal range, then the Brightness adjustment darkens the midpoint and forces more bits into the shadows while stretching the highlight range. This is a Good Thing, because as I explained in "Exposure and Linear Capture" back in Chapter 1, *Digital Camera Raw*, digital cameras capture a great deal more information in the highlights than they do in the shadows. In the version with Exposure at 0 and Brightness at 110, the opposite is happening—the data-rich highlight region is compressed, and the data-poor shadow region is stretched, by the Brightness adjustment. As you'll shortly see, this is a Bad Thing!

When I attempt to fine-tune the contrast using the Curve tab, the differences become more obvious. Figure 5-30 shows the highlight detail from both versions with the Curve tab at its default Medium Contrast setting.

Figure 5-30
Highlight detail at Curve tab default setting

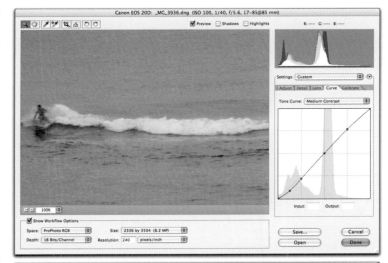

The image adjusted with the Exposure slider, top, has a lot more detail in the waves than the image adjusted with the Brightness slider, bottom.

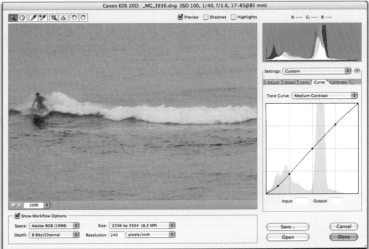

When I attempt to pull detail out of the highlights, I find that it's very easy to do so with the image that had the Exposure adjustment applied, and more or less impossible to do so with the one that had no Exposure adjustment but relied on the Brightness slider instead. The Exposure-adjusted image lets me easily shape the highlights with a couple of curve points, while in the other rendering, the best I can achieve is to change the overall shade of gray—the highlight compression induced by the Brightness move makes it impossible to pull out highlight detail without wrecking the overall contrast. See Figure 5-31.

Figure 5-31
Highlight detail after
curve adjustment

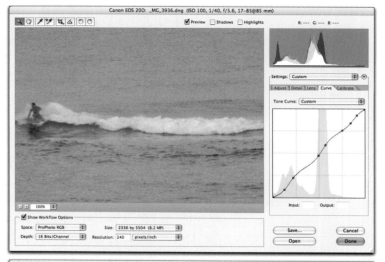

I can extract much more highlight detail from the image adjusted with the Exposure slider, top, than I can from the image adjusted with the Brightness slider, bottom.

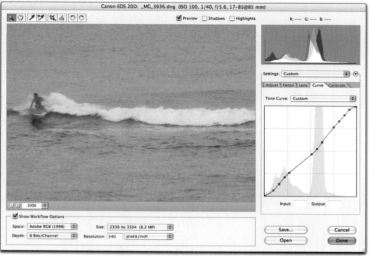

In the shadow range, the difference is, if anything, even greater. The image with the Exposure adjustment shows much more detail, simply because it has more levels describing the shadow values than does the image without the Exposure adjustment. The curve adjustments shown in Figure 5-32 are quite gentle on both images, but on the one without the Exposure adjustment I'm fighting posterization, and there's almost no detail in the grass, on the tree trunks, or in the leaves. Figure 5-33, on the next page, shows the images after the curve adjustments. The image with the Exposure adjustment has much better overall contrast and detail.

Figure 5-32
Shadow detail after
curve adjustment

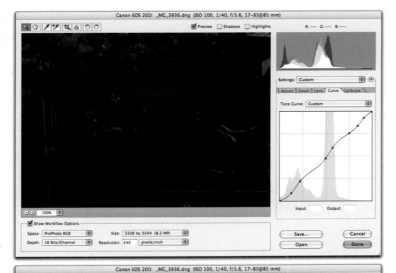

The image adjusted with the Exposure slider, top, preserves detail without pushing the contrast too far. The bottom image, without the Exposure adjustment, is on the verge of posterization.

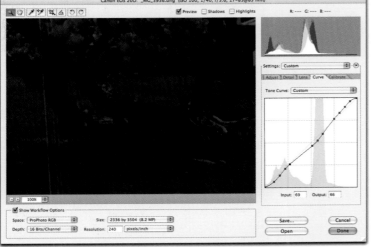

Figure 5-33
The final images

The final renderings of the image. The top image, which has the Exposure adjustment, shows better contrast and detail throughout the tonal range.

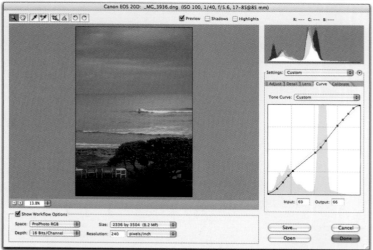

Many different combinations of Camera Raw adjustments can produce superficially similar results, but one combination invariably works better than the others. If this example is puzzling to you, revisit "Exposure and Linear Capture" in Chapter 1, *Digital Camera Raw*, and "Image Editing and Image Degradation" in Chapter 2, *How Camera Raw Works*. The approach that works best is always the one that makes most efficient use of the bits. If you make a practice of thinking about how you're moving the bits around as you operate the Exposure, Shadows, Brightness, and Contrast sliders, and you stretch and squeeze the right tonal ranges, you'll be able to accomplish fine-tuning with the Curve tab very easily.

Creative white balance. Often, we want an accurate white balance. In a studio shoot, probably the easiest way to get one is to include a Macbeth ColorChecker in the first shot, click-balance on the second-to-lightest gray patch, then apply that white balance to all the other images in the shoot—see "Synchronize Settings," later in this chapter, for an easy way to do so. But the white balance controls are also wonderful creative tools. Photoshop's PhotoFilter adjustment lets you approximate the effect of different white balances on converted images, but Camera Raw's white balance tools produce more natural-looking results with less image degradation, so if you want to take liberties with the white balance, Camera Raw is by far the best place to do so.

The image we've been looking at for the past several pages is a good candidate for some radical white balance reinterpretation. The Temperature slider provides the basic adjustment for warming and cooling, while the Tint control operates on the color axis that's perpendicular to the Temperature slider. You can think of Temperature as approximately blue to yellow-orange, and Tint as approximately green to magenta-red. Figure 5-34 shows the image after a significant warming adjustment.

Figure 5-34
A warming adjustment

A radical warming adjustment. This edit entails not only raising the Temperature value from the As Shot value of 6800 to 9500, but also increasing the Tint value from 6 to 30.

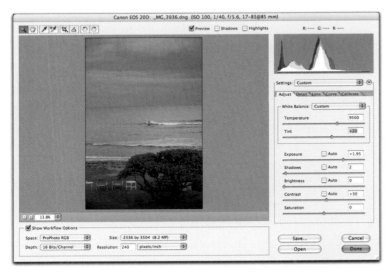

The same image lends itself equally well to a very different, much colder interpretation that appears equally plausible but tells a very different story—see Figure 5-35.

A radical cooling adjustment. I changed the Temperature value from the As Shot value of 6800 to 5500, and increased the Tint value from 6 to 12.

The Calibrate tab. I've already covered the intended use of the Calibrate tab controls—fine-tuning the color rendering for a specific camera—in detail earlier in this chapter. Here I'll look at some creative uses of the controls.

One non-obvious use of the Calibrate tab, which I must credit to Adobe evangelist, raconteur, bon vivant and demomeister Russell Brown, is in color-to-grayscale conversions. Start by reducing the Saturation control in the Adjust tab to -100, and then move to the Calibrate tab. The Hue sliders control the panchromatic response, while the Saturation controls let you modulate the strength of the Hue controls' effect. Figure 5-36 shows examples of different black and white conversions, along with the settings that produced them. Note that the ideal values will vary from camera to camera, but the ones shown here should get you in the ballpark.

These conversions approximate the use of traditional color filters, but you aren't limited to this approach—you can create intermediate settings or make image-specific conversions.

If you're going for natural color, it's probably a bad idea to use the Calibrate controls as selective color correction tools—selective color corrections are better left for Photoshop—but you can certainly use them for creative color effects like the one in Figure 5-37!

Figure 5-36
Color to grayscale

©2002 Jeff Schewe   *Color image*

Starting with the color image, reduce the Saturation slider in the Adjust tab to zero to get a grayscale image, and then adjust the Calibrate controls to vary the panchromatic response.

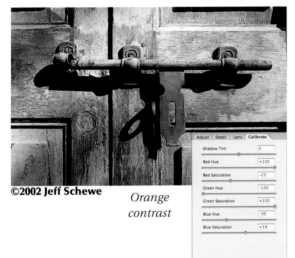

©2002 Jeff Schewe   *Orange contrast*

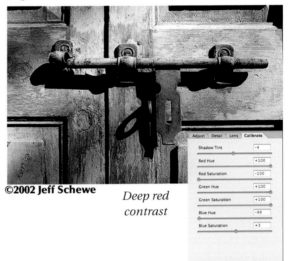

©2002 Jeff Schewe   *Deep red contrast*

©2002 Jeff Schewe   *Green contrast*

©2002 Jeff Schewe   *Blue contrast*

Figure 5-37
Creative Calibrate

The image before (above) and after
some radical Calibrate tab adjustments
(right).

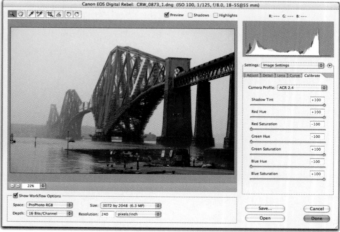

The image before (above) and after
some radical Calibrate tab adjustments
(right).

Filmstrip Mode

If you had to adjust every slider on every image, you might conclude that Camera Raw was an instrument of torture rather than a productivity tool. Fortunately, the combination of Camera Raw, Bridge, and Photoshop offers several ways of editing multiple images. One of these, often the most useful, is built right into Camera Raw itself. When you select multiple images to open, either by selecting them in Bridge or in the File>Open dialog box, Camera Raw opens them in filmstrip mode—see Figure 5-38.

Figure 5-38
Filmstrip mode

When you select multiple raw files to open, Camera Raw presents them in filmstrip mode, with the thumbnails arranged vertically down the left side of the Camera Raw dialog box.

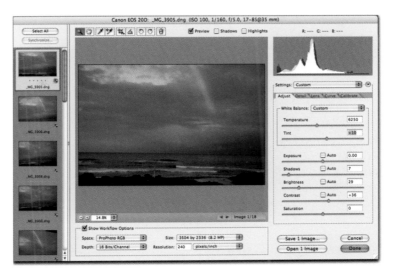

In filmstrip mode, Camera Raw offers a great deal of flexibility when it comes to editing multiple images. You can select all the open images using the Select All button, which makes all your edits apply to all the selected images. You can also select contiguous ranges of images by Shift-clicking, or discontiguous by Command-clicking. When the focus is on the filmstrip, you can navigate through the images using the up and down arrow keys, and select them all by pressing Command-A.

Tip: Match Zoom Percentage. If you want to view the images at a zoom percentage other than Fit in View (the default view), select all the images in the filmstrip, then choose the desired zoom percentage from the zoom menu or using the zoom tool. Then as you navigate through the images, each one is displayed at the zoom percentage you specified.

Synchronize Settings

When you select more than one image, the Synchronize Settings button becomes available. Synchronize Settings lets you apply all the settings or any subset of the settings for the image that's currently being previewed, to all the selected images. Obviously, this feature is of most use when you open a series of images that need similar corrections, but within that general mandate you have a great deal of flexibility in how you choose to work—see Figure 5-39.

Figure 5-39
Synchronizing settings

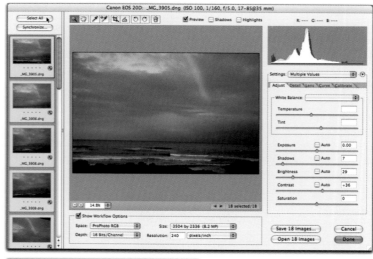

When you select multiple images, the Synchronize Settings button becomes enabled. Clicking it opens the Synchronize Settings dialog box, below.

The Synchronize Settings dialog box lets you apply all the current image's settings, a single setting, or any combination of settings to the selected images. The menu offers a quick way to select commonly used subsets.

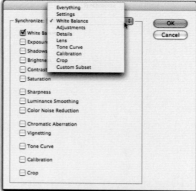

In the above example, I applied the same white balance to all the images in the series—the changing light and the varying amounts of whitecaps require different tonal adjustments. On a different series of images, I may synchronize the tonal adjustments, or the noise reduction, all the settings, or whichever combination of settings is most applicable. A general rule of thumb that works well is to start out by applying the settings that are applicable to the largest number of images, then whittle them down to smaller groups that can take the same corrections.

If you're willing to spend a little extra time planning your corrections, consider sorting the images in Bridge so that images that require identical corrections are grouped in order. That way, you can very quickly zip through large numbers of images, applying general corrections quickly, and doing fine-tuning only on those that require it.

Filmstrip mode also offers a quick way to examine raw images at actual pixels view without performing conversions. And since Camera Raw can be hosted by both Photoshop and Bridge, you can even open two separate Camera Raw sessions, one in Photoshop, one in Bridge, for those times when you need to see two images side-by-side at actual pixels view. It's not a particularly elegant or intuitive solution, and in the longer term I'd much prefer it if Bridge could show images at full resolution, but it's certainly better than nothing.

Saving Images in the Background

One of the major enhancements to Camera Raw 3.0 is the ability to save converted images directly to disk without having to first open them in Photoshop. Notice that when you have x images selected, Camera Raw's Open and Save buttons change to read "Open x images" and "Save x images," respectively. When you click Save x images, the Save Options dialog box appears, as shown in Figure 5-40.

Figure 5-40
Save Options dialog box

The Save Options dialog box lets you specify a location, a naming convention, and a file format for the files you save out of Camera Raw.

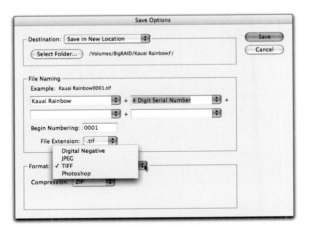

When you click Save, Camera Raw goes to work processing the images. The exact behavior depends on whether Bridge or Photoshop is hosting Camera Raw. When Photoshop hosts Camera Raw, you can continue to work in the Camera Raw dialog box during the save, but if you dismiss it, you'll see the Save Status dialog box shown in Figure 5-41, and you won't be able to do anything else in Photoshop until the save is completed.

Figure 5-41
Camera Raw Save Status
dialog box

*When Camera Raw hosted
by Photoshop is saving
files, you see this status
message.*

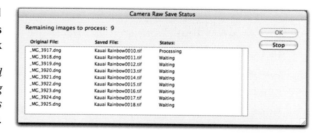

When Bridge hosts Camera Raw, the images are processed in the background. You can continue to work in the Camera Raw window, or you can dismiss it and do other work in a Bridge window (including launching a new Camera Raw session). While Camera Raw hosted by Bridge is saving files in the background, the only status message that appears is in the Camera Raw window itself—see Figure 5-42.

Figure 5-42
**Camera Raw Save
Status message**

*When Camera Raw
hosted by Bridge is
saving files, the only
status message is in the
Camera Raw window
itself, just above the
main control buttons.*

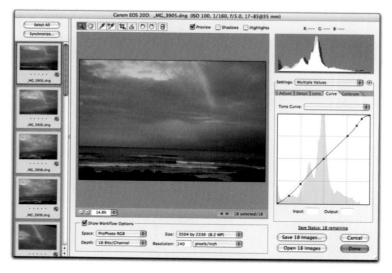

I'll discuss the workflow implications of Camera Raw's saving abilities under both hosts in much greater detail in Chapter 7, *It's All About the Workflow.* For now, I'll simply make the point that Camera Raw 3.0 offers much more workflow flexibility, with many more options, than did its predecessor.

Saving Image Settings

Depending on how you set Camera Raw's "Save image settings in:" Preference, the settings that comprise your edits to an individual image get saved either in the Camera Raw Database, or as individual sidecar .xmp files—see "The Camera Raw Menu," in Chapter 4, *Camera Raw Controls*. (The one exception is that if you use DNG files, the edits are saved inside the DNG file itself.) Each approach has its strengths and weaknesses.

Camera Raw Database

The Camera Raw database (filename is Adobe Camera Raw Database) lives in the Application Data folder as Document and Settings*user name*\Application Data\Adobe\Camera Raw on Windows systems, and in the user's Preferences folder as Users/*user name*/Library/Preferences on Mac OS.

If you want to do absolutely no file management, and you work on only one computer, the advantage of saving settings in the Camera Raw database is that they're indexed by file content rather than name. You can rename your raw images and move them anywhere on your computer, and Camera Raw will still associate the correct settings with each image.

The significant downside is that you then rely on a single file on a single computer to hold all your image settings. If you move the images to a different machine, or even just burn them on a CD, the settings won't travel with the images. So while settings saved in the Camera Raw database are easy to handle in terms of file management on a single machine, they're very inflexible. This inflexibility leads me to always set Camera Raw's Preferences to save my settings as sidecar .xmp files.

Sidecar .xmp Files

Adobe's XMP (Extensible Metadata Platform) is an open, documented, W3C-compliant standard for saving metadata (literally, data about data), including all the EXIF data generated by the camera; IPTC information such as captioning, keywording, and copyright notices; and, last but not least, all the settings you used in Camera Raw on a given image.

When you elect to save image settings as sidecar .xmp files, they're saved in a small file with the same name as the image and a .xmp extension. The sidecar file is automatically saved in the same folder as the image, which is usually what you want.

As you'll learn in the next chapter, Bridge automatically keeps the sidecar files with the raw images as long as you use Bridge to copy or move them. If you use some other software to move or copy your images, it's up to you to keep the sidecar files with the images. Since they're always saved in the same folder as the images, and the filenames match those of the images, this isn't hard to do.

Sometimes, though, it's useful to save multiple settings for the same raw image. It's often useful to combine two or more renderings of the same raw file—for example, you can tailor one rendering for the highlights and another for the shadows to increase the apparent dynamic range, or combine different white balances.

Often this takes some experimentation—the Open a Copy feature offered by Camera Raw hosted in Photoshop lets me tweak the settings and open a copy without burning those settings into the .xmp file or Camera Raw Database, and hence is useful for just this kind of experiment—but once I have settings that work, I generally want to save them. I do so by choosing Save Settings from the Camera Raw menu, adding some distinguishing text to the default "filename.xmp" name for the saved settings, such as "filename_shadows.xmp" and "filename_highlights.xmp," then saving them in the same folder as the raw file.

Figure 5-43 shows an example of combining different tonal mappings. This is an admittedly extreme example, shot almost directly into the sun, but it shows just how much you can accomplish by combining different versions of a single raw image in Photoshop.

Figure 5-44 shows an example of combining different white balances. I wanted to exaggerate the split between the warm highlights and cool shadows, which a single white balance wouldn't let me do. In this example, I did no masking in Photoshop—instead, I simply used the Blend If sliders in the Layer Options dialog box to make sure that the top, warm layer only applied to the highlights in the bottom cool layer, letting the cooler shadows from the bottom layer show through. Combining the two renderings is much quicker and easier than trying to edit a single rendering in Photoshop to produce the same result.

Figure 5-43
**Combining different
tone mappings**

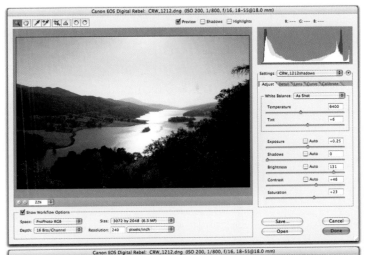

*The image rendered
for the shadows and
midtones*

*The image rendered
for the highlights*

*The renderings
combined as layers in
Photoshop. I loaded the
luminosity mask of the
highlight layer by
Command-clicking
on the RGB tile in the
Channels palette, then
added it to the highlight
layer as a layer mask.
Editing the layer mask
with Levels, and further
lightening the Shadow
layer with Screen
blending produced
this result.*

Figure 5-44
Combining different
white balances

*The image rendered
for the cool shadows*

*The image rendered
for the warm highlights*

*The combined
renderings. In this case
I chose to increase the
difference between the
warm highlights and
cool shadows, but you
can use the same
technique to achieve
the opposite effect.*

Save Settings Subset

When you edit an image, you generally want to save all the settings that apply to that image so that the settings get applied each time you open the raw file. But it's also useful to save and recall subsets of settings to speed editing, hence the Save Settings Subset command on the Camera Raw menu.

For example, if you create Calibrate settings, either for color calibration for different lighting conditions or for black-and-white conversions, it's useful to have them available at all times. You may also wish to save Exposure or White Balance settings, or noise reduction settings for different ISO speeds, so that you can simply choose them from the Settings menu instead of manipulating sliders. The Save Settings Subset command lets you choose exactly which settings you want to save—see Figure 4-18 in Chapter 4, *Camera Raw Controls.*

To make settings subsets constantly available, save them in the Camera Raw Settings folder (that's User/Library/Application Support/Adobe/Camera Raw/Settings (Mac), or Documents and Settings\User\Application Data\Adobe\Camera Raw\Settings (Windows)). Saving settings in the Settings folder is useful for two reasons.

► They appear automatically on Camera Raw's Settings menu, and on Bridge's Apply Camera Raw Settings submenu.

► Each saved setting is represented by a separate file, so when my Settings menu becomes unmanageably long, I can easily prune it by going into the Camera Raw Settings folder and trashing the files I no longer need rather than laboriously selecting each setting and then choosing Delete Current Setting from the Camera Raw menu.

Note that when you choose a settings subset from either of the aforementioned menus, only those settings that are actually saved in the settings file are applied to the image, so you can apply them freely without worrying about them overwriting other settings. If you consistently find yourself making the same setting over and over again, it's probably a good candidate for a preset. But if you save too many settings as presets, your Settings menu becomes unmanageably long. The bottom line is that we each need to arrive at our own ideal trade-off between the convenience of presets and the length of the Settings menu.

Beyond Camera Raw

Camera Raw has evolved into a powerful tool for tweaking and processing raw images, individually or in groups. But if you've just returned from a day's shoot with 700 images, Camera Raw really isn't the place to start. In this chapter, I've focused on the kinds of detailed edits you typically want to make to your selects, but even if you're the world's greatest photographer, it's unlikely that every image from a shoot will deserve this kind of attention.

Moreover, editing the pixel data is only part of the job. Before I open a single image from a shoot, I add metadata. At minimum, I'll add my copyright notice and a few select keywords. Then I go about the business of sorting the wheat from the chaff, and only after I've accomplished these tasks do I start optimizing images. So in the next chapter, we'll look at another key component of the workflow, Bridge.

Adobe Bridge

Your Digital Light Table

When the File Browser first appeared in Photoshop 7, I thought of it as a nice alternative to the File menu's Open command when dealing with a folder full of files, because it let me see thumbnails and previews of the images, letting me identify the ones I wanted quickly. In Photoshop CS, the File Browser became a mission-critical tool for anyone who shoots raw. In Photoshop CS2, the File Browser is replaced by a standalone application, Bridge, which incorporates all of File Browser's capabilities and adds new ones of its own.

You can make your initial selects from a shoot using Bridge as a digital light table. When you want to convert your images, you can host Camera Raw in Bridge, and have it convert images in the background. You can also use Bridge to add and edit metadata—one of the first things I do to a new folder of raw images is to add my copyright notice to each image. And while I admit to being less assiduous than I really should be, I also use Bridge to add keywords to images so that I can find them easily several years hence. See the sidebar "All About Metadata," later in this chapter.

Although it's a version 1.0 application, Bridge is pretty deep. So in this chapter I'll introduce you to its various parts, explain what they do, and show you how to use them to handle your images efficiently. But bear in mind that Bridge serves the entire Adobe Creative Suite, not just Photoshop, so don't expect a comprehensive Bridge reference guide here—I'm only going to talk about the features that apply to a digital raw workflow!

Launching Bridge

When I work on single-monitor systems, I usually keep Bridge hidden unless I'm actually using it. On dual-monitor systems, I keep Bridge open on the second monitor all the time.

The simplest way to launch Bridge is to do so the way you launch any other application on your platform of choice. However, you have the following additional options as shown in Figure 6-1:

▶ Choose Browse from Photoshop's File menu.

▶ Click the Go to Bridge button in the Options bar (it's the icon that looks like a magnifying glass over an open folder).

▶ Check Automatically Launch Bridge in Photoshop's Preferences> General tab—that way, whenever you launch Photoshop, Bridge automatically launches too.

Figure 6-1
Launching Bridge

Choose Browse from the File menu.

Click the File Browser icon in the Options bar.

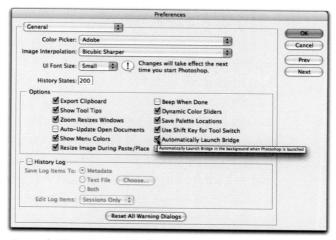

Launch Photoshop with the "Automatically Launch Bridge" Preference checked.

Bridge Windows

Where the File Browser was limited to a single window, in Bridge, you can open as many windows as you like. Each window shows the contents of a folder or volume (subfolders appear as folder icons). Curiously enough (remember that this is a 1.0 application), the windows don't show up on Bridge's Window menu. This makes managing Bridge windows a little complicated.

Arranging Windows

A few tricks can help you manage your Bridge windows.

▶ You can minimize windows to the Dock (Mac) or Taskbar (Windows).

▶ You can set windows to Compact mode.

▶ You can set windows to Ultra-Compact mode.

In Compact and Ultra-Compact modes, Bridge windows by default "float" above full-mode windows, so they're easily available—see Figure 6-2.

Figure 6-2
Bridge window modes

The icons in the upper-right corner of the window let you switch between Full, Compact, and Ultra-Compact window modes.

Full mode

Compact mode

Ultra-Compact mode

Full to Compact

Compact to Ultra-Compact

Ultra-Compact to Compact

Compact to Full

You can cycle through all the open Full-mode windows by pressing Command-~ (tilde) on the Mac and Alt-Tab on Windows, but the shortcut doesn't apply to Compact or Ultra-Compact windows, so it's just as well that they float by default. If the floating behavior annoys you, you can turn it off for individual Compact or Ultra-Compact windows from the flyout menu sported by those window modes, but be warned that doing so can make your Compact and Ultra-Compact-mode windows hard to find—see Figure 6-3.

Figure 6-3
Compact and Ultra-Compact window menu

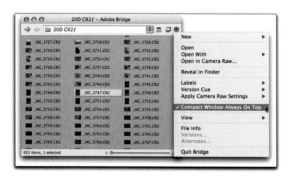

You can toggle between Full and Compact modes by pressing Command-Return (Mac) or Ctrl-Enter (Windows). The shortcut toggles between Full and either Compact or Ultra-Compact modes, depending on which of the compact modes you'd last applied to the window.

Tip: Select to Ensure the Right Window. One curious side effect of the floating compact windows is that Bridge can have multiple windows as the foreground window, and sometimes simply clicking on the one you want to switch from compact to full or vice versa doesn't work. If you select one or more thumbnails in that window, though, the shortcut will apply to that window.

Bridge Window Components

In Full mode, Bridge windows contains seven different areas, two of which, the tools and buttons, and the main window containing the thumbnails, are always visible. The five remaining components—the Folders, Favorites, Preview, Metadata, and Keywords palettes—are resizable and rearrangeable within the palette area at the left of the window—see Figure 6-4.

Figure 6-4
Full window components

Back/Forward buttons

Up One Level button

Unfltered menu

New folder

Rotate buttons

Delete button

Look In menu

Favorites panel tab

Folders panel

Preview panel

Size controls

Keywords panel tab

Metadata panel

Show/Hide panels toggle

Status display

Thumbnail size slider

Content display buttons

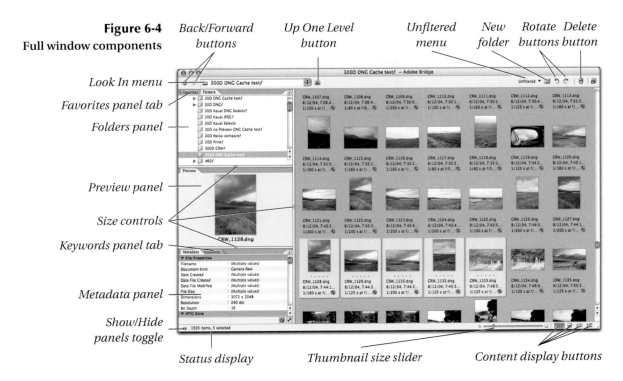

The main window holds thumbnails, which you can display at different sizes. The Folders palette lets you quickly browse through folders and also lets you move or copy files by dragging or Option-dragging their thumbnails to a Folder icon in the Folders palette. The Preview palette shows a preview of the selected image. The Metadata palette shows the metadata associated with the selected image—you can control which fields are displayed. The Keywords palette lets you create keywords and sets of keywords, assign them to images, and perform searches.

Bridge Tools and Buttons

Bridge's tools and buttons are arranged in three logical groups. The navigation controls are at the upper left of the window, the content controls are at the upper right, and the display controls are at the lower right.

Navigation controls. The Back/Forward buttons work like those in Web browsers, letting you move backward and forward through recently visited folders. The Look In menu shows the current folder and its path, the number of recently visited folders specified in Bridge's Preferences, and folders or volumes added to the Favorites list using the File>Add Folder to Favorites command or by dragging into the Favorites panel—see Figure 6-5. The Up One Level button lets you navigate upward through the folder hierarchy.

Figure 6-5
Bridge Look In menu

Content controls. The content controls are a somewhat loose logical grouping, but they all affect the main window content in some way. The Unfiltered/Filtered menu lets you choose which thumbnails are displayed based on their rank or label (but not both)—see Figure 6-6. I'll discuss using ranks and labels later in this chapter.

Figure 6-6
Bridge Unfiltered menu

The New Folder icon lets you create a new folder inside the folder you're currently browsing (you can do the same by pressing Command-Shift-N). The rotate left and rotate right tools (keyboard shortcuts are Command-[and Command-], respectively) rotate the selected thumbnails and previews, and instruct Camera Raw to apply the rotation to the raw file on open. The Trash icon (keyboard shortcut is Delete key) moves selected items to the Trash/Recycle Bin, but doesn't actually empty it.

Display controls. The thumbnail size slider lets you control the size at which Bridge's thumbnails are displayed, with the long side at a minimum of 16 pixels to a maximum of 512 pixels. The remaining buttons let you switch quickly between Thumbnails view, Filmstrip view, Details view, and for VersionCue users, Versions and Alternates view. VersionCue is outside the scope of this book and isn't readily applicable to a raw digital workflow.

Note that the view buttons apply only to the main window that shows the image thumbnails. They have no effect on the palettes—if the palettes are visible, switching views keeps the palettes visible, and if they're hidden, switching views keeps them hidden. Figure 6-7 shows the Thumbnails, Filmstrip, and Details views with the palettes hidden.

Figure 6-7
Bridge views

Thumbnails view shows the image thumbnails with up to three lines of additional metadata.

Filmstrip view shows the image thumbnails arranged along the bottom of the window with a large preview of the selected image displayed above.

Figure 6-7
Bridge views,
continued

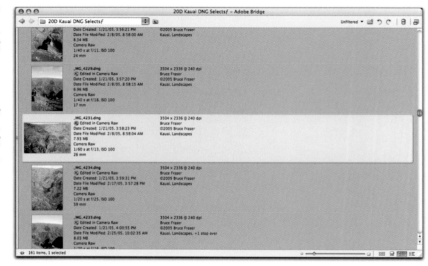

*Details view shows the
thumbnails as a list,
along with additional
metadata.*

If you're like me, you'll find that none of these views is quite what you
need at any given moment. Rest assured that Bridge is very tweakable—see
"The Window Menu and Bridge Configuration," later in this chapter.

Bridge Palettes

The Bridge Main window that holds the thumbnails lets you do a great deal
of your work, but the other palettes are useful for specialized tasks. The
Folders and Favorites palettes are primarily navigation aids, the Metadata
and Keywords palettes let you apply and edit metadata, and the Preview
palette offers a larger preview than the thumbnails at maximum size. Let's
look at them individually.

The Folders palette. The Folders palette displays the volume and folder
hierarchy, allowing you to navigate to different folders—see Figure 6-8. You
can navigate up and down the folders list using the up and down arrow
keys, and you can collapse and expand volumes or folders that contain
subfolders using the left and right arrow keys. Command-up arrow moves
you up to the next level in the folder hierarchy. The palette menu contains
but one command, Refresh.

The Favorites palette. As its name suggests, the Favorites palette is a handy
place for storing things that you often want to return to in a Bridge window.
In addition to actual volumes and folders, the Favorites palette can hold Col-

Figure 6-8
The Folders palette

lections, which are saved search criteria that act as "virtual" folders. It also contains an icon for Photoshop CS2. Clicking it transfers you to Photoshop CS2, launching it if it isn't already running. You can configure the preset items from Bridge's Preferences (see "Bridge Menu Commands," later in this chapter), and you can add items to it by dragging or by menu command. The Favorites palette has no menu of its own—see Figure 6-9.

Figure 6-9
The Favorites palette

The Preview palette. The Preview palette displays a preview for the selected image. Like the other palettes, you can collapse it by double-clicking on its tab and resize it by dragging its size controls, but it has no menu and no secrets.

The Metadata palette. The Metadata palette (see Figure 6-10) displays the metadata associated with the currently selected image or images (see the sidebar "All About Metadata, later in this chapter). When you have more than one image selected, many of the fields read "Multiple Values Exist."

Metadata fields that are editable appear in the palette with a pencil icon next to the title. To edit these fields, select the images or images whose metadata you wish to edit, and then either click the pencil icon or click directly in the text area to enter the new metadata. To confirm entries, click the Apply checkbox at the palette's lower-right corner, or press Enter (Mac) or Alt-Enter (Windows). The only IPTC field that isn't editable here is the Keywords field—to edit keywords, you need to use the Keywords palette.

Figure 6-10
The Metadata palette

The Metadata palette menu lets you launch a search using the Find command (press Command-F), which is replicated in Bridge's Edit menu; increase or decrease the font size used in the palette; and append or replace metadata from saved templates, which appear in the menu (see "File Info and the File Menu," later in this chapter). The Preferences command takes you directly to the Metadata panel of Bridge's Preferences (see "Bridge Menu Commands," later in this chapter). It's definitely worth taking the few minutes needed to decide which fields you want to display—very few Photoshop users need to see them all!

The Metadata palette contains two separate sets of IPTC (International Press Telecommunications Council) metadata. The older IIM (Information Interchange Model) set is there for compatibility with legacy images—it has been superseded by the new IPTC Core schema for XMP metadata. You can find out more about the IPTC standards at www.iptc.org. I'll discuss advanced handling of metadata in Chapter 8, *Mastering Metadata*.

The Keywords palette. The Keywords palette lets you create keywords (which you can group into categories called *keyword sets*), and apply them to a selected image or images. The keywords get written into the Keywords field of the IPTC metadata, so they're visible in the Metadata palette—you just can't edit or apply them there.

Keyword sets appear as folders—the triangle to the left lets you expand and collapse them. When they're expanded, you can see the list of keywords in the set (see Figure 6-11). To apply a keyword to selected images, click in the column at the left of the palette—a checkmark appears, indicating that the selected images contain this keyword. To apply all the keywords in a set, click beside the set name rather than beside the individual keyword. Icons at the bottom of the palette let you create a new keyword set or keyword, or delete an existing keyword set or keyword. Deleting keywords removes them only from the list, not from any files that contain them. You can also move keywords to a different set by dragging.

All About Metadata

Metadata (which literally means "data about data") isn't a new thing. Photoshop's File Info dialog box has allowed you to add metadata such as captions, copyright info, and routing or handling instructions, for years. But digital capture brings a much richer set of metadata to the table.

Most current cameras adhere to the EXIF (Exchangeable Image File Format) standard, which supplies with each image a great deal of information on how it was captured, including the camera model, the specific camera body, shutter speed, aperture, focal length, flash setting, and of course the date and time.

IPTC (International Press Telecommunications Council) metadata has long been supported by Photoshop's File Info feature, allowing copyright notices and the like. Other types of metadata supported by Photoshop CS include GPS information from GPS-enabled cameras (it's immensely cool that my good

friend Stephen Johnson's stunning landscape images include GPS metadata that will allow people to identify where they were shot 10 or 100 years from now, and note how the landscape has changed). You apply Camera Raw settings as metadata to instruct Photoshop how you want the image to be processed before actually doing the conversion. You can even record every Photoshop operation applied to the image as metadata using the History Log feature.

Adobe has been assiduous in promoting XMP (eXtensible Metadata Platform), an open, extensible, W3C-compliant standard for storing and exchanging metadata—all the Creative Suite applications use XMP, and because XMP is extensible, it's relatively easy to update existing metadata schemes to be XMP-compliant. However, it will probably take some time before all the other applications that use metadata, such as third-party digital raw converters, get

updated to handle XMP. But let's be very clear: XMP is not some proprietary Adobe initiative. It's an open, XML-based standard. So if you find that another application is failing to read XMP metadata, contact the publisher and tell them you need them to get with the program!

Right now, unless you're a programmer or a very serious scripting wonk, there may not be a great deal you can do with much of the metadata, at least, not automatically; but it likely won't be too long before you start seeing things like camera-specific sharpening routines that vary their noise reduction with ISO value and exposure time, to give just one example. The more information you have about an image, the better your chances of being able to do useful things to it automatically; and the more things you can do automatically, the more time you can spend doing those things that only a human can do, like exercising creative judgment.

Figure 6-11
The Keywords palette

The Keywords palette menu commands mostly replicate the functions of the control buttons, but the Rename command provides the sole path for renaming keywords or categories, and the Find command, which is only enabled when a keyword is selected, takes you to Bridge's Find dialog box with the selected keyword already loaded in the search criteria.

Bridge Menu Commands

Bridge serves not only Photoshop but the entire Creative Suite, so a good many of its menu commands aren't relevant to a digital raw workflow. Moreover, many of the menu commands offer relatively inefficient ways to accomplish tasks that can be performed more easily by other means. So rather than giving a blow-by-blow description of every single menu command, I'll give you an overview of the menus, along with details about the commands I find particularly useful and/or interesting.

Preferences and the Bridge Menu (Mac)

The Bridge menu, which is found only in the Mac version of Bridge, really contains only one important command, Preferences (press Command-K). The Camera Raw Preferences command that also appears on the Bridge menu simply replicates the one on Camera Raw's own menu (see "The Camera Raw Menu" in Chapter 4, *Camera Raw Controls*). On Windows, these commands are on the Edit menu.) Bridge's Preferences dialog box contains six different panels, each governing a different aspect of Bridge's behavior—see Figure 6-12.

Figure 6-12
Bridge Preferences,
General

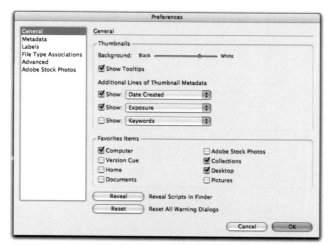

General Preferences. The controls in this panel let you set the shade of gray for the background on which thumbnails are displayed, hide or show tooltips, and specify up to three additional lines of metadata that are displayed under the thumbnail along with the filename. It also lets you specify items that always appear in the Favorites panel, and offers two control buttons, one of which reveals scripts in the Finder (Mac) or Explorer (Windows).

Metadata Preferences. These options let you specify which metadata fields are displayed on the Metadata palette. If you don't have a GPS-enabled camera, for example, you may as well hide all the GPS fields. This panel also offers the option to hide fields that are empty for the selected image or images automatically—see Figure 6-13.

Figure 6-13
Bridge Preferences,
Metadata

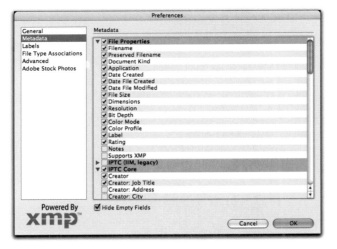

Labels Preferences. These options let you associate text labels with the label colors (you can't change the colors) to something more useful than the color names. The label text is searchable in Bridge, and can be displayed both in the Metadata palette and as an additional line of metadata accompanying the thumbnails if you choose that option in the General Preferences tab. If you change the label text in Preferences, images that have previously had labels applied lose the label color—it turns white—but the label text remains part of the image's metadata. See Figure 6-14.

Figure 6-14
Bridge Preferences,
Labels

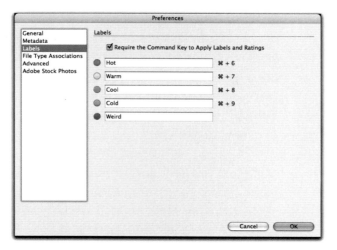

File Type Association Preferences. These options let you specify the default application for opening files from Bridge. It applies only to the behavior you get when opening files from Bridge, and has no effect on how files open from the Macintosh Finder or Windows Explorer—see Figure 6-15.

Figure 6-15
Bridge Preferences,
File Type Associations

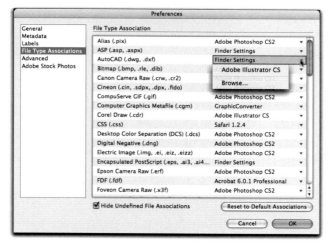

Advanced Preferences. This panel contains several unrelated but nevertheless important items. The Miscellaneous preferences are largely self-explanatory, with the exception of "Double-click edits Camera Raw settings in Bridge." When this preference is unchecked, which it is by default, double-clicking a raw's thumbnail opens it in Camera Raw hosted by Photoshop. When it's checked, doing the same thing opens the raw image in Camera Raw hosted by Bridge. This preference works as advertised, but has a non-obvious impact on some other file-opening keyboard shortcuts—see "Opening Images," later in this chapter. The other important setting in this panel is the choice of whether to use centralized or distributed cache files—see Figure 6-16.

Figure 6-16
Bridge Preferences,
Advanced

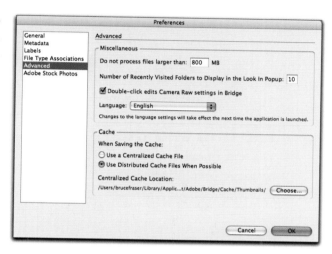

Bridge's cache holds the image thumbnails and previews, custom sort order, and, for file types that can't store metadata either in the file itself or in a sidecar .xmp file, label and rating information. For raw files, only the thumbnails, previews, and custom sort order are stored uniquely in the Bridge cache, but since the thumbnails and previews take some time to generate, they're pretty important.

The only advantage offered by using a centralized cache is simplicity—you know where all your cache files are. The significant disadvantages of the centralized cache are:

▶ If you move or rename a folder outside Bridge, the connection to the cache files is lost.

▶ When you burn a folder full of images to a CD or DVD, you first have to go through the extra step of exporting the cache. If you don't, the recipient of the CD or DVD will have to take the time to recache the folder, rebuilding thumbnails and previews, and any custom sort order will be lost.

Using a distributed cache avoids both problems. The cache files are written directly into the folder to which they pertain, and travel with the folder even when it's renamed or moved. Note, however, that if Bridge for some reason can't write a distributed cache (the volume may be read-only, or mounted on a server) it writes to the central cache instead.

The only real downside to using distributed caches is that every folder that Bridge has opened winds up containing two files named Adobe Bridge Cache.bc and Adobe Bridge Cache.bct. By default, Bridge hides these files, but the Macintosh Finder and Windows Explorer do not. I find that it's well worth suffering this small inconvenience to obtain the benefits of distributed caching, and besides, it's often useful to be able to see the cache files so that you can check that they're present and up-to-date.

File Info and the File Menu

The bulk of the commands on the File menu let you do things that are better accomplished via keyboard shortcuts—opening images, creating new windows, and so on. See Figure 6-17.

Figure 6-17
Bridge File menu

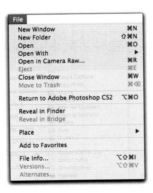

In the case of raw images, the subtle difference between "Open" (Command-O) and "Open in Camera Raw" (Command-R) is that the former opens the raw image or images in Camera Raw hosted by Photoshop, while the latter opens the raw image or images in Camera Raw hosted by Bridge. There are several easier ways to open images than choosing the menu commands, including the aforementioned keyboard shortcuts. I'll discuss these in "Opening Images," later in this chapter. I'll discuss the workflow implications of which application hosts Camera Raw in Chapter 7, *It's All About the Workflow.*

Most of the other commands are self-explanatory. However, the File Info command, which opens the File Info panel, deserves a closer look—see Figure 6-18.

Figure 6-18
Bridge File Info

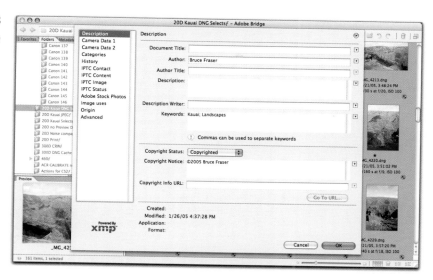

The first thing you'll notice when you open File Info in Bridge is that it's a modal panel (not a movable modal dialog box) that helpfully covers all the images. I find that this behavior makes File Info less useful than it could be!

While Bridge allows you to open File Info when multiple images are selected (the old File Browser did not), it's a relatively inefficient way to apply keywords and other metadata when compared to the Metadata and Keywords palettes. I use it to do three things:

▶ To add image-specific keywords that I don't want to save in a keyword set to small numbers of images.

▶ To examine metadata in something close to raw form—for example, to see exactly how the camera encodes things like shutter speed and aperture value, or the date and time shot—by looking in the Advanced panel of File Info under EXIF Properties.

▶ To save Metadata Templates that I can apply from the Metadata palette menu—see Figure 6-19.

To save a Metadata template, make the entries you want the template to contain in File Info, then choose Save Metadata Template from the File Info panel's flyout menu. This template applies the copyright flag and notice.

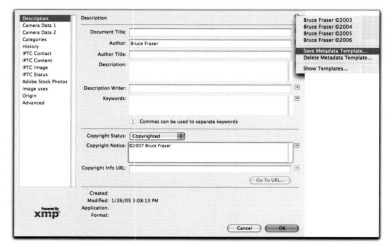

I'll discuss metadata, the File Info panel, and Metadata templates in much more detail in Chapter 8, *Mastering Metadata.*

Select, Find, and Edit with the Edit Menu

The Edit menu hosts Bridge's Preferences command on Windows, and offers the same functionality as the Mac version does on the Bridge menu. It also hosts the usual Copy, Paste, Cut, and Duplicate commands, as well as the Rotate commands whose functionality is replicated by Bridge's Rotate buttons. The important commands for the raw workflow are the various Select commands, the Find command, and the Apply Camera Raw Settings commands—see Figure 6-20.

Figure 6-20
The Edit menu

Selection commands

Find command

Apply Camera Raw Settings command

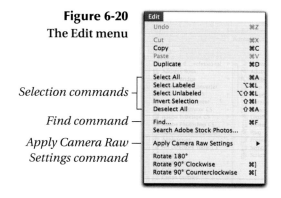

Let's look at these in turn.

The Select Commands. The Select commands offer quick ways to manipulate selections. Select All (press Command-A), Deselect All (press Command-Shift-A) and Invert Selection (press Command-Shift-I) do exactly what they say—Invert Selection deselects the files that were selected and selects those that weren't. The two remaining commands, Select Labeled and Select Unlabeled (press Command-Option-L and Command-Option-Shift-L, respectively), work in conjunction with Bridge's Label feature, which lets you apply one of five labels, or no label, to images. See "Labeling, Rating, and the Label Menu," later in this chapter.

The Find Command. The Find command lets you perform searches using up to 13 different search criteria—see Figure 6-21.

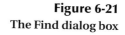
Figure 6-21
The Find dialog box

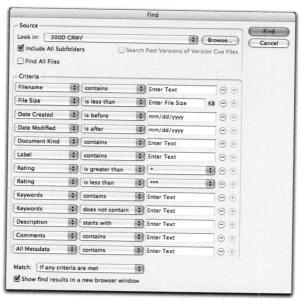

The Find command is undeniably powerful, but some of the things it lacks serve to remind us that Bridge is a version 1.0 application. For example, the "All Metadata" criterion does let you search on EXIF metadata or Camera Raw settings, but only up to a point. You can only search for values; you can't specify the metadata field to which they belong. That means you have to be very aware of exactly how the metadata is expressed. For example, searching for "300 mm" finds all my images shot at 300 mm focal length, but excludes images shot with my 28-300mm lens because the lens is expressed as "28.0–300.0 mm." Likewise, searching for "f/8" will find all images shot at f8. But there's no easy way to find all images shot at ISO 400—if you search on All Metadata contains "400" you'll find all your ISO 400 images, but also all images shot at 1/400 second, and all images with a white balance of 4000K.

Of course, there are workarounds. Figure 6-22 shows search criteria that will find ISO 400 images while excluding those shot at 1/400 second and those with a 4000K white balance. (Of course, this will also find all images whose keywords contain the string "400.")

Figure 6-22
Finding ISO 400 images

*These search criteria
find all images whose
metadata contains
the string "400", while
excluding those whose
metadata contains
"1/400" or "4000."*

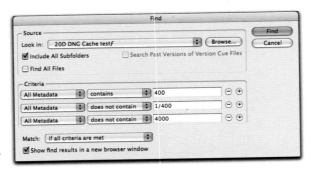

Even this search isn't perfect. It finds all ISO 400 images, but in my case it also finds an ISO 100 image shot at 1/250 second at f13, because my Canon EOS 20D recorded the aperture value in the EXIF data as "7400879/1000000." The bottom line is that if you plan to use metadata searches, you'll need to become quite familiar with the *exact* contents of the metadata—see Chapter 8, *Mastering Metadata*, for a much deeper discussion of working with metadata. (Unless it got fixed at the last minute, the online help indicates that you can use * as a wildcard character in search criteria. It's wishful thinking—you can't!) In addition to the criteria, the Find dialog box has the following important features.

► **Include All Subfolders** does what it says—it extends the search to include any subfolders in the folder specified in the Look In menu.

► **Find All Files** also does what it says (when you check this option, the selection criteria are grayed out). This feature is mostly useful in conjunction with the "Show find results in a new browser window" option when you've done a lot of work winnowing down files using ratings and labels, and you want to see all the images quickly in a new window.

▶ **The Match menu** lets you choose whether to find files if any criterion is met (equivalent to putting "or" between the criteria), or to find files only if all criteria are met (equivalent to putting "and" between the criteria).

▶ **Show find results in new browser window** also does what it says.

Save As Collection. When you perform a search, you have the option to save the search criteria as a collection. The slightly confusing element is that the option doesn't appear in the Find dialog, but rather in the results window—see Figure 6-23.

Figure 6-23
Save As Collection

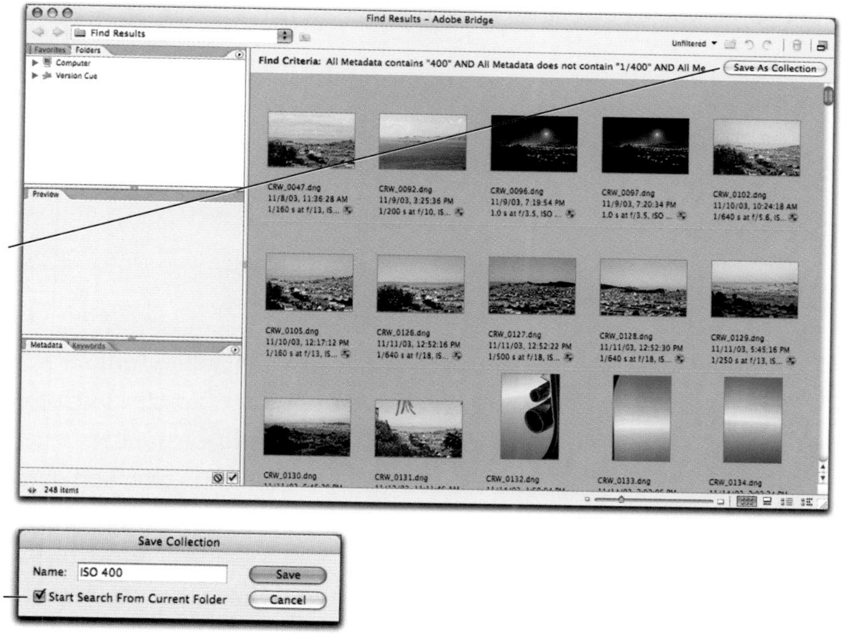

To save search criteria as a collection, click the Save As Collection button.

Check here if you want to apply the search to any folder. Leave unchecked if you always want to search the same folder.

When you save a collection, you can save it as an "absolute" search or a "relative" search. Absolute searches always search the folder you specified in the Find dialog box's Look In menu when you did the initial search that created the collection, while relative searches can be applied to any folder. Checking "Start Search From Current Folder" in the Save Collection dialog box creates a relative search; leaving it unchecked creates an absolute one. Collections are saved in User/Library/Application Support/Adobe/Bridge/Collections (Mac) or Documents and Settings\Username\Application Data\Adobe\Bridge\Collections (Windows).

If you enabled the Preference that displays Collections in the Favorites panel, you can navigate quickly to the Collections folder by clicking Collections in the Favorites panel. You'll see all your saved collections in the folder—see Figure 6-24.

Figure 6-24
Saved Collections

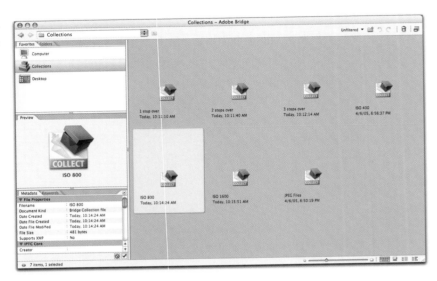

You can start absolute searches (ones that start from the folder used to create the collection) by double-clicking a collection in the folder. (If you start a search this way, it doesn't matter whether the "Start Search From Current Folder" checkbox was checked or unchecked when you saved the collection—the search always applies to the folder that was specified when you created the collection.) Applying the search to a different folder is a little trickier, and is only possible if you saved the collection with the "Start Search From Current Folder" checkbox checked.

First, drag the collection you want to use to the Favorites panel, then navigate to the folder to which you want the search to apply. Then, to start the search, single-click on the collection icon in the Favorites panel—see Figure 6-25.

The search is performed on the folder you selected in the Folders panel, including subfolders if you chose that option for the initial search that created the collection, and using the search criteria you specified when you created the collection. The results appear in the same window or in a new Bridge window depending on whether "Show find results in a new browser window" was checked or unchecked when you created the collection.

Figure 6-25
Searching a
different folder

Click the collection's
icon in the Favorites
panel to start a search
on the current folder
using the criteria saved
in the collection.

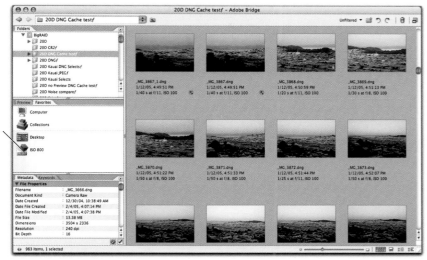

When the search results are displayed, a line of text showing the search criteria and the folder searched appears at the top of the window, but since it doesn't wrap, you often can't see most of it. The Edit Collection button lets you edit the search criteria—bear in mind that you're actually editing the collection itself, so any changes you make will be permanent—see Figure 6-26.

Figure 6-26
Search results

Search criteria

Edit Collection button

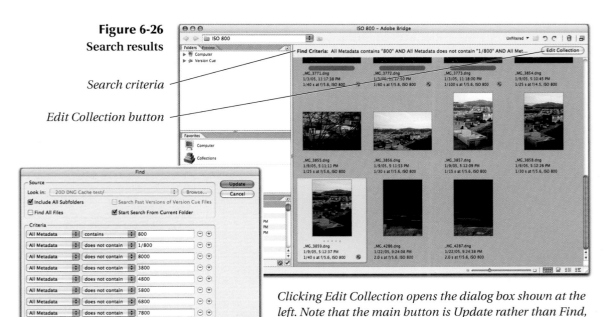

Clicking Edit Collection opens the dialog box shown at the left. Note that the main button is Update rather than Find, and the dialog box includes the "Start Search From Current Folder" checkbox.

Apply Camera Raw Settings. The Apply Camera Raw Settings submenu lets you apply Camera Raw Defaults or Previous Conversion (the last-used Camera Raw settings) to selected images. It also lets you copy settings from an image and apply them to others by pasting, or clear existing settings from an image. Finally, it lets you apply any saved settings that you've saved in Camera Raw's Settings folder (see "Loading and Saving Settings" in Chapter 4, *Camera Raw Controls*). Figure 6-27 shows the Apply Camera Raw Settings submenu.

Figure 6-27
Apply Camera
Raw Settings

Saved custom settings
appear at the foot of the
Apply Camera Raw
Settings submenu.

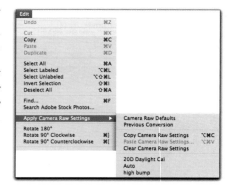

You may wonder what the difference is between applying Camera Raw defaults and clearing Camera Raw settings. The effect on the image is identical in both cases, but Bridge offers a useful piece of feedback that shows whether or not an image has settings applied to it—see Figure 6-28. When you apply Camera Raw defaults, Bridge treats the image as having had settings applied; when you clear the settings, Bridge treats the image as having no settings applied.

Figure 6-28
Apply Camera Raw
Defaults and Clear
Camera Raw Settings

When you choose Apply Camera Raw
Defaults, Bridge indicates that the
image has settings applied.

When you choose Clear Camera Raw
Settings, Bridge indicates that the
image has no settings applied.

The Copy Camera Raw Settings command (Command-Option-C) copies all the Camera Raw settings from the selected image. When you choose Paste Camera Raw Settings (Command-Option-V), the dialog box shown in Figure 6-29 appears, giving you the opportunity to choose all the settings, any individual parameter, or everything in between, to apply to the image or images to which you're pasting the settings.

Figure 6-29
Paste Camera
Raw Settings

The checkboxes let you apply individual settings; the menu lets you choose a group of settings quickly.

The ability to apply Camera Raw settings by pasting to multiple images offers an alternative to working directly in Camera Raw in filmstrip mode. I'll discuss the workflow implications of each approach in detail in Chapter 7, *It's All About the Workflow*.

Automation, the Cache, and the Tools Menu

The Tools menu provides access to several useful Photoshop-hosted automation features as well as Bridge's own Batch Rename, allows you to work with Bridge's cache files, and provides an alternative means of applying metadata templates if you don't want to use the Metadata palette menu—see Figure 6-30.

Figure 6-30
The Tools menu

Batch Rename. Bridge's Batch Rename feature looks nothing like Photoshop's, though it offers essentially the same functionality—see Figure 6-31. The inclusion of EXIF Metadata as a naming component is intriguing, but the potentially most-useful piece of metadata, Date Time Digitized, should be treated with some caution. The option looks in the metadata for DateTimeOriginal. If it's not present, it looks for DateTimeDigitized. If that too is not present, the feature uses the IPTC DateCreated property. It's possible for these three dates and times to be different, so test this option carefully and make sure you understand its behavior with your raw files before using it on live jobs—see Chapter 8, *Mastering Metadata*, for further discussion.

Figure 6-31
Batch Rename

Batch Rename offers options to rename images in place, rename and move to a different folder, or make renamed copies in a different folder.

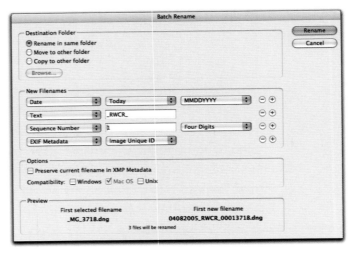

The option to preserve the current filename in XMP metadata actually adds a custom metadata tag containing the filename. If you've already applied Camera Raw settings before renaming, you can skip this option because the Camera Raw settings metadata already contains the original filename, but if you're renaming otherwise-untouched raw files, and you want the original filename to be retrievable, it's a good idea to check this option.

Tip: Undoing Renaming. One of the useful things that the aforementioned "Preserve current filename in XMP Metadata" option allows is easy undoing of batch renaming. Simply choose Batch Rename, and specify Preserved Filename. Your files will get renamed to their original filenames.

You can add up to 10 different sets of data for inclusion in the filename. Figure 6-32 shows an "exploded" view of the menus with all the possible choices.

Figure 6-32
Renaming options

This figure shows all the renaming options from the expanded menus. You can combine up to ten of these.

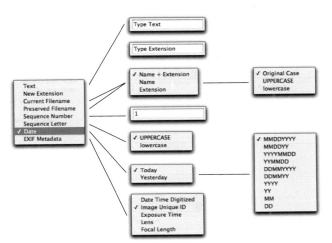

Since Bridge is eminently javascriptable, you can expect to see a variety of useful image-ingestion scripts, possibly including some from Adobe, that will likely include more flexible metadata-based renaming features, but Bridge's Batch Rename at least provides baseline functionality out of the box.

Photoshop. The Photoshop submenu (see Figure 6-33) provides access to several useful Photoshop automation features. If you want to run any of these automations using images selected in Bridge as the source, you *must* launch them from Bridge's Tools menu—if you try to launch them from Photoshop's File>Automate menu instead, you'll find that Bridge is either grayed out or simply unavailable as the source.

Figure 6-33
The Photoshop submenu

I'll discuss these features in much more detail in Chapter 9, *Exploiting Automation*, but here's an overview.

► **Batch** is the basic Photoshop automation feature. It lets you open images, run a Photoshop Action on them, and save them—in the case of raw files, you can't save over the original—while optionally renaming the files.

► **Contact Sheet II** lets you build simple but effective contact sheets from selected images. (If you also own InDesign, you can build fancier ones from Bridge using InDesign.)

► **Image Processor** is really Son of Dr. Brown's Image Processor. It differs from Batch in one important capability—it lets you save multiple versions of images, such as a full-resolution TIFF and a downsampled JPEG, each in its own folder, without writing insanely complicated actions.

► **Merge to HDR** lets you merge bracketed exposures of the same scene into a High-Dynamic-Range (HDR), 32-bit floating-point-per-channel image. HDR imaging is a brand-new feature in Photoshop CS2 that allows over-range encoding and hence preserves highlights that are brighter than pure white, often referred to as "overbrights." It has been primarily used in the movie industry, but its introduction in Photoshop may bring it more into the photographic mainstream. To use this feature successfully, my experience suggests that you'll benefit from a heavy tripod, a cable release, and mirror lockup if you want sharp HDR images.

► **PDF Presentation** lets you create either a multipage PDF with one image per page, or a PDF slideshow that's readable by anyone with the free Adobe Acrobat Reader. For slideshows, you can use any one of Acrobat's built-in transitions, but you can't add audio unless you edit the slide show in Acrobat.

► **Photomerge** is Photoshop's stitching routine for creating panoramas from a series of images.

► **Picture Package** lets you create a single page containing multiple versions of the same image, such as you typically get from a portrait studio. You can use one of the preset layouts, or edit a preset to create your own custom layout.

▶ **Web Photo Gallery** lets you build simple or not-so-simple Web galleries of selected images using one of 20 preset layouts. If you're comfortable editing HTML code you can edit the templates to customize them.

For all these automation features, the procedure for invoking them from Bridge is the same. You select the images you want processed through the automation, then choose that automation from the Tools>Photoshop submenu. Photoshop then goes to work, opening the images using the Camera Raw settings you've applied, or the camera-specific default settings if you haven't applied settings to the image, then processing them using the settings you've specified for the automation. You can continue to work in Bridge while Photoshop is processing the images.

Labeling, Rating, and the Label Menu

The Label menu offers a not-particularly-efficient alternative to the keyboard shortcuts for applying labels or ratings to your images (see Figure 6-34. The only things you can do from this menu that you can't do with keyboard shortcuts are to remove a label, or to apply the fifth label, which by default is called Purple, (though you can change the text but not the color in Bridge's Preferences). See "Labels Preferences," earlier in this chapter.

Figure 6-34
The Label menu

Labels and ratings are entirely separate. Labels apply the selected label color to the image thumbnail's label area, and write the label text into the image's metadata (in the Label field under File Properties). Ratings apply zero to five stars to the image thumbnail's rating area, and write the rating (from one to five) into the image's metadata (in the Rating field under File Properties). See Figure 6-35.

Figure 6-35
Labels and ratings

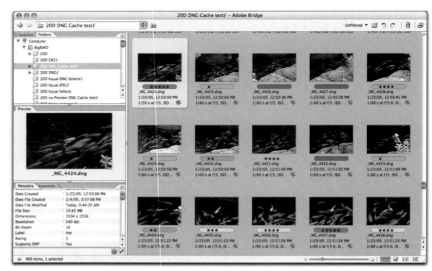

Labels appear as colored swatches beneath the thumbnails. Ratings appear as stars in the label area. Both the label text and the rating appear in the File Properties metadata.

You can search images by label and by rating, and sort images by label *or* by rating. Last but not least, you can use the Unfiltered/Filtered menu (on Bridge's tool bar, not on the menu bar) to filter which images are displayed in the Bridge window based on label, on rating, or by doing first one, then the other, on both.

Labels and ratings are simply arbitrary flags that you can apply to images. It's entirely up to you to decide what they mean. For my own work, I avoid using labels entirely because I dislike the extraneous color they introduce, and I find that six levels of rating (0 to 5 stars) is more than enough for my needs, but that's just my personal bias—what's important is that you come up with a system that works for you! But for some suggestions on how to use these features, see "Selecting and Sorting," later in this chapter.

Applying labels and ratings. By far the easiest way to apply labels or ratings is to use the keyboard shortcuts (most of which also work in Camera Raw). To apply red, yellow, green, and blue labels, press Command-6 through Command-9, respectively. To apply the purple label, or to remove labels, you must use the menu commands. (Inside Camera Raw, the purple label can be toggled using Command-Shift-0.)

To apply ratings, press Command-1 through Command-5 to apply that number of stars, and press Command-0 to remove ratings. (Inside Camera Raw, the shortcut is command-~ (tilde)—Command-0 fits the image in the preview. You can also press Command-. (period) to increase the rating by one star or Command-, (comma) to reduce it by one star. A slower alternative that is nevertheless occasionally convenient is to click and drag in the rating area of the thumbnail—dragging to the right increases the rating, and dragging to the left reduces it. Last but not least, for those who have grown to love the simplicity of the old File Browser's flagging mechanism, the old keyboard shortcut. Command-' (apostrophe), toggles one star on and off.

Bridge Display and the View Menu

The commands on the View menu offer a variety of controls over the way Bridge displays both its windows and the contents of its windows. In the former category, several of the commands replicate the functionality of the control buttons in Bridge's windows—Compact Mode, As Thumbnails, As Filmstrip, As Details, and As Versions and Alternates (the last is relevant for VersionCue users only). Others let you toggle the visibility of the individual panels—Favorites, Folders, Preview, Metadata, and Keywords. See Figure 6-36.

Figure 6-36
The View menu

Sort. The Sort command (see Figure 6-37) lets you sort the contents of the Bridge window based on the file properties listed in the Sort menu. The Manually item becomes checked when you sort images into a custom order by dragging their thumbnails—choosing it from the menu has no effect unless you've previously sorted your images manually, in which case it switches to the last manual sort order you used.

Figure 6-37
The Sort submenu

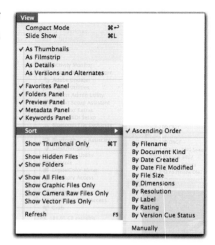

Show Thumbnail Only. The Show Thumbnail Only command (colloqui-ally known as the "Hide the crap" command thanks to the good offices of my friend and colleague Jeff Schewe) suppresses the display of the filenames and any other optional metadata displayed under the thumbnails. Press Command-T to toggle the metadata display on and off—see Figure 6-38.

Figure 6-38
Show Thumbnail Only

The Show Thumbnail Only command toggles the display of filenames and optional metadata under the image thumbnails. It doesn't hide the other panels.

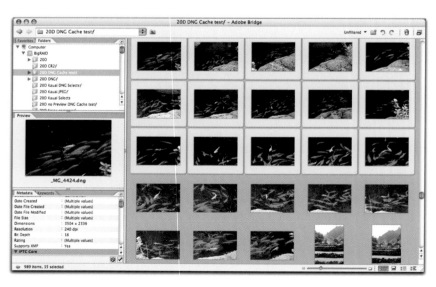

Note that despite its name, Show Thumbnail Only doesn't hide the other palettes. The easiest ways to do so are to click the Show/Hide panels button at the lower left of the window, or choose a Workspace that hides them from the Window>Workspace menu (see "The Window Menu and Bridge Configuration," later in this chapter).

Content filtering commands. Six commands on the View menu let you control the types of content Bridge displays in its windows.

▶ **Show Hidden Files** toggles whether or not Bridge displays sidecar .xmp files and Bridge cache files, as well as files that are normally hidden by the operating system, in its windows *and* in the Folders panel. By default, it's turned off.

▶ **Show Folders** toggles the display of subfolders. By default, it's turned on.

▶ **Show All Files** shows all file types *except* those that are governed by Show Hidden Files.

▶ **Show Graphic Files Only** shows most types of graphics files, including TIFF, JPEG, EPS, Photoshop, and Camera Raw. Curiously, it doesn't show PDF, even when the PDF is created by Photoshop.

▶ **Show Camera Raw Files Only** does exactly what it says. Use this when you only want to see raw files with no distractions from other file types—but don't forget that you've turned it on; otherwise you may waste some time in fruitless searches for your TIFFs and JPEGs!

▶ **Show Vector Files Only** shows Illustrator (.ai), EPS, and PDF files (including those PDFs that only contain pixels).

Of all these commands, the only one I truly find useful in a raw workflow is Show Camera Raw Files Only, but as the EPA is wont to say, your mileage may vary.

Slide Show. Slide Show (press Command-L) offers an alternative to Bridge's light table metaphor by presenting selected images as a slide show that also allows you to apply ratings and rotations while enjoying the benefits of a large image preview. If you prefer to review your selects as before-and-afters rather than (or as well as) side-by-sides, you'll find the new Slide Show feature extremely useful. Press H (with no modifier) to display all the keyboard shortcuts that apply in Slide Show mode. See Figure 6-39.

You can run the slide show in a window, or in full-screen mode with the image either scaled to fit the screen (the entire image is displayed at the maximum size that will fit your screen) or scaled to fill your screen (the image is cropped to the aspect ratio of your screen and displayed at maximum size).

Figure 6-39
Slide Show Options

Slide Show offers by far the easiest way to review and rank your raw images at full-screen resolution, and is a valuable addition to the workflow.

The Window Menu and Bridge Configuration

The Window menu is short and sweet (so short and sweet that it doesn't actually list the windows that are open in Bridge—maybe next time), and the one item you're likely to use again and again is the Workspace menu, which lets you save and recall custom Bridge configurations. Bridge ships with four preconfigured Workspaces—Lightbox, File Navigator, Metadata Focus, and Filmstrip Focus, shown in Figure 6-40—but if you're at all like me you'll probably find that none of them is exactly what you want.

Figure 6-40
Preset Workspaces

*Bridge's preconfigured
Lightbox Workspace*

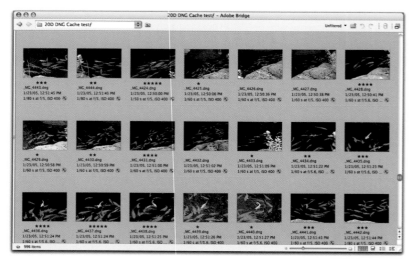

Figure 6-40
Preset Workspaces,
continued

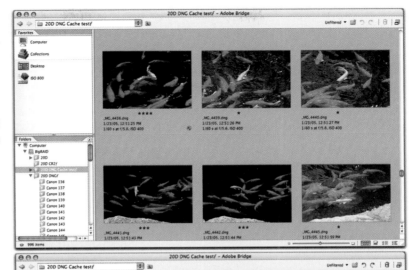

*Bridge's preconfigured
File Navigator Workspace*

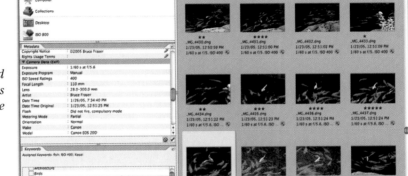

*Bridge's preconfigured
Metadata Focus
Workspace*

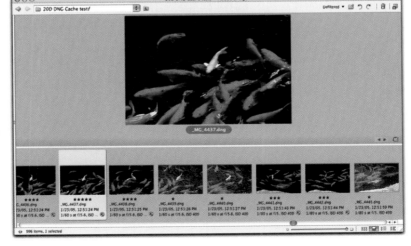

*Bridge's preconfigured
Filmstrip Focus
Workspace*

Fortunately, Bridge windows are eminently configurable, and you can save your custom configurations as Workspaces too. You can dock the panels as you wish, resize them by dragging their borders, remove panels you don't need using the View menu commands, or hide all the panels using the Show/Hide panels toggle. See Figure 6-4, earlier in this chapter, for the locations of the various window components.

Saving Workspaces in Bridge is easy. Configure the window the way you want the Workspace to appear, then choose Save Workspace from the Window>Workspace menu. Enter a name (and, optionally, a keyboard shortcut), then click Save, checking Save Window Location as Part of Workspace if you always want the window to appear in the same place (very useful on dual-monitor setups). Your saved Workspace is then added to the Workspace menu—see Figure 6-41.

Figure 6-41
Saving a Workspace

Configure the window the way you want the Workspace to behave. In this case, I'm displaying two maximum-size thumbnails side by side with filename and metadata hidden.

Choose Save Workspace from the Workspace submenu on the Window menu.

Name and save your Workspace.

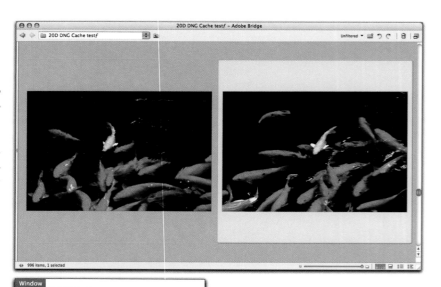

For those of you have to know where things get saved, Workspaces as saved as workspacename.workspace, and are stored in Users/username/Library/Application Support/Adobe/Bridge/Workspaces on Mac OS and in Documents and Settings\Username\Application Data\Adobe\Bridge\Workspaces on Windows.

Bridge Navigation

You can always navigate in Bridge with the mouse, but it's often more efficient to do so from the keyboard.

In the Folders panel, the up and down arrow keys move up and down one folder at a time. Adding the Command key moves up one level in the hierarchy. The right arrow key expands folders containing subfolders; the left arrow key collapses them.

In the Metadata panel, Tab advances to the next editable field, Shift-Tab to the previous one, and Enter commits an entry. In the Keywords panel, the up and down arrows move up and down the keywords list.

In the main window, the up, down, left, and right arrows move the selection to the next thumbnail in their respective directions. Adding Shift extends the selection to include the next thumbnail in that direction. (You can't, however, make discontiguous selections from the keyboard—you have to Command-click the thumbnails to add noncontiguous images to the selection.) Home selects the first thumbnail, and End selects the last one. Command-A selects all thumbnails, and Command-D deselects all thumbnails. Command-Option-L selects all labeled images, while Command-Option-Shift-L selects all unlabeled images. Last but not least, Command-Shift-I inverts the selection, deselecting the selected images and selecting the formerly unselected ones.

Opening Images

If you thought that opening an image is simply a matter of double-clicking its thumbnail, you're missing some important nuances of Bridge's behavior. First and foremost is the distinction between opening raws in Camera Raw hosted by Bridge, and opening raws in Camera Raw hosted by Photoshop.

I'll discuss the workflow reasons for choosing one or the other in the next chapter, *It's All About the Workflow*. Table 6-1 shows the mechanics.

Table 6-1
Opening raw images

To do this...	Press this
Open raw images in Camera Raw hosted by Bridge, leaving Photoshop unaffected.	**Mac** Command-R **Windows** Ctrl-R
Open raw images in Camera Raw hosted by Photoshop, bringing Photoshop to the foreground, and leaving Bridge visible in the background.	**Mac** Command-O, Return, or Command-down arrow **Windows** Ctrl-O, Enter, or Ctrl-down arrow
Open raw images in Camera Raw hosted by Photoshop, bringing Photoshop to the foreground, and hiding Bridge.	**Mac** Option-Return, or Command-Option-down arrow **Windows** Alt-Enter, or Ctrl-Alt-down arrow
Open raw images directly into Photoshop, bypassing the Camera Raw dialog box, bringing Photoshop to the foreground, and leaving Bridge visible in the background.	**Mac** Shift-Return, or Command-Shift-down arrow **Windows** Shift-Enter, or Ctrl-Shift-down arrow
Open raw images directly into Photoshop, bypassing the Camera Raw dialog box, bringing Photoshop to the foreground, and hiding Bridge.	**Mac** Option-Shift-Return, or Command-Option-Shift-down arrow **Windows** Alt-Shift-Enter, or Ctrl-Alt-Shift-down arrow

In addition, double-clicking thumbnails opens images in Camera Raw hosted by either Bridge or Photoshop depending on the setting of the Double-click edits Camera Raw settings in Bridge preference—see Figure 6-16, earlier in this chapter.

Various other keyboard shortcuts may or may not open raw images, depending on this preference setting. The ones listed above are unaffected by the preference setting, and encompass all the available behaviors!

Bridge Thumbnails

The primary function of Bridge thumbnails is to show you the images at whatever size up to the maximum of 512 pixels you prefer. But the thumbnails can also display some handy additional information. Bridge's General Preferences let you display up to three extra lines of metadata besides the filenames. Bridge's thumbnails also display icons that alert you to three conditions.

▶   The image is open in Photoshop.

▶   The image has been cropped in Camera Raw.

▶   The image has had Camera Raw settings applied.

Figure 6-42 shows a thumbnail with extra lines of metadata and all three icons.

Figure 6-42
Thumbnail information

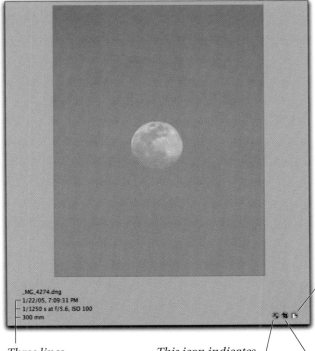

_MG_4274.dng
1/22/05, 7:09:31 PM
1/1250 s at f/5.6, ISO 100
300 mm

This icon indicates that the image is open in Photoshop.

Three lines of additional metadata

This icon indicates that the image has had settings applied in Camera Raw.

This icon indicates that the image was cropped in Camera Raw.

Working in Bridge

Camera Raw is a wonderful raw converter, and Bridge is a pretty capable image manager, but what really makes Photoshop CS2 a compelling solution for a raw digital workflow is the integration between the two. As soon as Bridge encounters a folder of raw files, Camera Raw kicks in automatically, generating thumbnails and generous-size previews that allow you to make good judgments about each image without actually converting it, so that you can quickly make your initial selects.

Note that the high-quality previews are based on Camera Raw's default settings for your camera. If you find that they're consistently off, it's a sign that you need to change your Camera Default settings—see "Loading and Saving Settings" in Chapter 4, *Camera Raw Controls*.

Then, when you've decided which images you want to work with, Bridge lets you apply conversion settings from Camera Raw by writing them to the image's metadata, again without doing an actual conversion, using either the Apply Camera Raw Settings command or, if you need to see larger zoomable previews, in Camera Raw itself.

When I do conversions other than quick one-offs, I almost always do so as batch processes, incorporating other actions—I might set up one batch to produce high-res JPEGs for client approval, another to produce low-res JPEGs for e-mailing, and still another to prepare images for localized editing in Photoshop, with adjustment layers already added so that much of the grunt work is already done for me. Then, when the computer is busy doing my work for me, I go off and lead my glamorous life….

In the next chapter, *It's All About the Workflow*, I'll examine the process from bringing images into Bridge to producing final images in much more detail, but here's a thumbnail sketch of the kinds of work you do in Bridge.

Selecting and Sorting

One of the biggest bottlenecks in a raw digital workflow is in making your initial selects from a day's shoot. Bridge helps in getting past this bottleneck with the Rating and Label features.

I start by copying the files from the camera media to my hard drive—I've learned from bitter experience to avoid opening images directly from the camera media in all but the direst emergency. Then I point Bridge at the folder full of raw images and wait the few minutes while it builds the thumbnails and previews and reads the metadata.

Next, I enter my copyright notice on all images by pressing Command-A to Select All and either using a metadata template from the Metadata palette menu or clicking in the copyright field in the IPTC section of the Metadata palette and typing in the notice manually—see Figure 6-19.

Yes/No sorting. For simple binary sorts, I load Bridge's Filmstrip View workspace, and then I use the arrow keys to advance from one image to the next. For the keepers, I press Command-1 or Command-' (apostrophe) to apply a single-star rating. The rest I simply bypass (though I may rotate images that need it by pressing Command-[or Command-] to rotate them left or right, respectively).

When I've gone through all the images, I choose Show 1 or More Stars (Command-Option-1) from the main window's Unfiltered/Filtered menu, so that I can start processing the keepers without being distracted by the rejects. (Of course, later on I'll probably choose Show Unrated Items Only from the same menu for a more nuanced look at the rejects.)

Further Ratings. If a yes/no/maybe approach appeals to you more than a straight binary choice, you can take a second pass through the 1-star-rated images, and add one or more stars to those images that deserve them. You can also make use of Bridge's Label feature to add another layer of differentiation that you can use separately from or in addition to the star ratings.

Sequencing. Last but not least, if you're the type who thinks in terms of sequences of images rather than single images, you can drag the thumbnails into the order you want, just as you did with film on a light table. Once you've sequenced the images, you can use Batch Rename to rename the files, including a numbering scheme that reflects your custom sort order.

At this stage, I'll often look at the images using Slide Show mode for a quick reality check. I find that I sometimes notice things in the slide show that weren't obvious from looking at the Preview panel or the thumbnails, and I may adjust ratings accordingly.

Applying Camera Raw Settings

The slowest possible way to process raw images in Photoshop CS2 is to open them one by one, make adjustments in Camera Raw, click OK to open the image in Photoshop, and then save it. Unless you're working for an hourly rate, I don't recommend this as a workflow.

Instead, I open images that require similar edits simultaneously in Camera Raw, then I use the Synchronize button to apply the edits to multiple images. If I feel unusually confident, I may do a rough edit pass by editing one image in Camera Raw, and then use Copy/Paste Camera Raw Settings from Bridge's Edit menu to apply that image's settings to others, but seeing a large zoomable preview in Camera Raw is often invaluable.

Processing images. Once I've applied settings to the images, I either save them by opening them in Camera Raw, selecting them all, and clicking Save x Images, or I use Batch to convert the images and also run an action. I'll discuss Batch in more detail in Chapter 9, *Exploiting Automation*.

Of course, some images deserve more attention than others, and hence get processed more than once. One of the problems that digital makes worse rather than better is never knowing when you're finished! The key to working efficiently is to go from the general to the specific, starting out by making all the candidate images look good rather than great, and applying general metadata and keywords to large numbers of images. Then you make more detailed edits and more specific metadata entries to smaller numbers of images until you're left with the ones that genuinely deserve and demand individual treatments. With planning and forethought, you can handle huge numbers of images relatively painlessly.

It's Smart to Be Lazy

Any way you slice it, shooting digital virtually guarantees that you'll spend more time in front of the computer and less time behind the lens. But the power of automation is there to let you make sure that when you *are* sitting in front of the computer, you're doing so because your critical judgment is required.

One of the great things about computers is that once you've figured out how to make the computer do something, you can make it do that something over and over again. You can save yourself a great deal of work by teaching Photoshop how to do repetitive tasks for you. That way, you can concentrate on the exciting stuff. I'll look at automation in detail in Chapter 9, *Exploiting Automation*. But an efficient workflow takes more than automation. It also takes planning. So before tackling automation, I'll look at workflow and strategy in the next chapter, *It's All About the Workflow*.

It's All About the Workflow

That's Flow, Not Slow

In the previous chapters, I've shown you how to drive Camera Raw and Bridge in detail (some might say exhaustive detail). But knowing what buttons to push to get the desired result just means you know how to do the work. To turn that understanding into a practical *workflow*, you need to understand and optimize each part of the process. So this chapter will contain plenty of details, but I'll put them in the context of the big picture.

There are four basic stages in a raw workflow. You may revisit some of them—going back and looking at the initial rejects, or processing the images to different kinds of output file—but everything you do falls into one of four stages.

▶ **Image ingestion.** You start by copying the raw images to at least one hard disk on the computer.

▶ **Image verification.** You point Bridge at the newly copied images and let it cache the thumbnails, previews, and metadata.

▶ **Preproduction.** You work with the images in Bridge, selecting, sorting, applying metadata, and editing with Camera Raw.

▶ **Production.** You process the raw images to output files.

In this chapter, I'll look at all four stages of the workflow, but the major emphasis is on the preproduction stage—the work you do in Bridge—because about 80 percent of the actual work happens in this stage, even if it only takes about 20 percent of the time spent. But all four stages are, of course, vital.

Image ingestion. If you screw up during the ingestion phase, you run the significant risk of losing images, because at this stage, they only exist on the camera media.

Image verification. If you're tempted to skip the second stage, image verification, you may not find out that you've lost images until it's too late to do anything about it. Whenever possible (with the full recognition that it isn't always possible), I don't touch an image until I know that I have two good copies that aren't resident on the camera media. I may be paranoid, but I've yet to lose a single image! If you allow Bridge to verify the images before you reformat the camera media, you'll have a chance of recovering your images if something goes awry in the ingestion phase. If you shoot new images over the old ones and the copies are bad, those images are gone forever.

Preproduction. The preproduction phase is where most of the work takes place, though it's not where you spend the most time. Preproduction generally means doing the minimum number of things to the maximum number of images so that you can get to the point where you can pick the hero images that are truly deserving of your time, while leaving the rejects ready for revisiting.

Production. The production phase is where you hand-polish the select images that deserve the bulk of your time and attention, hand-tuning the Camera Raw settings, and bringing the images into Photoshop for the kinds of selective corrections that Camera Raw simply isn't designed to do. The exercise of your creative judgement is one aspect of the workflow that you can't automate, but automation can and will speed up the execution of that creative judgment.

Before looking at the individual phases, though, you need to make some strategic decisions, and to make those, you need to absorb two basic principles of workflow efficiency.

Workflow Principles

There are likely as many workflows are there are photographers—maybe more! One of the wonderful things about Bridge, Camera Raw 3.0, and Photoshop CS2 is the incredible workflow flexibility that they offer. The price of this flexibility is, of course, complexity. There are multiple ways to accomplish almost any task, and it may not be obvious at first glance which way is optimal in a given situation.

In this chapter, I'll look at the different ways of accomplishing the basic workflow tasks and explain the implications of each. That's the tactical level. But to make a workflow, you also need strategy that tells you how and when to employ those tactics.

Even an individual photographer may need more than one workflow. There's a big difference between the workflow you need to follow when you're on a shoot, the client is looking over your shoulder, and you need to agree on the hero shots before you strike the lighting and move on, and the workflow you'd like to follow when you're reviewing personal work with no deadlines attached. These two scenarios represent extremes, and there are many points on the continuum that lies between them.

I can't build your workflow for you, since I don't know your specific needs, or your preferences. What I *can* do is introduce you to the components that address the different workflow tasks, and offer two key principles of workflow efficiency that can guide you in how to employ them.

▶ Do things *once,* efficiently.

▶ Do things automatically wherever possible.

Doing Things Once

When you apply metadata such as copyright, rights management, and keywords to your raw file, the metadata is automatically carried through to all the TIFFs, JPEGs, or PSDs that you derive from that raw file, so you only need to enter that metadata once.

By the same token, if you exploit the power of Camera Raw to its fullest, many of your images may need little or no work postconversion in Photoshop, so applying Camera Raw edits to your images is likewise something that can often be done only once.

A key strategy that helps you do things once, and once only, is to start with the general and proceed to the specific. Start with the things that can be done to the greatest number of images, and proceed to make increasingly more detailed treatments of ever-decreasing numbers of images, reserving the full treatment—careful hand-editing in Camera Raw and Photoshop, applying image-specific keywords, and so on—to those images that truly deserve the attention.

Do Things Automatically

Automation is a vital survival tool for simply dealing with the volumes of data a raw workflow entails. One of the great things about computers is that once you've told them how to do something, they can do that something over and over again. Photoshop actions are obvious automation features, but metadata templates and Camera Raw presets are automations too, albeit less obvious ones.

I rarely open an image from Camera Raw directly into Photoshop unless I'm stacking multiple renderings of the raw file into the same Photoshop image. Even then, I take advantage of the Option-Open shortcut that opens the images as copies so that I don't have to rename them manually in Photoshop—that too is an automation feature!

In the vast majority of cases, when I create converted images that Photoshop can open, I do so using either Batch or Image Processor, and I apply actions that do things like sharpening and creating adjustment layers so that when I do open the image in Photoshop, it's immediately ready for editing without my having to create layers first.

I'll discuss automation in more detail in Chapter 9, *Exploiting Automation,* but the workflow message is, if you find yourself doing the same things over and over again, they're good candidates for automation.

Be Methodical

Once you've found a rhythm that works for you, stick to it. (Emergencies will happen, and sometimes circumstances will force you to deviate from established routine, but that's the exception rather than the rule.) Being methodical and sticking to a routine makes mistakes less likely, and allows you to focus on the important image decisions that only you can make.

For better or worse, computers always do *exactly* what you tell them to, even if that's jumping off a cliff. Established routines help ensure that you're telling the computer to do what you really want it to.

Planning and Strategy

An efficient workflow requires planning. Photoshop CS, Bridge, and Camera Raw 2.x offered a limited amount of workflow flexibility. Photoshop CS2, Bridge, and Camera Raw 3.x offer many more options. You can flail around and try everything—it's actually not a bad way to get your feet wet, though I hope you'll use the information in this chapter to make your flailing somewhat methodical—but at some point, you have to decide what works, and stick with it.

Among the things you need to decide, and stick with, are the following:

▶ **Bridge cache.** You can use a centralized cache, or use distributed caches. Each has its strengths and weaknesses, but your life will be simpler, and your workflow more robust, if you pick one approach and stick to it.

▶ **Camera Raw settings for individual images.** You can save the Camera Raw settings for each image in the Camera Raw database, in sidecar .xmp files, or in the case of DNG format, in the DNG file itself. It's slightly easier to switch from one approach to another in Bridge with Camera Raw 3.x than it was with File Browser and Camera Raw 2.x, but doing so requires considerable work and a great deal of care.

▶ **File naming conventions.** After much wrestling with the subject, I no longer rename my raw files—I rely on keywords and other metadata to help me find my images. But that isn't an approach that works for everyone. If you do rename your raw files, though, pick a naming convention that makes sense to you, and stick with it.

▶ **Labels and ratings.** The labels and ratings you apply in Bridge or Camera Raw are simply arbitrary flags. Labels and ratings give you two sets of flags, each of which contains six possible values when you include no label and no rating. It's entirely up to you what they mean. Again, pick a system that makes sense to you, and stick with it!

You'll need to make plenty of decisions when you're working on your images. It's a Bad Idea to start making decisions about any of the above when you're working on a deadline, because doing so introduces complexity (of which you already have enough) and increases the chance of unintended consequences (which you want to avoid).

Who Has the Cache?

Bridge's cache performs the important task of storing image thumbnails, previews, and sort order. (For file types that can't support sidecar .xmp files, it also stores keywords and metadata, but that doesn't apply to raw formats.) Bridge's Advanced Preferences let you choose whether to use a central cache or distributed caches (see the Advanced Preferences section under "Preferences and the Bridge Menu (Mac)" in Chapter 6, *Adobe Bridge*).

The only downside to using distributed cache files is that you wind up with two cache files in every folder that Bridge ever sees. If that drives you crazy, by all means use a central cache instead, but do so with the clear knowledge that you run the risk of losing thumbnails, previews, and custom sort orders when you do any of the following:

▶ Rename a folder outside of Bridge.

▶ Copy a folder outside of Bridge.

▶ Burn a folder to removable media such as CD-ROM or DVD.

▶ Copy a folder to a different computer.

You can work around these limitations of the central cache by making sure that you use the Export Cache command from Bridge's Tools>Cache submenu, but you're introducing complexity that is unnecessary with distributed caches, and hence creating more opportunities for operator error. If you're downloading images to a laptop computer in the field, with the eventual goal of transferring them to a desktop machine back in the studio for further processing, I'll come straight out and say that it's just crazy to use a central cache on the laptop. (Using a central cache on the desktop I deem merely eccentric.)

A second argument against a central cache is that when you use it, you're putting all your eggs in one basket. You can control where the central cache gets stored, so you don't have to store it in the default location on your startup drive where it's vulnerable to permissions issues and other ills, but like pets, all hard drives die, eventually, and storing all your caches in one folder incurs the risk that you'll lose them all. With distributed caches, every folder contains a cache automatically, you can copy and rename your folders without having to think about it, and when the inevitable does happen, you've only lost what was on that drive (which was of course backed up).

Strategies for Settings

You can save Camera Raw settings either in the Camera Raw Database or in sidecar .xmp files. Superficially, it may seem that the same arguments apply to the Camera Raw Database as apply to the centralized Bridge cache, but in fact it's not that simple.

The Camera Raw Database indexes images by their content, not by their filenames, so you can copy, move, or rename them willy-nilly without losing track of your raw settings—but only as long as the images remain on the same computer as the Camera Raw Database. Move them to another machine, and the settings are gone (or, rather, they're still on the originating computer where they'll do absolutely no good). You can work around this limitation by always remembering to use Camera Raw's Export Settings command to write out a sidecar .xmp file for the image, and always remembering to include the sidecar file with the image. But that's a lot of "always remembering."

If you use sidecar .xmp files instead, Bridge does its best to keep track of them. As long as you use Bridge to copy, move, and rename your raw files, the sidecar files travel with them automatically. But if you copy, move, or rename your raw files *outside* of Bridge, it's up to you to keep track of your sidecar files and move them with the images manually. Again, it's not an ideal solution.

There's a third alternative, which is to use the DNG format instead. This is a topic that's sufficiently nuanced to deserve its own discussion, so see the sidebar "Working with DNG" on the following page. Those of you with sharp eyes will doubtless have noticed that all the screen shots in this book use DNG images. My personal opinion is that unless you like to bounce back and forth between Camera Raw and your camera vendor's proprietary raw converter, a DNG workflow makes more sense than one based on proprietary raws. The convenience of having all the metadata, including Camera Raw settings, stored right in the file itself outweighs the one-time speed bump entailed in converting the raws to DNG. But if you want to use your camera vendor's converter, and your camera doesn't write DNG, you should stick with proprietary raws for your working files, at least for now. You may, however, want to consider using DNG with the original raw embedded as an archival format. See "Archiving Images," later in this chapter.

Working with DNG

The DNG format is, as previously noted, Adobe's proposed standard for a documented, open, nonproprietary raw format.

From a workflow standpoint, DNG files offer at least one major advantage: they're designed to be metadata-friendly, so if you use DNG files, you don't need sidecar .xmp files to hold your Camera Raw settings or other metadata. Instead, all these things get written directly into the DNG file, so they can't get lost or dissocciated from the image.

DNG Downsides

There are really only two downsides to the DNG format.

▶ You have to convert your proprietary raw files to DNG, which takes time.

▶ The DNG files can't be opened by your proprietary raw converter.

If, like me, you're perfectly happy with Camera Raw and don't plan on using your camera vendor's proprietary raw software, the second point is moot, but if you like to bounce back and forth between Camera Raw and the proprietary converter, DNG isn't well suited to doing so. You can embed the original raw in a DNG, but you have to take the time to extract it before you can work with the proprietary raw, so DNG with original raw embedded is intended more

as an archival format than as one suited for everyday use.

That leaves the first point. The slow way to get to DNG is to run all your proprietary raws through the Adobe DNG Converter application before you start working on your images. That's not always an acceptable solution since it takes some time.

A better method, the one I favor, is to make selects and initial edits on the proprietary raw files, then to use Camera Raw hosted by either Bridge or Photoshop, depending on which application I want to continue using, to batch-save the raws to DNG. Once I've saved everything as DNG, I make an archive using DNG with the original raw images embedded. Then I simply discard the proprietary raw files.

DNG Advantages

I do this to exploit the advantages of the DNG format. First and foremost, all the information in the proprietary raw files' sidecar .xmp files—Camera Raw settings, keywords, copyright and rights management notices—gets saved directly into the DNG so I no longer need to worry about sidecar files.

A second benefit of DNG is that it can contain a full-size or medium-size JPEG preview that third-party asset managers can use instead of having to spend time parsing the raw data before it can display

the image. Photoshop and Bridge make use of the embedded preview in a very limited way—Photoshop displays the preview in the File>Open dialog box, and Bridge uses it to display the initial thumbnail before building its high-quality previews. One reason that Photoshop and Bridge don't make greater use of the embedded previews is that Camera Raw 3.0 doesn't update the preview when you edit a DNG in Camera Raw, although it does when you save a new, edited DNG. Obviously this is not an ideal situation for those who want to use DNG with third-party asset managers, so here's some late-breaking news.

Camera Raw 3.1

By the time you read this, however, Camera Raw 3.1 will likely be available for download from Adobe's Web site. In addition to providing support for new cameras such as Nikon's D2X and Canon's EOS Digital Rebel XT, Camera Raw 3.1 introduces two new preferences that are relevant only in a DNG workflow—see Figure 7-1.

The first new preference item, Ignore sidecar ".xmp" files, addresses a relatively obscure situation that arises only when you have a DNG and a proprietary raw version of the same image in the same folder, and they're identically named except for the extension. If you edit the proprietary raw file, Camera Raw 3 also applies the edits to the DNG, to maintain compatibility with Photoshop CS and Photoshop Elements 3, both of which write sidecar files for DNG. The preference setting lets you tell Camera Raw 3.1 to ignore sidecar files and leave the DNG alone in this situation.

The second preference item, Update embedded JPEG previews, lets you tell Camera Raw 3.1 to always update the preview when you edit a DNG. The penalty for doing so is that you take a speed hit because the previews take time to build and save. The advantage is that the embedded previews accurately reflect the current state of the image.

You can also defer the speed hit by working with this preference turned off. Then, when you want to update the previews, choose Export Settings from the Camera Raw menu. You'll see the dialog box shown in Figure 7-2, which allows you to update the Medium SIze or Full Size preview.

You can skip the dialog box by pressing Option or Alt when you choose Export Settings, in which case Camera Raw will update the preview size you selected the last time you opened the dialog box.

Preview Size

When you choose Full Size preview, Camera Raw 3.1 actually embeds both Full Size and Medium Size previews, so smart applications can extract only the amount

Figure 7-1
Camera Raw 3.1 Preferences

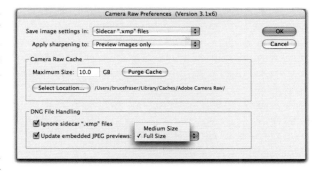

Figure 7-2
Export Settings for DNG

of data they need for thumbnails while allowing you to zoom to see the actual pixels. The only downsides to Full Size previews are that they take slightly longer to build and make a slightly larger file. If you need only thumbnail support in a third-party application, you can save yourself a little time by using the Medium Size option, but the savings are small, and if you change your mind later and decide you need full-size previews, any savings are wiped out.

Full Size gets you the best of both worlds, and since Camera Raw 3.1 is flexible about when you take the speed hit, it's the option I prefer.

Bear in mind too that you can choose which application, Bridge or Photoshop, gets tied up building the previews so that you can continue working in the other application while the one hosting Camera Raw builds the previews in the background.

You may have noticed that all the screen shots in this book use images in DNG format. When I initially made the decision to use DNG in the book, I confess that I did so partly for political reasons. But now that I've come to enjoy the benefits of the DNG workflow, and the absence of sidecar files, I'll never go back to proprietary raws.

What's in a Name?

I don't, personally, make a practice of renaming my raw files, simply because I haven't found a compelling reason to do so. That said, I know a good many photographers whose sophisticated naming schemes are a core part of their workflow, so I'm not in any way against the practice.

If you *do* want to make a practice of renaming your raw files, I suggest the following two simple rules:

▶ Adopt a naming convention that makes sense to you, and stick to it (in other words, be methodical).

▶ What's in a name? Anything you want, but if you want that name to be consistently readable across platforms and operating systems, stick to alphanumeric characters—no spaces (underscore works everywhere), and no special characters.

   The only place a period should appear is immediately in front of the extension—today's OSs have a tendency to treat everything following a period as an extension, and promptly hide it, so periods in the middle of filenames are very likely to cause those filenames to be truncated. Many special characters are reserved for special uses by one or another operating system. Including them in filenames can produce unpredictable results, so don't!

Aside from these two simple rules, file naming conventions are limited only by your ingenuity. Don't overlook metadata as a source for naming elements, and expect to see ingestion scripts that offer more metadata-related naming features than Bridge's Batch Rename (see Figure 6-32 in Chapter 6, *Adobe Bridge*) both from Adobe and from third-party scripters.

Ratings and Labels

Bridge and Camera Raw offer two independent mechanisms, labels and ratings, for flagging images. Each mechanism offers six possible values: if you use them in combination, you can have 36 possible combinations of ratings and labels, which is almost certainly more than most people need!

If you think you can use a system with 36 values productively, knock yourself out. Otherwise, I suggest keeping things simple. I prefer to avoid using labels because they introduce large blobs of color into an environment where the only color I want to see is the color in my images, so I use ratings instead.

The ratings system was designed to mimic the time-honored practice of making selects on a light table by marking the keepers from the first round with a single dot, adding a second dot to the keepers from the second round, and so on. That's how I use it—it's simple and effective.

I do make limited use of labels for various esoteric purposes. For example, I've applied the purple label (which I've renamed "weird") to the ever-growing collection of high-ISO sodium-vapor-lit nighttime cityscapes that I use for testing noise reduction techniques, and hide most of the rest of the time. Labels are handy for this kind of use because they can operate completely independently of the star-based rating system. If you can think of uses for them, go ahead and use them, but don't feel that just because a feature exists, you have to use it.

Remember that if you want to use labels to communicate something about images to someone else, you and they need use the same definitions of the labels. If they're different, the recipient will get a bunch of images with white labels, indicating that a label has been applied, but with different label text than is currently specified in their Labels preferences. (See Figure 6-14 in Chapter 6, *Adobe Bridge.*) They can search the metadata for your label text, but since labels are meant to be an easy visual way to identify *something* about the images, you'd likely be better off using keywords instead.

Simplicity Is Its Own Strategy

Camera Raw, Bridge, and Photoshop offer an amazing number of options. Only a genius or a fool would try to use them all. If, like me, you're neither, I recommend keeping things as simple as possible without making any overly painful compromises.

The four issues that I've called out in this section—Bridge cache, Camera Raw settings, naming conventions, and rating/labeling strategies—are things that can't be changed without going through considerable pain. You can certainly spend some time trying out the options before setting your strategies in stone, but once you've found the approach that works best for you, don't change it arbitrarily. If you do, it's entirely likely that you'll lose work, whether it's Camera Raw edits, Bridge thumbnails, ratings, or simply winding up with a bunch of incomprehensibly named files. Any of these violates the first workflow principle—do things once, efficiently—and you pay for it with that most precious commodity, your time.

The Image Ingestion Phase

Transferring your images from the camera to the computer is one of the most critical yet often one of the least examined stages of your workflow. It's critical because at this stage, your images exist only on the camera media. It's not that Compact Flash, Secure Digital, or microdrives are dramatically more fragile than other storage media, it's simply that there's only one copy! Losing previews or camera raw settings is irritating, but you can redo the work. If you make mistakes during ingestion, though, you can lose entire images.

The following ground rules have stood me in good stead for several years—I've had my share of equipment problems, but thus far, I've yet to lose a single image.

▶ Don't use the camera as a card reader. Most cameras will let you connect them to the computer and download your images, but doing so is a bad idea for at least two reasons. Cameras are typically very slow as card readers, and when the camera is being used as a card reader, you can't shoot with it.

▶ Never open images directly from the camera media. It's been formatted with the expectation that the only thing that will write to it is the camera. If something else writes to it, maybe nothing will happen, but then again, maybe something bad will.

▶ Don't rely on just one copy of the images—always copy them to two separate drives before you start working.

▶ Don't erase your images from the camera media until you've verified the copies—see "The Image Verification Phase," later in this chapter.

▶ Always format the cards in the camera in which they will be shot, never in the computer.

Following these rules may take a little additional time up front, but not nearly as long as a reshoot (assuming that lost images can in fact be reshot).

Camera Media and Speed

All CF cards (or SD cards, or microdrives) are not created equal, but vendor designations like 4x, 24x, 40x, 80x, Ultra, and Write Accelerated aren't terribly reliable guides as to the performance you'll get with your personal setup.

There are two distinctly different aspects to CF card speed.

▶ Your burst shooting rate is dictated by the speed with which the CF card writes images in the camera.

▶ Your image offloading speed is dictated by the speed with which images can be read from the CF card onto your computer's hard disk.

In either case, the bottleneck may be the CF Card, or it may be the hardware used to write to it (your camera) or read from it (your card reader).

Compact Flash write speed. Most of today's high-speed CF cards can write data as fast as the camera can send it. However, older cameras may not be able to deliver the data fast enough to justify the premium prices the fastest cards command.

The best source I know for comparative data on different cameras' write speeds to different cards can be found on Rob Galbraith's Web site, www.robgalbraith.com—look for the CF Database link on the front page. Note that the database no longer gets updated for some older cameras, so if the notes say something to the effect of "this camera will benefit from the fastest card available," look in the table to check which card that actually was and when that page was last updated.

Compact Flash read speed. The card reader and even the operating system can play an equal role in determining read speed to that of the card itself. Card readers almost invariably use one of three interfaces: USB 1.1, USB 2.0, or FireWire.

Almost any card available today can max out the speed of a USB 1.1 reader. In theory, USB 2.0 is faster than FireWire, but in practice, as the EPA says, "your mileage may vary"—I've generally found FireWire to be both faster and more reliable than USB 2.0, particularly with fast cards such as the SanDisk Ultra II and Extreme and the Lexar 80x product lines.

Mac OS X users should take note that OS X versions prior to Panther (OS 10.3) were very slow at reading 2GB and larger cards that use FAT-32 formatting. Panther fixed the problem.

Microdrives. In addition to solid-state Compact Flash cards, microdrives—miniature hard disks in Compact Flash form factor—are also available. Microdrives were introduced when solid-state CF cards were still quite limited in both speed and capacity.

Today, solid-state CF cards have outstripped microdrives in both capacity and speed, and they also have enormous advantages in durability. Like all hard drives, microdrives use moving parts machined to very fine tolerances, so they don't respond well to impacts—it's easy to destroy both the data and the drive itself by dropping it. Solid-state CF cards are a great deal more robust—while I don't recommend abusing them in any way, I have one that survived being run over by a Ford Explorer!

Microdrives may make a comeback, with much higher capacities than before, but right now such designs are still on the drawing board.

Secure Digital (SD) cards. If microdrives are the wave of the past, Secure Digital (SD) cards are the wave of the future, though at the time of this writing only a handful or so of cameras support them. The main impetus behind the development of SD is the built-in encryption, which is inviting for the music and movie industries, since it will let them distribute copyrighted material digitally.

For camera use, SD is still pretty new, and relatively few cameras use it—the Canon EOS 1DsMkII lets you use both CF and SD, but the SD card seems intended as a spare for when the CF card gets full. The capacities of the current generation are still lower than the largest CF cards—at the time of writing, 1GB cards are common and we're just starting to see 2GB SD cards—but the fastest SD cards are slightly faster in the camera than are the fastest CF cards, though they're considerably slower at transferring data from the card to the computer. Both of these statements are subject to change. All the recommendations for handling and using CF cards apply equally to SD.

Formatting Camera Media

Always format your camera media, whether CF card, microdrive, or SD card, in the camera in which it will be used! Your computer may appear to let you format the card while it's loaded in the card reader, but it's quite likely that it will either do so incorrectly or offer you a set of options from which it's easy to make the wrong choice.

Formatting CF cards on Windows systems can, at least in theory, be done correctly, but the only time I'd recommend doing so is if you've used software supplied by the card vendor to perform data recovery or diagnostics *and* the software recommends formatting. Formatting CF cards under any flavor of the Mac OS is a recipe for disaster. Formatting cards in the camera in which they will be used is always safe and guarantees that the format will be the one your camera can use.

Tip: When Disaster Strikes. If you wind up with a card that's unreadable but contains data you want to recover (it's rare, but it can be caused by doing things like pulling the card out of the reader without first ejecting it in software), *do not* format it! Doing so will guarantee that any data that was still on the card will be permanently consigned to the bitbucket. Major CF card vendors such as SanDisk and Lexar include data-recovery software with the cards (which for my money is sufficient reason to stick with those brands). Before attempting anything else, try the recovery software. If that fails, and the data is truly irreplaceable, several companies offer data recovery from CF cards, usually at a fairly hefty price—a Google search for "Compact Flash Data Recovery" will turn up all the major players.

Camera Card Capacities

Bigger isn't always better, and in the case of CF cards, large capacities often come at premium prices. A 4GB card will generally cost more than twice as much as a 2GB one, and so on.

Using two smaller cards rather than one big one offers an immediate workflow advantage. When the first card is full, you can switch to the second one to continue shooting while the first card is being copied to the computer. By the time the second card is full, the first one will have finished copying, and you can format it in the camera and continue shooting.

Ingesting Images

I always copy images onto a hard drive before attempting to open them. (Actually, I always copy the images onto two different hard drives. I may be paranoid, but I've yet to lose a digital capture.)

It's possible to connect the camera to your computer and actually open the images while they're still on the CF card. It's likewise possible to put the CF card in a card reader and open the images directly from the CF card. But "possible" doesn't mean it's a good idea! It's possible to run a Porsche on kerosene or to perform brain surgery with a rusty Phillips screwdriver, and I consider either one about as advisable as opening images directly from the camera media.

I always copy to two hard drives for the simple reason that hard drives break, usually at the least convenient moment they could possibly choose to do so. If you simply can't take the time to make two copies, consider setting up a mirrored (not striped) RAID array. Mirrored RAID arrays copy the data to two drives simultaneously, so unless both drives fail simultaneously (which is extremely unlikely), you'll always have a copy of the data. RAID level 5 (distributed parity) offers a good compromise between speed and reliability—the data is distributed with parity bits across three drives, so even if one drive fails, the array can be rebuilt (though it takes a while to do so).

You can even kill two birds with a single stone by using a casing that allows hot-swapping of the drives, and use the drive mechanisms themselves, suitably boxed, to archive the data—hard disks are much faster than CD-R or DVD-R; will almost certainly last at least as long, particularly if they're simply being stored; and can cost less than a dollar per gigabyte—see the next section, "Archiving Images."

When I'm shooting in the field and using a laptop to offload the images, I carry a portable 100GB FireWire drive, and make a second copy of all the images on the portable drive. When time permits, I make both copies directly from the camera media. Failing that, I make one copy from the camera media, then copy from one hard drive to the other. When there's absolutely no time to spare, I may work from a single copy of the images, but in that situation, I always verify the images by letting Bridge build previews before I format the camera card from which they came.

However you choose to accomplish the task, my overriding recommendation is that you wait until the copy from camera media to hard drive is complete and verified before you try to do anything at all to the images.

Archiving Images

I've heard of photographers who don't bother to archive their raw images once they've processed them to gamma-corrected color ones. That seems about as sensible to me as throwing out all your negatives because you've made prints that you like! Given the huge amount of processing that goes into converting a digital raw capture and the fact that the techniques for doing said conversions are only likely to get better, it seems extraordinarily short-sighted at best not to archive your raw captures. The issues then become when, in what form, and on what media you archive them.

When to archive. When I first copy the raw images to the computer, I almost always copy them to two different drives. One copy becomes my working copy; the other serves immediately as a short-term backup and then, after conversion to DNG with the original raw file embedded, as a long-term archive.

Once I've done my selecting, sorting, ranking, and renaming, I've applied initial Camera Raw edits, and I've saved the files in DNG format to bind the metadata, I archive these too. Yes, it makes for a heavy storage requirement, but storage space is relatively inexpensive, time is expensive, and images are irreplaceable.

What to archive. You should archive anything you want yourself or someone else to be able to retrieve at some unspecified time in the future. It's really that simple.

Don't confuse archives and backups. Backups are usually automated, incremental copies that reflect the current state of your system. Archives are long-term storage, designed to remain undisturbed unless and until the data is required. An archive isn't a substitute for backups, and backing up isn't a substitute for archiving!

Archive media. Strictly speaking, there's no such thing as an archival medium for digital storage—any of the even slightly convenient solutions available for recording ones and zeroes will degrade over time. Archives must be maintained!

There are really two problems in archival storage. The obvious one is the integrity of the storage medium. The less obvious but equally critical one is the availability of devices that can read the storage medium. There's probably still magnetic tape from 1970s mainframes that has good data on it, but good luck finding a drive that can read it.

Any archiving strategy *must* include periodic refreshing of the data onto new media, preferably taking advantage of improvements in technology. I've migrated most of my early-'90s CD-ROMs onto either DVD-Rs or to large-capacity hard disks, and unless something better comes along I'll probably refresh that data onto the even larger, faster, and cheaper hard disks that will be available in the future with capacities measured in tera-bytes rather than gigabytes.

Burnable CDs and DVDs, both read-only and rewritable, differ from commercially pressed CDs and DVDs in an important way. In the com-mercially manufactured disks, the data is stamped on a foil layer made of metal. (It's about the same thickness as the foil in a cigarette pack, but it's metal nonetheless.) Burnable CDs and DVDs use a photosensitive dye layer to record the data—the dye changes color when the laser writes to it. Photographers should be well aware of the fragility of dyes.... So use whatever storage medium you find convenient, but recognize that it *will* fail, and plan accordingly.

The Image Verification Phase

Once you've copied the raw files to your hard disk, the next thing to do is to point Bridge at the folder containing the raw images. Bridge is command central for dealing with hundreds of images. You'll use it to make your initial selects, to apply and edit metadata including Camera Raw settings, and to control the processing of the raw images into a deliverable form.

But before you start doing any of these things, it's a good idea to give Bridge a few minutes to generate the thumbnails and previews and to read the image metadata. The old File Browser was pretty much unusable while it was building previews. As a standalone multithreaded application Bridge is much more responsive while it's building previews, but whenever possible, it's still a good idea to let it finish building the cache for the folder before you start working.

The reason is simple. While you can identify raw images as soon as the thumbnail appears, and open them in Camera Raw, the thumbnails are generated by the camera, and Bridge simply reads them. To build the high-quality previews, though, Camera Raw actually reads the raw data.

Verifying Images

If Camera Raw has any problem reading the images, the problems will only show up on the high-quality thumbnail and preview. The initial thumbnails are the camera-generated ones, and they don't indicate that the raw file has been read successfully. The high-quality ones *do* indicate that the raw file has been read successfully, so wait until you see them before you erase the raw image files from the camera media.

If there's a problem with the raw data, you won't see a high-quality preview, so the preview-building process verifies that the raw data has been copied correctly. It's the first time you actually see a processed version of the raw image created from the raw file on the computer.

If you see a problem at this stage, check the second copy (if you made one) or go back to the camera media—you haven't reformatted it yet, right? It's fairly rare for the data to get corrupted in the camera (though it does sometimes happen, particularly in burst-mode shooting), so the first suspect should be the card reader.

If you have only one reader available, try copying the problem images one by one. If you have a second reader available, try copying the files using the second reader. If this copy fails, try running the rescue software provided by the card vendor. If none of these suggestions work, your options are to reshoot, to accept the loss and move on, or to resort to an expensive data-recovery service.

Feeding the Cache

Bridge's cache holds the thumbnails, previews, and sort order information for each folder at which you point it. (In the case of other file types, the cache may contain additional information, but with raw files, the thumbnails, previews, and sort order are the only pieces of data that are uniquely stored in the Bridge cache.) With a brand-new folder of images, there's no custom sort order, so the caching process consists of reading the thumbnails and EXIF metadata, and building the high-quality previews.

This is a two-pass process. The first pass reads the thumbnails and metadata, the second pass actually uses Camera Raw to build the high-quality previews—it's this second pass that lets you verify the raw images. When you point Bridge at a folder of raw images for the first time, it goes to work. The first thing you'll see is a message that reads "Examining folder contents"—see Figure 7-3.

Figure 7-3
Examining folder
contents

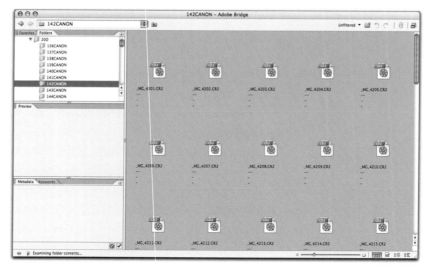

With the typical hundred images per folder that cameras write, the "Examining folder contents" message flashes by so quickly that if you blink, you may miss it. The second message that appears is "Getting *filename* thumbnail." This second pass takes a little longer, because it's extracting the camera-created thumbnail and metadata from the raw images—see Figure 7-4.

Figure 7-4
Getting thumbnails

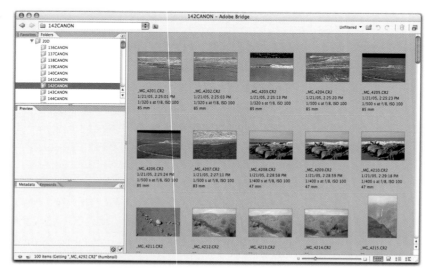

The last phase of the initial cache-building process is also the most crucial one—generating previews. In this phase, Bridge uses Camera Raw to build higher-quality thumbnails than the ones that appear initially. (They're downsampled versions of the result you'd get if you processed the raw file using the current Camera Default settings for the camera that shot the images in Camera Raw.) If you look closely, you can see the thumbnails updating. (Even in print at this small size, you can see the difference between the thumbnails in Figure 7-4 and the ones in Figure 7-5.) The status message reads "Generating *filename* preview"—see Figure 7-5.

Figure 7-5
Generating previews

Once Bridge has completed the process of generating the previews, it displays a message that states the number of images in the folder, indicating that it's ready for you to proceed to the preproduction phase. Large previews appear instantly when you advance from one image to another, so you can work quickly.

Interrupting the Cache

In an ideal scenario, you'll follow the procedures described in the previous section, but in the real world, scenarios are often less than ideal. In this section, I'll cover a couple of ways to start work while Bridge is still building its cache. You're still verifiying the images, just not necessarily in the order in which Bridge loaded them.

If you need to see and start working with a specific image right now, you can force Bridge to read all the data and build the preview by selecting the thumbnail in the Bridge window. Bridge gives preference to that image, and generates a preview before moving on to the other images, even if you do so during the thumbnail pass. However, this approach doesn't work with multiple images—Bridge builds the preview for the first selected image, then carries on reading thumbnails. You can also scroll the Bridge window to give preference to a series of images—Bridge always builds previews for those images whose thumbnails are currently visible in the main window first.

But the most effective way of getting images while Bridge is still caching is to select the thumbnails, then press Command-O to open the images in Camera Raw filmstrip mode hosted by Photoshop. Camera Raw builds the previews very quickly, and because it's hosted by Photoshop, it doesn't have any effect on Bridge's caching performance. You can apply ratings or labels in Camera Raw in addition to editing the images. The only thing you can't do is to apply keywords, or metadata other than labels, ratings, and Camera Raw settings.

Tip: Download to Your Fastest Drive. The cache-building process is largely dependent on disk speed, so the faster the drive to which you download the raw images, the faster Bridge builds the cache. Consider dedicating a partition on your fastest drive, the same size as your camera media, for downloading and caching your raw images. If you use distributed caches in Bridge, you can then copy the folder to another drive without having to do anything else to keep your thumbnails and previews intact.

Caching Multiple Folders

Most cameras create subfolders on the camera media with 100 images in each. If you use larger-capacity cards, you may have three or four image folders. The fastest way to deal with multiple folders is to copy all the image folders to a single enclosing folder. Then, when the copy is complete, point Bridge at the enclosing folder and choose Build Cache for Subfolders from Bridge's Tools>Cache menu. Bridge builds a cache for each subfolder in the enclosing folder, reading the thumbnails and metadata and generating previews for all the images contained in the subfolders. It displays a status message so you'll know when it's done.

The Preproduction Phase

The absolute order in which you perform tasks like selecting, sorting, re-naming, keywording, and so on, isn't critical, so the order in which I'll discuss them is, I freely admit, arbitrary. But in those cases where the result of one task depends on the prior completion of another, I'll point that out. I do, however, offer one golden rule.

Start with the operations required by the largest number of images, and complete these before you start handling individual images on a case-by-case basis. For example, the first thing I always do with a folder full of new raw images is to select all the images and enter my copyright notice by applying a metadata template.

Similarly, if you know that you want to add the same keyword or keywords to all the images in a shoot, you can do it now (see "Applying Keywords and Metadata," later in this chapter). But if you don't care about copyrighting or keywording your rejects, you can make your initial selects first.

Selecting and Editing

Some photographers like to do a rough application of Camera Raw settings on all the images before they start making selects by flagging or ranking. Then they look at a large preview for each image and apply a flag or rank accordingly. Others may take a quick scan of the thumbnails and weed out any obvious junk before proceeding. Still others may want to do key-wording and metadata editing before they start making selects. Bridge can accommodate all these different styles.

So start out by loading a Bridge configuration that works for the task you want to start with—if you need to refresh your memory on configuring Bridge's layout for different tasks and saving those layouts as workspaces, see "The Window Menu and Bridge Configuration" in Chapter 6, *Adobe Bridge*.

Selecting by thumbnail. If the thumbnail view lets you see enough detail to make initial selects, choose an all-thumbnail view, then click-select the keepers or the rejects, whichever is easier. Shift-clicking selects all contiguous files between the last-selected image and the one on which you click, Com-mand-clicking selects noncontiguous images one at a time. See Figure 7-6. You can apply a label or rating as you go—see "Rating and Labeling," later in this chapter.

Figure 7-6
Selects by thumbnail

Click to select.

Shift-click to extend the selection contiguously.

Command-click to add or subtract non-contiguous images from the selection.

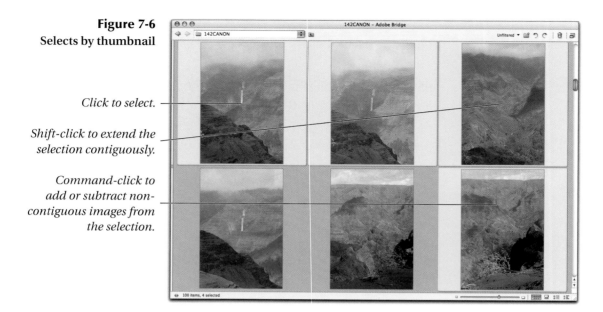

Selecting by preview. To see more detail, you can look at each image's preview. Bridge's Filmstrip view lets you see a large preview with a single row of thumbnails. The left and right arrow keys let you navigate from one thumbnail to the next and display the corresponding preview—see Figure 7-7.

Figure 7-7
Selects by preview

Press right arrow to go to the next image.

Press left arrow to go to the previous image.

With this method, it's easier to apply a label or rating as you go than to rely on selecting thumbnails—see "Rating and Labeling," later in this chapter.

Selecting in Slide Show. Bridge's Slide Show view lets you review images one at a time at up to full-screen resolution. Slide Show offers the largest preview you can get without opening the image in Camera Raw and zooming. You can't select images in Slide Show view, but you can apply labels or ratings.

Comparing images. When you're making selects, you often need to compare images. In Slide Show view you can see before-and-afters, but I offer two techniques for comparing images side by side.

▶ To compare using thumbnails, set your Bridge window to show two largest-size thumbnails side by side. It's often easier to open a new Bridge window to do this, and use another window showing the same folder with smaller thumbnails to navigate.

▶ If you need to compare the actual image pixels at full resolution, you can do so by opening the same images in Camera Raw *twice*, with one Camera Raw session hosted by Photoshop and the other hosted by Bridge. (Press Command-O to open the selected images in Camera Raw hosted by Photoshop, then return to Bridge and press Command-R to open them again in Camera Raw hosted by Bridge.) Then arrange the two Camera Raw windows so that you can see the preview in each one.

Figure 7-8 shows a Bridge window with side-by-side thumbnails. Figure 7-9 shows two simultaneous Camera Raw sessions.

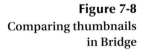
Figure 7-8
Comparing thumbnails
in Bridge

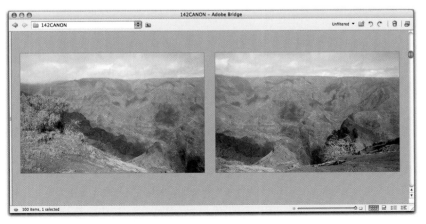

Figure 7-9
Simultaneous Camera
Raw sessions

*Camera Raw hosted
by Photoshop*

*Camera Raw hosted
by Bridge*

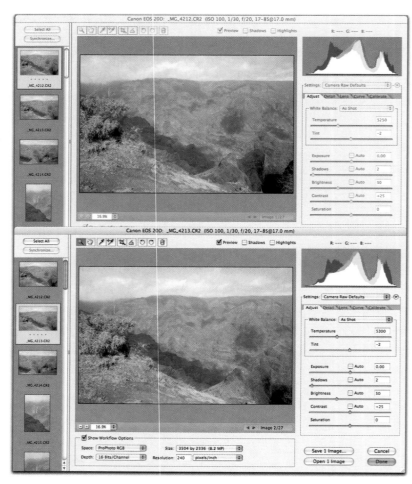

If you use this technique, remember that the settings that get applied to the image are those written by the last copy of Camera Raw to touch it.

Rating and Labeling

Physically selecting thumbnails is certainly one way to distinguish keepers from rejects, but it's ephemeral. A better method, which can be used with any of the techniques described in the previous section, is to use ratings or labels. Ratings and labels become part of the image's metadata that you can use to search and to filter which images get displayed (see "Labeling, Rating, and the Label Menu" in Chapter 6, *Adobe Bridge*).

As I mentioned earlier in this chapter, I prefer using ratings to labels, but the choice is entirely up to you. In this section I'll discuss the mechanics of applying and using labels and ratings.

One-star rating for binary sorts. If you've become accustomed to using the old File Browser's flagging mechanism for binary, yes/no sorting and selecting, you'll be happy to find that the old keyboard shortcut, Command-' (apostrophe), now lets you toggle a one-star rating on and off.

If you've selected a mixture of images, some of which have a one-star rating and some of which are unrated, pressing Command-' works the same as the old File Browser's Flag command—the first application adds one star to the unrated images and preserves the one-star rating for those that already have it. When all the selected images have the same attribute (all rated with one star, or all unrated), the command acts as a toggle, adding a star to unrated images or removing it from ones rated with one star.

However, if the selection also contains images rated with more than one star, pressing Command-' will apply a one-star rating to these images, so you need to be a little careful with your selections.

If you have no old habits, or if you're happy to unlearn those that you have, Command-1 applies a one-star rating to all selected images, and Command-0 removes the rating for all selected images. You can apply the rating to one image at a time (which is the most convenient method in Filmstrip view, and the only possible method in Slide Show view), or to multiple selected images (which is often convenient in Thumbnails view).

Once you've applied the one-star rating, you can segregate the rated and unrated images in any of the following three ways—see Figure 7-10.

▶ Choose Show 1 or More Stars (press Command-Option-1) from Bridge's Unfiltered/Filtered menu (this will also display images that have more than one star rating, but if you're using this mechanism for an initial yes/no select, none of your images will have more than one star as yet).

▶ Choose Show Unrated Items Only from Bridge's Unfiltered/Filtered menu, then choose Invert Selection (press Command-Shift-I) from Bridge's Edit menu to invert the selection.

▶ Choose Find (press Command-F) from Bridge's Edit menu, then in the Find dialog box, choose Rating is equal to * (one star). If some of the images in the folder already have a rating of more than one star, this is the only way to display only those images that have exactly one star as their rating.

Figure 7-10
Separating rated and
unrated images

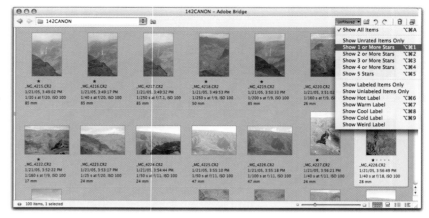

Choose Show 1 or More
Stars from the Unfiltered/
Filtered menu, or...

...choose Show Unrated
from the Unfiltered/
Filtered menu, then choose
Invert Selection from the
Edit menu, or...

...choose Find from the
Edit menu, then use
the selection criteria
shown at right.

One-star is great for making quick, yes/no, binary decisions—keep or reject—but for more nuanced choices, you can add stars to the rating.

Multistar Ratings. The techniques for applying multistar ratings are the same as those for applying a single star. Command-0 removes the rating, and Command-1 through Command-5 apply one to five stars. Command-. (period) adds a star to the current rating, and Command-, (comma) reduces it by one star.

There are basically two ways to approach rating your images. Use whichever one works for you.

► Make an initial one-star pass, then go through the one-star images and apply an additional star to those images that deserve it, then go through the two-star images, and apply a third star to those that deserve it. Many photographers find that four levels (unrated, one, two, or three stars) is enough, but you can go all the way to five if you see the need.

► Apply all your ratings in a single pass.

If you're collaborating with others in determining the hero shots, the first approach is probably the more suitable. The second approach lends itself better to situations where you're the only person making the call.

The techniques shown in Figure 7-10 are equally applicable to multi-star ratings as they are to single-star ones. The Unfiltered/Filtered menu commands let you find all images that have a minimum number of stars, while the Find command lets you find images that have a specific number of stars.

Labels. The main reason I don't use labels is that they introduce extraneous color in Bridge windows. But the Label mechanism is also less well suited to rating images than is the star-based ratings system. It's intuitively obvious that a five-star rating is either better or worse than one star, while there's no clear comparison between, say, yellow and green.

The stars are incremental, but the labels are not—they're simply arbitrary labels. You can apply any of the first four labels using Command-6 through Command-9, but there's no concept of promoting or demoting images from one label to another.

Labels are also less portable than ratings. Your labels will show up as white on any machine that uses a different label definition than yours, which is almost certain to happen if you use something other than the default label definitions (red, yellow, green, blue, and purple), and reasonably likely to happen even if you do use the default definitions, since the recipient may not. They can always search for your label text, but it's probably simpler just to use ratings.

Applying Camera Raw Settings

There are basically three ways to approach the task of applying rough Camera Raw edits to multiple images. Remember, at this stage in the workflow, you're simply aiming for good, not perfect. (Perfect comes later, when you've whittled the images down to the selects you'll actually deliver.)

To work efficiently, look for and select images that require approximately the same edit. Once you've done so, you can apply the edits in any of the following three ways—you can mix and match techniques as required.

Edit by example in Bridge. Select the first of the images that need the same edit, then open it in Camera Raw. The choice of host application—Bridge or Photoshop—depends on what else is going on. If Photoshop is busy batch-processing files, host Camera Raw in Bridge. If Bridge is busy building the cache, host Camera Raw in Photoshop. If they're both busy, host Camera Raw in Bridge—Bridge's multithreading lets you work in Camera Raw with surprisingly responsive performance even while Bridge itself is busy doing other tasks.

Make your edits—white balance, exposure, whatever the image needs—and then dismiss the Camera Raw dialog box by clicking Done (it's the default option in Camera Raw hosted by Bridge, but not in Camera Raw hosted by Photoshop).

Choose Apply Camera Raw Settings>Copy Camera Raw Settings from Bridge's Edit menu, or press Command-Option-C. Then select all the other images that need the same edit and choose Apply Camera Raw Settings>Paste Camera Raw Settings from Bridge's Edit menu (press Command-Option-V). If necessary, select the combination of subsets or settings you want to apply from the Paste Camera Raw Settings dialog box, then click OK. See Figure 7-11.

This approach works well when you need to apply the same settings to a large number of images that are identifiable by relatively small thumbnails, because you can select them quickly. But if you need to make small changes to the settings for each image, the following two approaches are better suited.

Figure 7-11
Copy and Paste
Camera Raw Settings

Edit the first image in the series, then choose Copy Camera Raw Settings.

Select the remaining images in the series, then choose Paste Camera Raw Settings. Choose the settings you want to apply from the Paste Camera Raw Settings dialog box, shown at right.

The Camera Raw settings you chose are applied to the selected images.

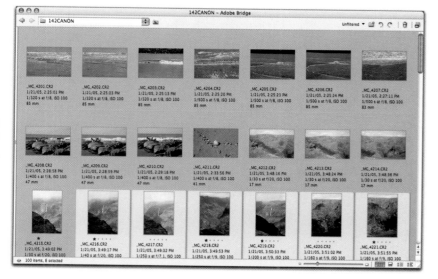

Edit by presets. If you've saved presets for Camera Raw in Camera Raw's Settings folder—see "Loading and Saving Settings" in Chapter 4, *Camera Raw Controls,* if you need a refresher—you can apply them to all the selected images by choosing Apply Camera Raw Settings from Bridge's Edit menu, then choosing the settings or settings subsets from the submenu. See Figure 7-12.

Saving Settings Subsets as presets is particularly powerful, because you can simply choose them in succession. Each one affects only the parameters recorded when you saved it, so you can load a preset for white balance, followed by one for Exposure, for Brightness, for Contrast, for Calibrate settings, and so on.

This approach is useful for fine-tuning results after a rough edit accomplished using Copy/Paste Camera Raw settings, or for applying very general settings, such as lighting-specific Calibrate adjustments, that you don't want to include in your default settings.

Figure 7-12
Choosing saved presets

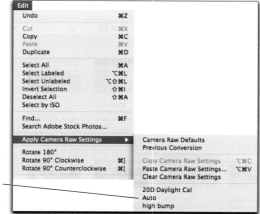

Saved settings appear at the foot of the Apply Camera Raw Settings submenu.

Edit in Camera Raw. The method that offers the most flexibility, and the one I prefer, is to open multiple images in Camera Raw. There's probably a limit to the number of images you can open simultaneously in Camera Raw, but I haven't yet found it—I've been able to open 1500 images simultaneously in Camera Raw and while it took a couple of minutes to launch, it worked perfectly.

That said, it's more practical to work with smaller sets of images. If you open 10 or more images, you'll get a dialog box asking if you really want to open 10 files. I recommend clicking the Don't show again checkbox, and cheerfully opening as many images as your machine can reasonably handle without bogging down—if the hardware is at all recent, it's almost certainly a considerably larger number than 10.

When you open multiple images, Camera Raw works in filmstrip mode. The current image is one whose preview shows in the preview window—see Figure 7-13.

Figure 7-13
Camera Raw in filmstrip mode

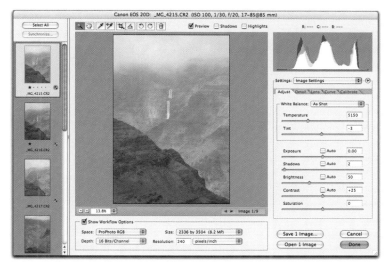

The current image is the one whose preview appears in the preview window.

Camera Raw in filmstrip mode offers two basic methods for editing multiple images besides the obvious one of editing images one by one.

▶ **Select multiple thumbnails.** When you select multiple thumbnails in Camera Raw, only the first (chronologically) selected image shows in the preview, but any edits you make apply to all the selected images, so you are in effect editing multiple images simultaneously. You'll see yellow warning triangles appear on the thumbnails while Camera Raw is updating them to reflect the edits, then disappear when the new thumbnail is built. Camera Raw's title bar displays the filename of the image that's being previewed.

When you're working with multiple selected images in Camera Raw, the up and down arrow keys move through the selected thumbnails, ignoring the unselected ones. The current image has a slightly heavier border than the others, but the filename in the title bar is a more obvious guide as to which image is the current one. See Figure 7-14.

Figure 7-14
Editing multiple images
in Camera Raw

Selected images

The current image

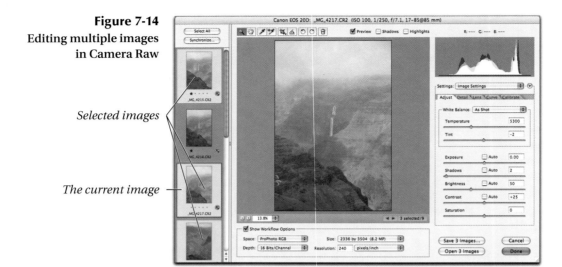

▶ **Use Synchronize.** Camera Raw's Synchronize feature is similar to copying and pasting Camera Raw settings. The Synchronize button lets you
apply the settings of the current image to all the other selected images,
so you need to pay attention to which image is in fact the current one!

When you click the Synchronize button, the Synchronize dialog box
(which is identical to the Paste Camera Raw Settings dialog box in all
but name) appears, allowing you to choose which settings will be applied to the selected images—see Figure 7-15. To skip the dialog box
and apply all the settings, Option-click the Synchronize button.

Figure 7-15
Synchronize Camera
Raw setting

The Synchronize button
and dialog box let you
synchronize the selected
images' settings to those
of the current image.

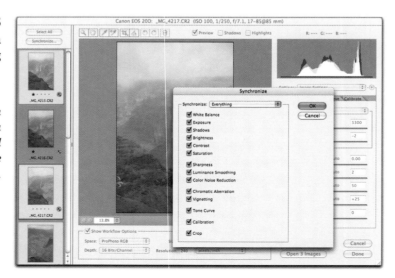

You can mix and match both of these approaches, while enjoying the benefits of zoomable previews, and Undo. (And if you simply can't resist the temptation, you can fine-tune individual images too.) Of all the methods of editing multiple raw images, I find this one the most powerful and the most flexible.

Sorting and Renaming

By default, Bridge sorts images by filename, so new raw images appear in the order in which they were shot, because the camera applies consecutive numbering to each image. You can vary the sort order by choosing any of the options on Bridge's View>Sort submenu—see Figure 7-16.

Figure 7-16
The Sort menu

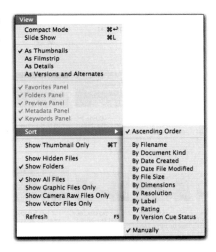

You can also create a custom sort order by dragging the thumbnails, just as you would with chromes on a light table. When you do so, the Manually item on the Sort menu is checked. The manual sort order is stored only in the Bridge cache for the folder. If you use distributed caches, you can move or rename the folder and Bridge will still remember the sort order. But if you combine images from several folders into a different folder, you have in effect created a new sort order, and it may well not be the one you wanted. So a simple way to preserve that order is to use Batch Rename to rename the images including a numbering scheme that reflects your custom sort order.

Or you may wish to batch-rename your raw images using some other scheme entirely. For example, my friend and colleague Seth Resnick, who has put more sheer ingenuity into building his workflow than anyone else I know, uses a sophisticated naming scheme that, to the initiated, at least, conveys a great deal of information at a glance.

For example, he might rename a raw file called 4F3S0266.tif to 20050423STKSR3_0001.tif. This decodes as follows. 20050423 defines the date on which the image was shot (April 23, 2005), so the files are automatically sorted by date order. STK indicates that the image was shot for stock, and SR indicates that it was shot by Seth Resnick. The number 3 indicates that it belonged to the third assignment or collection of images of the day, while the 0001 indicates that it was the first image in the collection. The .tif is the file extension that defines the file type. Figure 7-17 shows how to set up the either Bridge's Batch Rename or Photoshop's Batch dialog box to accomplish this renaming. Unless you want to run an action on the raw files and save them, it makes more sense to use Bridge's Batch Rename than Photoshop's Batch, but when the goal is to produce renamed converted images, Photoshop's Batch is the way to go.

Figure 7-17
Batch renaming

Bridge's Batch Rename
dialog box

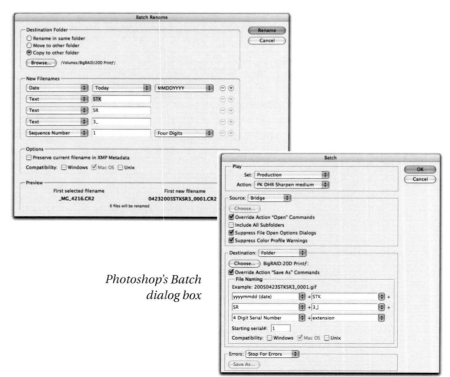

Photoshop's Batch
dialog box

Tip: Always Include the Extension as the Last Item. When you use proprietary raw files, each image is accompanied by a sidecar .xmp file that differs in name from the raw file only by the extension. If you include the extension as the last element, the sidecar files will get renamed correctly along with the raw files. If you fail to do so, the batch rename will fail with a message saying "file already exists."

Tip: Process JPEGs Separately. The Batch Rename command is smart enough to handle sidecar .xmp files, but if you shoot raw and JPEG, and you have three files whose names are distinguished only by their extension rather than two, you need to do a little more work. First, use the search tool to search for all the JPEGs, and run the batch rename on them. Then use the search tool again to find all the raws and run the same batch rename. You'll wind up with correctly named raws, JPEGs, and sidecar .xmp files for each image.

Tip: Be Careful with Length and Special Characters. To remain compatible with today's operating systems, your filenames should be no longer than 31 characters, including the extension. Some antediluvian systems may limit you to an 8.3 (eight characters plus a three-character extension) filename, but those are fortunately getting rarer with each passing moment. For cross-platform compatibility, limit yourself to the lower 128 characters of the ASCII character set and avoid characters that have a reserved use in the operating system such as \ / : * ? < > or |. If you limit yourself to lowercase and uppercase alphabetic characters, numerals, underscores, and hyphens, and only use the period immediately before the extension, you'll be safe.

Applying Keywords and Metadata

The key to being efficient with keywords and metadata is the same as that for being efficient with applying Camera Raw edits. Look for and select images that need the same treatment, and deal with them all at once.

IPTC metadata. The only metadata that is editable in Bridge (or in Photoshop, for that matter) is the IPTC metadata. For recurring metadata such as copyright notices, metadata templates provide a very convenient way to make the edits—see Figure 6-19 in Chapter 6, *Adobe Bridge*.

Alternatively, you can select multiple images and then edit the metadata directly in the Metadata palette. Click in the first field you want to edit, and type in your entry. Then press Tab to advance to the next field. Continue until you've entered all the metadata shared by the selected images, and then click the checkmark icon at the lower right of the palette, or press Enter or Return, to confirm the entries.

Keywords. Keywords show up in the IPTC section of the Metadata palette, but you can't enter or edit them there—you have to use the Keywords palette. The Keywords palette contains individual keywords grouped into sets (represented by the folder icons). The default keywords and sets are pretty useless unless you know a lot of people called Julius and Michael, but you can easily replace them with ones that are more useful for your purposes.

To apply a keyword, select one or more images and then click in the column to the left of the keyword. A check mark appears in the column, and Bridge writes the keyword to each file's sidecar.xmp file. To remove a keyword, select the images and then uncheck the checkmark.

Deleting a keyword from the Keywords palette doesn't delete the keyword from any images to which it has been applied; it only deletes it from the palette. So I find that it makes sense to keep only keywords I know I'll use a lot stored in the palette. For keywords that apply only to the current session, I create them in a set called Temp and delete them when I'm done, to keep the palette manageable.

Keyword sets let you organize keywords, but they also offer a very useful functionality—they let you apply all the keywords in the set to selected images by clicking next to the set name rather than the keyword names. When you click next to a keyword to apply it, Bridge starts writing it to the selected images. If you then add another keyword, Bridge will write both keywords to the images it hasn't yet touched, but then it has to go back and add the second keyword to the images it had already processed.

Tip: Sets Are Not Set in Stone. My Temp set also serves to add multiple keywords. When I want to apply multiple keywords to a set of images, I drag any existing keywords I want to use into the Temp set and create any new ones I want to apply inside the Temp set. Then I click beside the Temp set icon to apply all the keywords it currently contains to all the selected images—see Figure 7-18.

Figure 7-18
Adding multiple
keywords

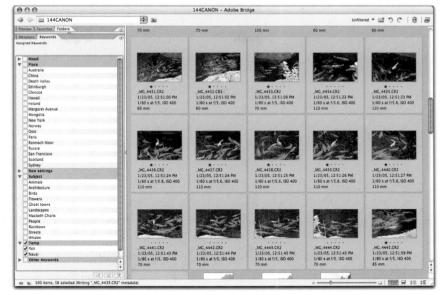

To add multiple
keywords quickly and
efficiently, drag them
all into the same set,
then click next to the set
name to apply all the
keywords in the set.

All the work you do in Bridge is aimed at setting things up to produce converted versions of your chosen raw images, with the correct Camera Raw settings to get the tone and color you want, and including all the metadata you've entered. So let's look at this last stage of the workflow, actually converting your raw images.

The Production Phase

When it comes to efficiency in converting raw images, actions are the key. I almost always convert raw images in batches using actions rather than simply opening them in Photoshop. Final deliverable images almost always require some handwork in Photoshop, but for the intermediate phases I'll often save images either directly out of Camera Raw, or using Photoshop's Image Processor if I need both a JPEG and a TIFF version of the images.

Even when I anticipate significant handwork in Photoshop, I try to work as efficiently as possible. Even in worst-case scenarios, such as when you need to stack multiple renderings of the same image, there are more and less efficient ways to do the job. I'll discuss the various built-in automation features in detail in the next chapter, *Exploiting Automation*, but here's the strategic overview.

Background Processing

One of the most useful additions to the raw workflow toolkit is the capability of Camera Raw 3.0 to save images in the background, hosted either by Photoshop or Bridge—see "The Main Control Buttons" in Chapter 4, *Camera Raw Controls*, and "Saving Images in the Background" in Chapter 5, *Hands-On Camera Raw*.

I use background saving for two distinct purposes.

► When I've completed my initial rough edits, metadata addition and keywording, I open the whole folder in Camera Raw, select all the images, click Save x Images, and save them as DNG using the Compressed (lossless) option, with Full Size JPEG preview. I save the DNGs to a new folder, then I either discard the proprietary raw files, or run them through the DNG Converter application to create DNG files with the original raw file embedded, as an archive.

In both cases, all the metadata, including Camera Raw settings, and any keywords I've applied are written into the DNG files, so I no longer need to worry about sidecar files. The choice of which application hosts Camera Raw for background saving depends entirely on which application I want to use while the files are being saved in the background.

► When I need to save a bunch of JPEGs or, less commonly, TIFFs without running any actions on them, I change the file format in camera Raw's Save Options dialog box to the one I need, and save the files in the background. Again, the choice of which application hosts Camera Raw's background saving depends on what I want to do during the save process.

Bear in mind that when Camera Raw is tied up doing saves in one application, it's still available for use in the other.

Automated Conversions

Background saving is useful when you've done everything the image needs in Camera Raw, but Camera Raw can't do everything *I* need to most images. For example, I always sharpen in Photoshop using PhotoKit Sharpener, and I often perform selective corrections to parts of the image in Photoshop, which Camera Raw simply can't do. But when I do so, I don't open the image in Photoshop and start editing. Instead, I use one of the options on Bridge's Tools>Photoshop menu to do as much of the work as possible. I'll discuss these in much greater detail in Chapter 9, *Exploiting Automation*, but for now I'll give you the 30,000-foot overview.

Batch. This is the Big Daddy of all the automation features, and is capable of doing just about anything that Photoshop can be made to do. To run Batch using selected images in Bridge as the source, you *must* invoke Batch from Bridge's Tools>Photoshop menu. If you try to launch Batch from Photoshop, you'll find that Bridge is grayed out as a source. The basic idea is that Batch takes selected images in Bridge as its source and opens them in Photoshop using the Camera Raw settings for each image. Then it runs an action on the images in Photoshop, and either leaves them open in Photoshop, saves them in a destination folder (optionally renaming them in the process), or, a potential big hurt-me button, saves and closes the files in place.

Most raw files are read-only in that Photoshop can't write the raw formats, but some cameras create their raw files as TIFF. If you have one of these cameras, avoid Save and Close like the plague, because it will overwrite your raw originals with the processed versions!

PDF Presentation. This option lets you create a slide show in PDF format or a multipage PDF with one image per page. For the slide show, you can specify how long each image stays on screen and choose a transition, but you can't add captions or copyright notices. It's quick and easy, but limited.

Image Processor. This option lets you save up to three versions of the selected images, a JPEG, a TIFF, and a Photoshop file, each in their own folders. You can resize the image independently for each format, run an action on the images, and embed a copyright notice (though in my opinion, you should already have done so long before you launched Image Processor). Image Processor is the easiest way to save a low-res JPEG and a high-res TIFF in the same operation.

Contact Sheet II. This option lets you build a contact sheet. You can specify a page size, select how many images appear per page, choose whether to preserve rotation or orient all images the same way for best fit, and choose whether or not to include filenames as captions, with the choice of font and size.

Picture Package. This option lets you produce a package of each image, with multiple copies and sizes of the image on the same page—for example, on an 8x10 page, you could specify one 5x7, two 2.5x3.5, and four 2x2.5 inch versions.

You can customize the layout and add captions—automated options are any one of filename, copyright notice, description, credit, or title, all picked up from the IPTC metadata, or a custom text string. This is a surprisingly deep little feature.

Web Photo Gallery. This option is like a contact sheet for the Web, but since it's a digital contact sheet, it offers the option of including feedback links. Like Picture Package, this feature has surprising depths, which I'll look at in detail in Chapter 9, *Exploiting Automation.*

All the work you do in Bridge forms the foundation for future automation. Images are converted using the right Camera Raw settings at the correct orientation, and the converted images contain all the metadata you attached to the original raws. Since this work is so important, you should understand how it gets saved and stored, and that means knowing a little about Bridge's cache.

Opening Multiple Iterations

Fairly often, I find it useful to combine differently converted versions of the same raw image in Photoshop, combining different tonal treatments to extend the apparent dynamic range, combining different white balances, or even combining different noise reduction strengths.

In Photoshop CS, this was a fairly painful process for two reasons.

▶ Once an image was open in Photoshop, I couldn't open a second version unless I first renamed the one that was already open.

▶ Camera Raw always saved the last-used settings into the image's metadata, which often was not what I wanted, so I had to manually save my "master" settings, then go back and reapply them.

Camera Raw hosted by Photoshop addresses both of these issues neatly with its Open Copy feature. When you press Option, the Open button changes to the Open Copy button. Open Copy opens the image in Photoshop without updating the Camera Raw settings, and if a copy is already open, it appends a number to the document name—if the first copy opens as *filename*, the second copy opens as *filename-2*, and so on.

Remember—this feature is only available in Camera Raw hosted by Photoshop (which, since it's where you want the image to go, makes perfect workflow sense).

Tethered Shooting

I hesitated to include this because I don't claim to have tested the process with a large number of cameras, and it's not a workflow that's sanctioned by any of the vendors involved. But if you wish Camera Raw offered tethered shooting, you may want to give this a try.

► Use your camera vendor's software to control the camera.

► Set it up to shoot to a folder on your hard drive.

► Point Bridge at that hard drive.

In theory, this should work. In practice, it *has* worked with both (Canon) cameras I've tried, so this comes with no warranties, expressed or implied. It doesn't take long to determine if it works or not with your camera. When it does, you can open the image in Camera Raw without even waiting for Bridge to read the thumbnail—as soon as the icon appears, you can open the image.

Make the Work Flow

Bridge is a deep, complex, and very powerful tool that puts you in charge of an even deeper, more complex, and more powerful workflow system. Bridge lets you do many things once, and once only, so that you don't need to keep doing them over and over again, whether it's applying Camera Raw settings, entering copyright notices, or rotating and cropping images. The time you spend in Bridge will be amply repaid further down the line.

You can make the work flow even faster if you plan it. Bridge lets you carry out operations in any order you choose; but the most efficient way is to proceed from the general to the specific, starting with the operations that every image needs (such as a copyright notice) and continuing with the more individualized and specific needs of progressively smaller numbers of images.

Some things, such as entering descriptions or captions, you'll have to do image by image, and you'll almost certainly want to fine-tune the Camera Raw settings for your hero images on an individual basis. But you probably don't need to hand-tune every single image that you shoot. Instead, use Bridge to whittle down the large collection of raws to the images that truly deserve individual attention, and save the handwork for those.

8 Mastering Metadata

The Smarter Image

Metadata, which literally means "data about data," isn't a new idea by any means. Library catalogs are good examples of long-established metadata systems—the data is what lies between the covers of the book, while the metadata includes information *about* the book—who wrote it, who published it, when both parties did so, what it's about, and where in the library it's located, for starters.

Metadata isn't new to photography either. Photojournalists have long relied on the metadata properties specified by the IPTC (International Press Telecommunications Council) to make sure that their images get delivered correctly with the appropriate photo credit. But two factors are bringing metadata to the front burner for all photographers, not just photojournalists.

▶ Digital cameras embed a wealth of useful metadata right in the raw file.

▶ Adobe is in the process of using its considerable clout to promote XMP (Extensible Metadata Platform) as a documented, open, extensible standard for creating, storing, and sharing metadata.

Digital captures are already rich in metadata straight out of the camera, but one of the problems that has plagued early adopters has been a plethora of proprietary and often incompatible methods of writing and storing metadata. This is an ongoing battle.

243

The EXIF (Exchangeable Image File Format) "standard," for example, is sufficiently vague that the exchangeability pretty much applies exclusively to JPEGs. Camera vendors are allowed a great deal of freedom ("too much freedom" is a phrase I rarely use, but it applies here) to use private proprietary fields in EXIF to encode important information.

For example, it seems to bring no conceivable benefit to Nikon shooters if the image White Balance settings are recorded by the camera in such a way that only Nikon software can read them directly, but that's how some current Nikon cameras work. This is not to single out Nikon—there's more than enough blame to go around, and almost every vendor who produces cameras that shoot raw does something similar with one or another piece of metadata.

Moreover, the EXIF standard contains quite a few redundancies: ExposureTime and ShutterSpeedValue tags both record the same information but use different encodings, as do the FNumber and ApertureValue tags. Some vendors use one, others use the other, entirely at their own whim—in short, the EXIF standard is a textbook example of what happens when a group of vendors whose sole aim in life is to compete with one another get together to make a standard.

Bridge's metadata panel tries to protect you from the EXIF mayhem by always reporting values consistently—for example, it always reports an Exposure value as shutter speed and aperture setting. If you need to see the original EXIF data, or if you're simply wondering why some other image browser doesn't report things in exactly the same way, you can see the original untranslated EXIF data by choosing File Info from either Bridge's or Photoshop's File menu, then clicking Advanced and opening the EXIF properties list—see Figure 8-1.

The intent here isn't to beat up on the camera vendors (well, not much), but rather to demonstrate just how badly we need a standard framework for handling metadata as well as pixel data. That's why XMP is so important to the future not only of photography, but of all the enterprises that consume photography: XMP is to metadata what DNG is to raw pixel data—a great idea waiting to happen. Until such time as XMP (or some other standard that's *really* standardized) comes into play, we're all pioneers, and recognizable as such by the collection of arrows protruding from our backs!

Figure 8-1
Metadata mayhem

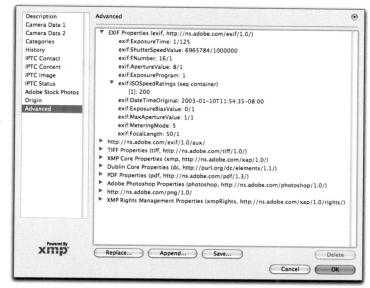

File Info's EXIF properties list in the Advanced panel shows the raw EXIF metadata.

Bridge's Metadata panel translates the raw EXIF metadata into a more friendly and more useful format.

What Is XMP, and Why Should I Care?

XMP is an Adobe initiative to promote a standard for metadata, but it's not a proprietary initiative. Instead, it's an open standard, it's documented, it's extensible, and it's even somewhat readable by humans. It is, in fact, a subset of XML (Extensible Markup Language), which is turn a subset of SGML (Standard Generalized Markup Language), the international standard metalanguage for text markup systems recorded in ISO 8879.

If you want to delve deeply into XMP, I suggest you start by looking at the available documentation. You can find several useful documents, including one on building custom File Info panels, at www.adobe.com:80/products/xmp/main.html.

I'm not going to teach you how to write XML code in this chapter (it's a bit more difficult than writing actions, but a good bit easier than writing JavaScripts), but I *will* show you what XMP metadata looks like and show you some of the ways in which you can work with it.

Growing Pains

Because XMP is still relatively new, you'll almost certainly encounter some growing pains if you try to work with a mixture of applications, some that support XMP, and others that as yet do not. There are two things you can do to lessen, if not eliminate, the pain.

► Ask the vendors of those applications that don't yet support XMP to do so.

► Learn how Photoshop and other Adobe and non-Adobe applications use XMP to record metadata, and find out just which files contain which pieces of information.

The first is up to you. The second is the core topic of this chapter. The metadata that you enter in Bridge for your raw files will persist through all the converted images that you create from the raw files, unless you take deliberate steps to remove it. This is mostly a huge advantage to photographers—you can enter the information once, for the raw file, and know that it will be present in all the variants that you create from that raw file, not as a sidecar file (those are only necessary with read-only raws) but embedded directly in the .tif, .psd, .jpg, or .eps image.

You know that your copyright notice will be embedded in the image, and, even better, you know that if you deliver the image on read-only media like CD-ROM or DVD-ROM, you can prove willful violation of the Digital Millennium Copyright Act of 1998 should someone else remove it. However, you may not always want to provide your clients with all that metadata. Some benighted souls still have attitude when it comes to digital capture: it's doubtful that they could identify the source of the image from the pixels, but they can do so easily from the metadata.

Metadata may seem mysterious at first, but with only minimal effort, you can gain a great deal more control over it. And if you're willing to do some serious heavy lifting, you can accomplish magic!

XMP Is Text

The first important thing to learn is that .xmp files are simply text files, readable by any text editor or word processor, that conform to a specific syntax and are saved with a .xmp extension. So it's easy to read and, if necessary, edit XMP metadata.

The second important thing to learn is how the user interface in Camera Raw and Bridge relates to the .xmp files that get stored in various locations on your computer. When you apply keywords or copyright notices, where does that data actually get stored? The answers may surprise you, but if you're at all curious, it's highly instructive to take a peek at sidecar .xmp files, saved Camera Raw Settings and Settings Subsets, and Metadata Templates with a text editor.

For the truly motivated, the third lesson involves the things you can do by customizing .xmp files. For example, when you save a custom Metadata Template, you may be surprised to see all the junk that by default gets saved in it. Judicious pruning with a text editor can make these important files more reliable. If you're really gung-ho, you can actually use XMP to make your own Custom File Info Panels. The IPTC schema, for example, is very much tailored to the needs of editorial shooters. You can use Custom File Info Panels to make it easy to add metadata to your images that more closely suits your own needs.

XMP Uncovered

Thus far, the discussion has been a little on the abstract side. So let's bring things down to earth and actually look at some XMP metadata. We'll start with a sidecar .xmp file.

Figure 8-2 shows an image, and Figure 8-3 shows what its accompanying sidecar .xmp file looks like when it's opened in a text editor.

At first glance, the metadata file may seem overwhelming, but once you break it down into its various components, things start to make a bit more sense. So I'll spend the next several pages walking you through the different chunks of text in the sidecar file and showing you the corresponding elements in Photoshop's user interface. Once you see the relationship between the two, things will start to make more sense.

Figure 8-2
The image

Figure 8-3
The sidecar .xmp file

```
<x:xmpmeta xmlns:x='adobe:ns:meta/' x:xmptk='XMP toolkit 3.0-28, framework 1.6'>
<rdf:RDF xmlns:rdf='http://www.w3.org/1999/02/22-rdf-syntax-ns#' xmlns:
iX='http://ns.adobe.com/iX/1.0/'>
 <rdf:Description rdf:about=''
  xmlns:crs='http://ns.adobe.com/camera-raw-settings/1.0/'>
  <crs:Version>3.0</crs:Version>
  <crs:RawFileName>CRW_1101.CRW</crs:RawFileName>
  <crs:WhiteBalance>Custom</crs:WhiteBalance>
  <crs:Temperature>5800</crs:Temperature>
  <crs:Tint>+11</crs:Tint>
  <crs:Exposure>+1.15</crs:Exposure>
  <crs:Shadows>0</crs:Shadows>
  <crs:Brightness>39</crs:Brightness>
  <crs:Contrast>+60</crs:Contrast>
  <crs:Saturation>0</crs:Saturation>
  <crs:Sharpness>25</crs:Sharpness>
  <crs:LuminanceSmoothing>0</crs:LuminanceSmoothing>
  <crs:ColorNoiseReduction>15</crs:ColorNoiseReduction>
  <crs:ChromaticAberrationR>0</crs:ChromaticAberrationR>
  <crs:ChromaticAberrationB>0</crs:ChromaticAberrationB>
  <crs:VignetteAmount>0</crs:VignetteAmount>
  <crs:ShadowTint>0</crs:ShadowTint>
  <crs:RedHue>-1</crs:RedHue>
  <crs:RedSaturation>+24</crs:RedSaturation>
  <crs:GreenHue>-12</crs:GreenHue>
  <crs:GreenSaturation>-18</crs:GreenSaturation>
  <crs:BlueHue>+5</crs:BlueHue>
  <crs:BlueSaturation>-13</crs:BlueSaturation>
```

Figure 8-3
The sidecar .xmp file,
continued

```
<crs:ToneCurveName>Custom</crs:ToneCurveName>
<crs:ToneCurve>
 <rdf:Seq>
  <rdf:li>0, 0</rdf:li>
  <rdf:li>34, 16</rdf:li>
  <rdf:li>70, 53</rdf:li>
  <rdf:li>121, 122</rdf:li>
  <rdf:li>184, 214</rdf:li>
  <rdf:li>255, 255</rdf:li>
 </rdf:Seq>
</crs:ToneCurve>
<crs:CameraProfile>ACR 2.4</crs:CameraProfile>
<crs:HasSettings>True</crs:HasSettings>
<crs:HasCrop>False</crs:HasCrop>
</rdf:Description>

<rdf:Description rdf:about=''
 xmlns:exif='http://ns.adobe.com/exif/1.0/'>
 <exif:ExposureTime>1/100</exif:ExposureTime>
 <exif:ShutterSpeedValue>6643856/1000000</exif:ShutterSpeedValue>
 <exif:FNumber>8/1</exif:FNumber>
 <exif:ApertureValue>6/1</exif:ApertureValue>
 <exif:ExposureProgram>2</exif:ExposureProgram>
 <exif:DateTimeOriginal>2004-08-12T06:57:52-07:00</exif:DateTimeOriginal>
 <exif:ExposureBiasValue>0/1</exif:ExposureBiasValue>
 <exif:MaxApertureValue>4/1</exif:MaxApertureValue>
 <exif:MeteringMode>5</exif:MeteringMode>
 <exif:FocalLength>28/1</exif:FocalLength>
 <exif:ISOSpeedRatings>
  <rdf:Seq>
   <rdf:li>200</rdf:li>
  </rdf:Seq>
 </exif:ISOSpeedRatings>
 <exif:Flash rdf:parseType='Resource'>
  <exif:Fired>False</exif:Fired>
 </exif:Flash>
</rdf:Description>

<rdf:Description rdf:about=''
 xmlns:aux='http://ns.adobe.com/exif/1.0/aux/'>
 <aux:SerialNumber>0660217086</aux:SerialNumber>
 <aux:Lens>18.0-55.0 mm</aux:Lens>
</rdf:Description>

<rdf:Description rdf:about=''
 xmlns:pdf='http://ns.adobe.com/pdf/1.3/'>
</rdf:Description>

<rdf:Description rdf:about=''
 xmlns:photoshop='http://ns.adobe.com/photoshop/1.0/'>
</rdf:Description>

<rdf:Description rdf:about=''
 xmlns:tiff='http://ns.adobe.com/tiff/1.0/'>
 <tiff:Make>Canon</tiff:Make>
 <tiff:Model>Canon EOS DIGITAL REBEL</tiff:Model>
```

Figure 8-3
The sidecar .xmp file,
continued

```
<tiff:Orientation>6</tiff:Orientation>
<tiff:ImageWidth>3072</tiff:ImageWidth>
<tiff:ImageLength>2048</tiff:ImageLength>
<tiff:PhotometricInterpretation>2</tiff:PhotometricInterpretation>
<tiff:XResolution>240/1</tiff:XResolution>
<tiff:YResolution>240/1</tiff:YResolution>
<tiff:ResolutionUnit>2</tiff:ResolutionUnit>
<tiff:BitsPerSample>
 <rdf:Seq>
  <rdf:li>16</rdf:li>
  <rdf:li>16</rdf:li>
  <rdf:li>16</rdf:li>
 </rdf:Seq>
</tiff:BitsPerSample>
<tiff:DateTime>2004-08-12T06:57:52-07:00</tiff:DateTime>
</rdf:Description>

<rdf:Description rdf:about=''
 xmlns:xap='http://ns.adobe.com/xap/1.0/'>
 <xap:ModifyDate>2004-08-12T06:57:52-07:00</xap:ModifyDate>
 <xap:MetadataDate>2005-03-25T16:27:25-08:00</xap:MetadataDate>
 <xap:Rating>0</xap:Rating>
</rdf:Description>

<rdf:Description rdf:about=''
 xmlns:xapRights='http://ns.adobe.com/xap/1.0/rights/'>
 <xapRights:Marked>True</xapRights:Marked>
</rdf:Description>

<rdf:Description rdf:about=''
 xmlns:dc='http://purl.org/dc/elements/1.1/'>
 <dc:creator>
  <rdf:Seq>
   <rdf:li>Bruce Fraser</rdf:li>
  </rdf:Seq>
 </dc:creator>
 <dc:rights>
  <rdf:Alt>
   <rdf:li xml:lang='x-default'>©2004 Bruce Fraser. All Rights Reserved</rdf:li>
  </rdf:Alt>
 </dc:rights>
 <dc:subject>
  <rdf:Bag>
   <rdf:li>Glencoe</rdf:li>
   <rdf:li>Scotland</rdf:li>
   <rdf:li>Flowers</rdf:li>
  </rdf:Bag>
 </dc:subject>
 <dc:description>
  <rdf:Alt>
   <rdf:li xml:lang='x-default'>lichen and heather in Glencoe</rdf:li>
  </rdf:Alt>
 </dc:description>
</rdf:Description>

</rdf:RDF>
</x:xmpmeta>
```

Sidecar .xmp Decoded

The first few lines say that this is a .xmp metadata document, identified by means of a *namespace*. A namespace is the secret decoder ring for a particular XMP *schema*, which is the collection of properties the document deals with. Namespaces avoid conflicts between properties with the same name but different meanings in different schemas. For example, the "Creator" property in one schema may be the human who created a resource, while in another it refers to the application used to create the resource.

Schema names look like URLs, but they're actually URIs—Uniform Resource Indicators—that may or may not point to a Web page. The second chunk of text, shown in Figure 8-4, contains the Camera Raw settings.

Figure 8-4
Sidecar .xmp
camera raw settings

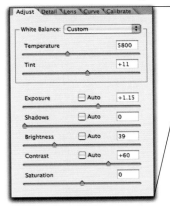

The boxed lines are the Camera Raw Adjust tab settings. The Detail, Lens, and Calibrate tab settings follow, then the Curve tab, then the Camera Raw profile, the flag that tells Bridge that the image has settings applied, and the crop.

```
<rdf:Description rdf:about=''
  xmlns:crs='http://ns.adobe.com/camera-raw-settings/1.0/'>
  <crs:Version>3.0</crs:Version>
  <crs:RawFileName>CRW_1101.CRW</crs:RawFileName>
  <crs:WhiteBalance>Custom</crs:WhiteBalance>
  <crs:Temperature>5800</crs:Temperature>
  <crs:Tint>+11</crs:Tint>
  <crs:Exposure>+1.15</crs:Exposure>
  <crs:Shadows>0</crs:Shadows>
  <crs:Brightness>39</crs:Brightness>
  <crs:Contrast>+60</crs:Contrast>
  <crs:Saturation>0</crs:Saturation>
  <crs:Sharpness>25</crs:Sharpness>
  <crs:LuminanceSmoothing>0</crs:LuminanceSmoothing>
  <crs:ColorNoiseReduction>15</crs:ColorNoiseReduction>
  <crs:ChromaticAberrationR>0</crs:ChromaticAberrationR>
  <crs:ChromaticAberrationB>0</crs:ChromaticAberrationB>
  <crs:VignetteAmount>0</crs:VignetteAmount>
  <crs:ShadowTint>0</crs:ShadowTint>
  <crs:RedHue>-1</crs:RedHue>
  <crs:RedSaturation>+24</crs:RedSaturation>
  <crs:GreenHue>-12</crs:GreenHue>
  <crs:GreenSaturation>-18</crs:GreenSaturation>
  <crs:BlueHue>+5</crs:BlueHue>
  <crs:BlueSaturation>-13</crs:BlueSaturation>
  <crs:ToneCurveName>Custom</crs:ToneCurveName>
  <crs:ToneCurve>
   <rdf:Seq>
    <rdf:li>0, 0</rdf:li>
    <rdf:li>34, 16</rdf:li>
    <rdf:li>70, 53</rdf:li>
    <rdf:li>121, 122</rdf:li>
    <rdf:li>184, 214</rdf:li>
    <rdf:li>255, 255</rdf:li>
   </rdf:Seq>
  </crs:ToneCurve>
  <crs:CameraProfile>ACR 2.4</crs:CameraProfile>
  <crs:HasSettings>True</crs:HasSettings>
  <crs:HasCrop>False</crs:HasCrop>
 </rdf:Description>
```

This chunk of text is what Photoshop and Bridge use to keep track of the custom settings for each raw image. It contains the image's Camera Raw settings in human-readable form. The next two chunks of text hold the EXIF data from the raw file. They correspond to the second and third entries you see in the Advanced panel of File Info—EXIF Properties, and the auxiliary EXIF data in http://ns.adobe.com/exif/1.0/aux/—see Figure 8-5.

Figure 8-5
EXIF data

```
<rdf:Description rdf:about=''
 xmlns:exif='http://ns.adobe.com/exif/1.0/'>
 <exif:ExposureTime>1/100</exif:ExposureTime>
 <exif:ShutterSpeedValue>6643856/1000000</exif:ShutterSpeedValue>
 <exif:FNumber>8/1</exif:FNumber>
 <exif:ApertureValue>6/1</exif:ApertureValue>
 <exif:ExposureProgram>2</exif:ExposureProgram>
 <exif:DateTimeOriginal>2004-08-12T06:57:52-07:00</exif:DateTimeOriginal>
 <exif:ExposureBiasValue>0/1</exif:ExposureBiasValue>
 <exif:MaxApertureValue>4/1</exif:MaxApertureValue>
 <exif:MeteringMode>5</exif:MeteringMode>
 <exif:FocalLength>28/1</exif:FocalLength>
 <exif:ISOSpeedRatings>
  <rdf:Seq>
   <rdf:li>200</rdf:li>
  </rdf:Seq>
 </exif:ISOSpeedRatings>
 <exif:Flash rdf:parseType='Resource'>
  <exif:Fired>False</exif:Fired>
 </exif:Flash>
</rdf:Description>

<rdf:Description rdf:about=''
 xmlns:aux='http://ns.adobe.com/exif/1.0/aux/'>
 <aux:SerialNumber>0660217086</aux:SerialNumber>
 <aux:Lens>18.0-55.0 mm</aux:Lens>
</rdf:Description>
```

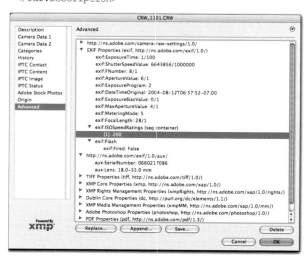

EXIF metadata in a raw file isn't editable by any means short of opening the raw image file with a hex editor, which is such a dangerous operation that I wouldn't even contemplate it. If you edit the EXIF data in the sidecar file, it simply gets overwritten by the EXIF data baked into the raw file the next time you open it. I'm opposed to anything that would allow changing the EXIF metadata—it's an essential part of the image's provenance, and we should be able to rely on its veracity.

Tip: Stripping Metadata. You can't strip EXIF metadata from a raw file, but if you don't want EXIF data in your final file, simply copy the image pixels in Photoshop, then paste them into a new document. This strips *all* metadata, not just EXIF, so make sure you add back any metadata you want to preserve in the delivered image.

Next comes the PDF Properties section, followed by the Photoshop Properties section. Notice that the File Info contains entries that the metadata does not—they're aliased from other areas in the sidecar .xmp file. By now, you may have noticed that the URI that starts each section of metadata points to one of the categories in the Advanced panel of File Info—it shows the URIs in parentheses right after the category—see Figure 8-6.

Figure 8-6
PDF and Photoshop Properties

```
<rdf:Description rdf:about=''
  xmlns:pdf='http://ns.adobe.com/pdf/1.3/'>
</rdf:Description>

<rdf:Description rdf:about=''
  xmlns:photoshop='http://ns.adobe.com/photoshop/1.0/'>
</rdf:Description>
```

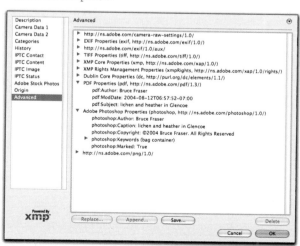

TIFF Properties comes next. Here you'll find the camera make and model, the pixel dimensions, the image orientation, and the default resolution and bit depth for the converted image, set in Camera Raw. You'll find the corresponding entries in the Advanced File Info listing under TIFF Properties. Again, notice that the File Info entries for TIFF Properties contain items—the Artist, Copyright Notice, and Image Description entries—that are aliased from entries that appear later in the sidecar .xmp file. See Figure 8-7.

Figure 8-7
TIFF Properties

```
<rdf:Description rdf:about=''
  xmlns:tiff='http://ns.adobe.com/tiff/1.0/'>
  <tiff:Make>Canon</tiff:Make>
  <tiff:Model>Canon EOS DIGITAL REBEL</tiff:Model>
  <tiff:Orientation>6</tiff:Orientation>
  <tiff:ImageWidth>3072</tiff:ImageWidth>
  <tiff:ImageLength>2048</tiff:ImageLength>
  <tiff:PhotometricInterpretation>2</tiff:PhotometricInterpretation>
  <tiff:XResolution>240/1</tiff:XResolution>
  <tiff:YResolution>240/1</tiff:YResolution>
  <tiff:ResolutionUnit>2</tiff:ResolutionUnit>
  <tiff:BitsPerSample>
   <rdf:Seq>
    <rdf:li>16</rdf:li>
    <rdf:li>16</rdf:li>
    <rdf:li>16</rdf:li>
   </rdf:Seq>
  </tiff:BitsPerSample>
  <tiff:DateTime>2004-08-12T06:57:52-07:00</tiff:DateTime>
</rdf:Description>
```

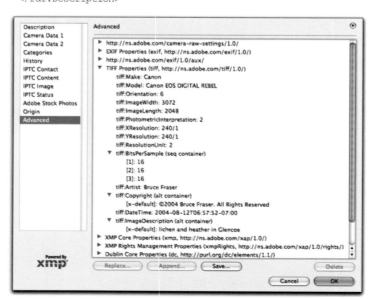

The next two sections generate the XMP Core Properties and XMP Rights Management entries in File Info. The XMP Core Properties holds the modification and metadata dates, along with any ranking or labeling information applied in Bridge. The XMP Rights Management section contains the copyright flag and copyright URL, if any. See Figure 8-8.

Figure 8-8
XMP Core and XMP
Rights Management
Properties

```
<rdf:Description rdf:about=''
 xmlns:xap='http://ns.adobe.com/xap/1.0/'>
 <xap:ModifyDate>2004-08-12T06:57:52-07:00</xap:ModifyDate>
 <xap:MetadataDate>2005-03-25T16:27:25-08:00</xap:MetadataDate>
 <xap:Rating>0</xap:Rating>
</rdf:Description>

<rdf:Description rdf:about=''
 xmlns:xapRights='http://ns.adobe.com/xap/1.0/rights/'>
 <xapRights:Marked>True</xapRights:Marked>
</rdf:Description>
```

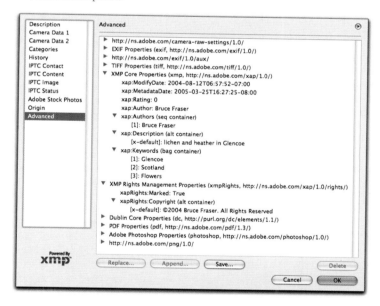

The last very important section of the text generates the Dublin Core Properties entry in File Info (Dublin is the name of the XMP schema). It holds all the key IPTC metadata such as Creator, Title, Description, and Copyright notice, and all the keywords you applied to the image in Bridge. Last but not least, it's the source of all the aliased entries you saw in the Photoshop Properties, TIFF Properties, XMP Core Properties, and XMP Rights Management Properties in File Info. So the Dublin Core Properties section is one of the most important areas in the sidecar .xmp file—see Figure 8-9.

Figure 8-9
Dublin Core Properties

```
<rdf:Description rdf:about=''
 xmlns:dc='http://purl.org/dc/elements/1.1/'>
<dc:creator>
 <rdf:Seq>
  <rdf:li>Bruce Fraser</rdf:li>
 </rdf:Seq>
</dc:creator>
<dc:rights>
 <rdf:Alt>
  <rdf:li xml:lang='x-default'>©2004 Bruce Fraser. All Rights Reserved</rdf:li>
 </rdf:Alt>
</dc:rights>
<dc:subject>
 <rdf:Bag>
  <rdf:li>Glencoe</rdf:li>
  <rdf:li>Scotland</rdf:li>
  <rdf:li>Flowers</rdf:li>
 </rdf:Bag>
</dc:subject>
<dc:description>
 <rdf:Alt>
  <rdf:li xml:lang='x-default'>lichen and heather in Glencoe</rdf:li>
 </rdf:Alt>
</dc:description>
</rdf:Description>
```

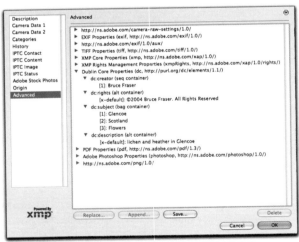

Why, you may quite reasonably ask, am I torturing you with this kind of information? My purpose for showing you all this is twofold.

► Understanding the contents of the metadata files makes the whole process by which you enter and store metadata a great deal less mysterious.

► It's often easier to use a text editor to remove metadata selectively from images than it is to do so using Photoshop or Bridge.

Image sidecar .xmp files aren't the only kinds of files that you can usefully manipulate outside of Photoshop and Bridge. It's often quicker and easier to use a text editor to make Camera Raw Settings Subset files. For example, Figure 8-10 shows a saved settings subset that sets Camera Raw's Exposure slider to +0.25.

Figure 8-10
Camera Raw
Settings Subset

```
<x:xmpmeta xmlns:x='adobe:ns:meta/' x:xmptk='XMP toolkit 3.0-28, framework
1.6'>
<rdf:RDF xmlns:rdf='http://www.w3.org/1999/02/22-rdf-syntax-ns#' xmlns:
iX='http://ns.adobe.com/iX/1.0/'>

 <rdf:Description rdf:about=''
  xmlns:crs='http://ns.adobe.com/camera-raw-settings/1.0/'>
  <crs:Version>3.0</crs:Version>
  <crs:Exposure>+0.25</crs:Exposure>
  <crs:HasSettings>True</crs:HasSettings>
 </rdf:Description>

</rdf:RDF>
</x:xmpmeta>
```

If you want to make a series of Exposure adjustment presets, it's much quicker to change the value in the .xmp file and save it under a new name in the Camera Raw settings folder than it is to change the slider and save the settings subset out of Camera Raw itself. This technique is applicable to any Camera Raw settings or settings subsets you want to create.

Meddling With Metadata

Back in Chapter 7, I showed you how to save and use metadata templates. If you save and apply them through Photoshop's or Bridge's user interface, they'll almost certainly work seamlessly better than 99 percent of the time. But if you open one of your saved metadata templates in a text editor, you may be in for a surprise.

When you do so, the first thing you'll see is the usual line or two describing what kind of file the template is. The second thing you'll see is a copy of the Camera Raw settings for the image that was selected when you saved the template—Thomas Knoll actually had to build special code into Camera Raw to ignore this entirely bogus data. This behavior was also present in Photoshop CS, and some pundits have suggested that the best way to create a metadata template is to start from a brand-new Photoshop document.

However, as you'll see in Figure 8-11, even this approach isn't perfect. You won't get bogus Camera Raw settings, but the template includes dates and image IDs that I'd much rather weren't there!

Figure 8-11
Unedited
metadata template

The unedited metadata template contains a good deal of extraneous data. The entries that are actually needed to make the template perform its task are the boxed ones— the rest can safely be deleted.

```
<?xpacket begin="Ô ª ø" id="W5M0MpCehiHzreSzNTczkc9d"?>
<x:xmpmeta xmlns:x="adobe:ns:meta/" x:xmptk="3.1.1-111">
    <rdf:RDF xmlns:rdf="http://www.w3.org/1999/02/22-rdf-syntax-ns#">
        <rdf:Description rdf:about=""
            xmlns:dc="http://purl.org/dc/elements/1.1/">
            <dc:format>application/vnd.adobe.photoshop</dc:format>
            <dc:creator>
                <rdf:Seq>
                    <rdf:li>Bruce Fraser</rdf:li>
                </rdf:Seq>
            </dc:creator>
            <dc:rights>
                <rdf:Alt>
                    <rdf:li xml:lang="x-default">©2007 Bruce Fraser. All Rights
                    Reserved.</rdf:li>
                </rdf:Alt>
            </dc:rights>
        </rdf:Description>
        <rdf:Description rdf:about=""
            xmlns:xap="http://ns.adobe.com/xap/1.0/">
            <xap:CreatorTool>Adobe Photoshop CS2 Macintosh</xap:CreatorTool>
            <xap:CreateDate>2005-03-27T17:02:23-08:00</xap:CreateDate>
            <xap:ModifyDate>2005-03-27T17:02:23-08:00</xap:ModifyDate>
            <xap:MetadataDate>2005-03-27T17:02:23-08:00</xap:MetadataDate>
        </rdf:Description>
        <rdf:Description rdf:about=""
            xmlns:xapMM="http://ns.adobe.com/xap/1.0/mm/">
            <xapMM:DocumentID>uuid:3447AB0D9F9B11D998CAFE202EB90405</xapMM:
            DocumentID>
            <xapMM:InstanceID>uuid:3447AB0D9F9B11D998CAFE202EB90405</xapMM:
            InstanceID>
        </rdf:Description>
        <rdf:Description rdf:about=""
            xmlns:photoshop="http://ns.adobe.com/photoshop/1.0/">
            <photoshop:History/>
            <photoshop:ColorMode>3</photoshop:ColorMode>
            <photoshop:ICCProfile>sRGB IEC61966-2.1</photoshop:ICCProfile>
        </rdf:Description>
        <rdf:Description rdf:about=""
            xmlns:xapRights="http://ns.adobe.com/xap/1.0/rights/">
            <xapRights:Marked>True</xapRights:Marked>
        </rdf:Description>
    </rdf:RDF>
</x:xmpmeta>
<?xpacket end="w"?>
```

Cleaning Up Metadata Templates

Metadata templates saved as is from File Info in Bridge or Photoshop seem to work seamlessly in Bridge or Photoshop. But having a template that contains erroneous metadata simply worries me—maybe I'm just paranoid, but I don't want to take the risk of third-party software stumbling over extraneous junk. So let's take a look at the best-case-scenario metadata template shown in Figure 8-11, and go through the process of slimming down so it only contains the information that's really needed.

When you save Metadata Templates, Photoshop saves them in a dedicated folder. Rather than typing the lengthy path names for both Mac and Windows, I'll show you the simplest way to find your saved templates. Just select a file, choose File Info from the File Browser's File menu, and then, in the File Info dialog box, pull down the flyout menu at the upper right and choose Show Templates—see Figure 8-12.

Figure 8-12
Show Templates

The easiest way to find saved metadata templates is to choose Show Templates from the File Info dialog box's popout menu.

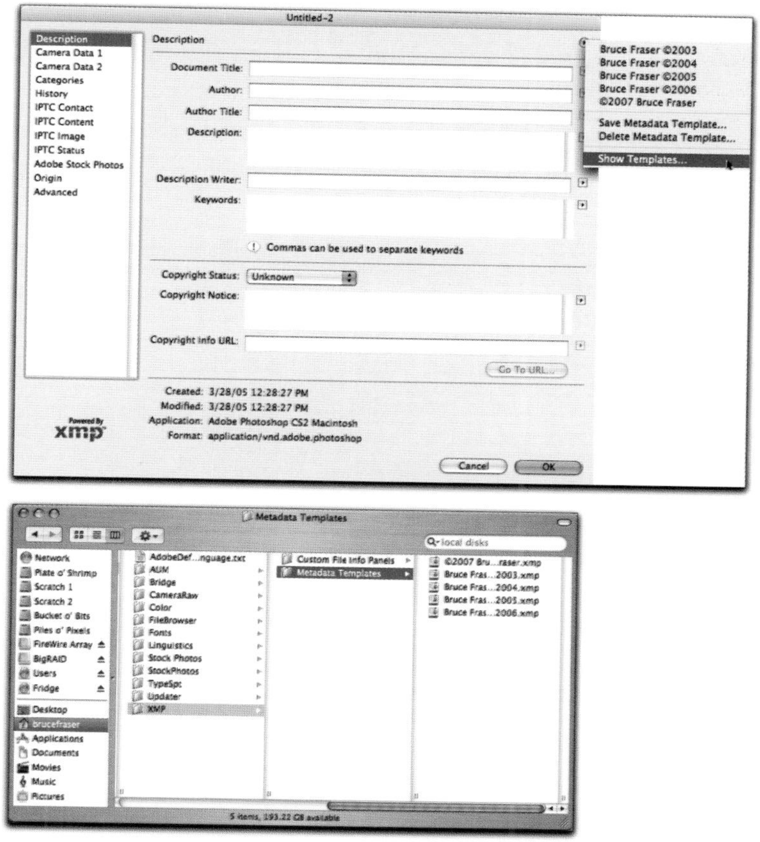

Once you've located your templates, open one in the text editor of your choice. Figure 8-11 shows a newly saved metadata template created from a new, blank Photoshop document that has never been saved. All I want it to do is to set the Copyright Status flag to Copyrighted, enter my name in the Author field, and set the Copyright Notice to ©2007 Bruce Fraser (I believe in being prepared). In practice, that is in fact all it does, at least when everything is working properly.

But as computers and software get ever more complicated, we all at some point learn the hard lesson that things don't always work as designed. One rule that's always stood me in good stead is to keep extraneous junk to a minimum! So the only entries that need to be in the template are the Dublin Core Properties and XMP Rights Management entries, and the enclosing entries that say what kind of .xmp file this is. All the others can safely be deleted.

Once the template is stripped down, it becomes apparent that the easy way to create copyright notices for different years is not to go back into File Info and make the entries there, but simply to change the year on the relevant line using the text editor and then save each one with an appropriate name. Figure 8-13 shows the edited metadata template—it's a whole lot more manageable.

Figure 8-13
Edited metadata template

```
<?xpacket begin="Ô³ø" id="W5M0MpCehiHzreSzNTczkc9d"?>
<x:xmpmeta xmlns:x="adobe:ns:meta/" x:xmptk="3.1.1-111">
   <rdf:RDF xmlns:rdf="http://www.w3.org/1999/02/22-rdf-syntax-ns#">
      <rdf:Description rdf:about=""
            xmlns:dc="http://purl.org/dc/elements/1.1/">
         <dc:format>application/vnd.adobe.photoshop</dc:format>
         <dc:creator>
            <rdf:Seq>
               <rdf:li>Bruce Fraser</rdf:li>
            </rdf:Seq>
         </dc:creator>
         <dc:rights>
            <rdf:Alt>
               <rdf:li xml:lang="x-default">©2007 Bruce Fraser. All Rights
               Reserved.</rdf:li>
            </rdf:Alt>
         </dc:rights>
      </rdf:Description>
      <rdf:Description rdf:about=""
            xmlns:xapRights="http://ns.adobe.com/xap/1.0/rights/">
         <xapRights:Marked>True</xapRights:Marked>
      </rdf:Description>
   </rdf:RDF>
</x:xmpmeta>
<?xpacket end="w"?>
```

Once you become comfortable with editing .xmp files, you'll find that it's often faster and easier to accomplish your goals using a lowly text editor than it is to do so by tunneling through the many dialog boxes and palettes presented by Photoshop.

Custom File Info Palettes

The panels that appear in File Info are actually created by .xmp files. They're stored in Library/Application Support/Adobe/XMP/Custom File Info Panels on the Mac OS, and in Program Files\Common Files\Adobe\ XMP\Custom File Info Panels on Windows.

In that folder, you'll find .xmp files that create many of the panels for the File Info dialog box (ignore the .dat files; the .txt files are the relevant ones). If you open these in a text editor, you'll get a fairly good idea of the level of complexity you're in for if you want to contemplate making your own File Info panels.

This is not an undertaking for the casual user. The syntax is unforgiving—it's either right or it doesn't work at all—and you'll need to read and digest the documentation referenced earlier in this chapter. In the previous edition of this book, I offered various clever tricks for embedding secret metadata that wasn't readily searchable or editable by anyone who didn't have the Custom File Info Panel that created it. In CS2, the rules have changed: any user-added metadata can be found using Bridge's Find command, and changed or removed by another user by editing it in File Info's Advanced panel. So the only reason to use Custom File Info Panels is to simplify adding custom metadata that doesn't fit easily into the fields provided in File Info.

MetaLab

If you feel that you could make use of Custom File Info Panels, but you're less than enthused about the steep learning curve, a reasonable solution is MetaLab, a free application from Pound Hill Software (www.poundhill. com). The same company also offers industrial-strength metadata tools, but MetaLab is a free and easy way to get your feet wet.

MetaLab-generated Custom File Info Panels are limited to 10 total fields, of which up to two can be popup menus and up to two can be checkboxes. If you can work within these limitations, it's all you need, and if you want to embark on more ambitious Custom File Info Panels, MetaLab is a handy learning tool for doing so. Figure 8-14 shows a Custom File Info Panel created in MetaLab, and the entries as they appear in File Info's Advanced panel on a machine that doesn't have the Custom File Info Panel installed.

Figure 8-14
Custom File Info Panel
generated by MetaLab

This Custom File Info Panel, generated by MetaLab, lets me track use of my images in my published work.

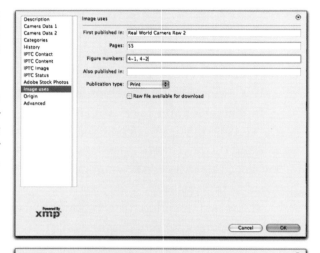

Without the Custom File Info Panel installed, the metadata appears in cryptic form in File Info's Advanced panel under the poundhill schema.

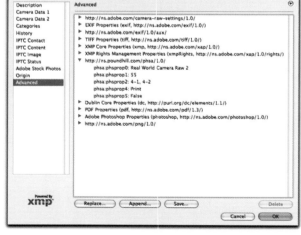

The XMP code that generated this Custom File Info Panel is shown in Figure 8-15. It may seem dauntingly complex, but if you work through it methodically you'll find that it's fundamentally simple, but detailed.

Figure 8-15
Custom File Info Panel
XMP code

```
<?xml version="1.0">
<!DOCTYPE panel SYSTEM "http://ns.adobe.com/custompanels/1.0">
<panel title="$$$/CustomPanels/Panels/PoundHill/PanelName=Image uses"
version="1" type="custom_panel">
        group(placement: place_column, spacing: gLargeSpace, horizontal:
        align_fill, vertical: align_top) {
                group(placement: place_row, spacing: gSpace, horizontal:
                align_fill, vertical: align_top, reverse: rtl_aware) {
                        static_text(name: '$$$/CustomPanels/Panels/Pound
                        Hill/phsprop0=First published in:', font: font_big_
                        right, vertical: align_center);
                        edit_text(horizontal: align_fill, font: font_big,
                        vertical: align_top, xmp_ns_prefix: 'phsa', xmp_
                        namespace: 'http://ns.poundhill.com/phsa/1.0/',
                        xmp_path: 'phsprop0');
                }
                group(placement: place_row, spacing: gSpace, horizontal:
                align_fill, vertical: align_top, reverse: rtl_aware) {
                        static_text(name: '$$$/CustomPanels/Panels/Pound
                        Hill/phsprop1=Pages:', font: font_big_right, verti
                        cal: align_center);
                        edit_text(horizontal: align_fill, font: font_big,
                        vertical: align_top, xmp_ns_prefix: 'phsa', xmp_
                        namespace: 'http://ns.poundhill.com/phsa/1.0/',
                        xmp_path: 'phsprop1');
                }
                group(placement: place_row, spacing: gSpace, horizontal:
                align_fill, vertical: align_top, reverse: rtl_aware) {
                        static_text(name: '$$$/CustomPanels/Panels/Pound
                        Hill/phsprop2=Figure numbers:', font: font_big_
                        right, vertical: align_center);
                        edit_text(horizontal: align_fill, font: font_big, ver
                        tical: align_top, xmp_ns_prefix: 'phsa', xmp_
                        namespace: 'http://ns.poundhill.com/phsa/1.0/',
                        xmp_path: 'phsprop2');
                }
                group(placement: place_row, spacing: gSpace, horizontal:
                align_fill, vertical: align_top, reverse: rtl_aware) {
                        static_text(name: '$$$/CustomPanels/Panels/Pound
                        Hill/phsprop3=Also published in:', font: font_big_
                        right, vertical: align_center);
                        edit_text(horizontal: align_fill, font: font_big, ver
                        tical: align_top, xmp_ns_prefix: 'phsa', xmp_
                        namespace: 'http://ns.poundhill.com/phsa/1.0/',
                        xmp_path: 'phsprop3');
                }
                group(placement: place_row, spacing: gSpace, horizontal:
                align_fill, vertical: align_top, reverse: rtl_aware) {
                        static_text(name: '$$$/CustomPanels/Panels/Pound
                        Hill/phsprop4=Publication type:', font: font_big_
                        right, vertical: align_center);
                        popup(items: '$$$/CustomPanels/Panels/PoundHill/
                        phsprop4=Print{Print};Online{Online};CD/DVD{CD/
                        DVD};', xmp_ns_prefix: 'phsa', xmp_namespace:
                        'http://ns.poundhill.com/phsa/1.0/', xmp_path:
                        'phsprop4');
                }
                group(placement: place_row, spacing: gSpace, horizontal:
                align_fill, vertical: align_top, reverse: rtl_aware) {
                        static_text(name: '$$$/CustomPanels/Panels/Pound
                        Hill/phsprop5=', font: font_big_right, vertical:
                        align_center);
                        check_box(name:'$$$/CustomPanels/Panels/PoundHill/
                        phsprop5=Raw file available for download', initial_
                        value:true, margin_width : 10, xmp_ns_prefix: 'phsa',
                        xmp_namespace: 'http://ns.poundhill.com/phsa/1.0/',
                        xmp_path: 'phsprop5');
                }
        }
</panel>
```

*This is the XMP code
that generates the
Custom File Info Panel
shown in Figure 8-14.*

Making Images Smarter

Metadata has been around in one form or another for a long time, but in many ways it's still in its infancy. Having a standard in the form of XMP is one factor that will doubtless accelerate its evolution, and the ready availability of basic shooting parameters from the EXIF data is another.

Today, photographers can gain a considerable measure of security by knowing that their copyright and rights management notices are embedded right in the image. In the future, you can reasonably expect to see software that makes more intelligent use of metadata—automatically applying the right lens corrections based on focal length, or the right noise reduction based on ISO speed, for example. You can also look forward to seamless integration with XMP-compliant asset managers and databases.

You'll doubtless encounter speed bumps along the way, but if you understand how image metadata works, you'll be in a much better position to troubleshoot any problems you encounter than those who just treat the whole thing as incomprehensible magic. I hope this chapter provides a starting point for further metadata explorations.

9 Exploiting Automation

Working Smarter, Not Harder

The goal of doing all the work I've discussed so far in this book is to set up your raw images with the correct Camera Raw settings and the right metadata so that you can produce deliverable processed images with the minimum amount of effort. The minimum amount of effort, in this case, means taking full advantage of Photoshop's rich automation features, so that you can simply press a button, walk away, and let the computer do your work for you.

One of the great things about a computer is that once you've made it do something, you can make it do that something over and over again, exactly the same way, automatically, without coffee or bathroom breaks. Tapping the power of automation is key to building an efficient workflow, so in this chapter I'll show you how to leverage the work you've done in Bridge and Camera Raw to produce deliverable images in a variety of formats.

Bridge serves as command central for all the operations I'll discuss in this chapter. They all boil down to a two-step process.

► You select the images that you want to process in Bridge.

► You run one of the options from Bridge's Tools>Photoshop menu to produce converted images. (When you want to use images selected in Bridge as source, you *must* call the automations from Bridge rather than Photoshop.)

The Photoshop submenu offers a variety of useful routines for creating images in a deliverable form, but by far the most powerful and flexible is the Batch command.

Batch Processing Rules

The Batch command is one of Photoshop's most powerful features. It's conceptually very simple. You point it at a batch of images, it runs an action on them, it (optionally) renames the images, and then it does one of the following:

▶   Saves new files

▶   Delivers open images in Photoshop

▶   Saves and closes, overwriting the source files

As you'll see shortly, though, the devil is in the details, and some of the details in the Batch dialog box are distinctly counterintuitive. Figure 9-1 shows the Batch dialog box before customizing any of the settings.

Figure 9-1
The Batch dialog box

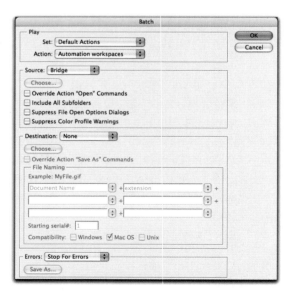

The dialog box is split into four different sections, each of which controls a different aspect of the batch process's behavior.

▶ **Play** lets you choose an action from an action set that will be applied to all the images.

▶ **Source** lets you designate the source—the images on which the batch will be executed—and also lets you choose some very important options whose functionality will become apparent later.

You can run a batch on a designated folder that you choose in the Batch dialog box by clicking the Choose button; on opened files; on images imported through the Photoshop File menu's Import command; or, when Batch is called from Bridge's Tools>Photoshop menu, on the images that are currently selected in Bridge. For processing raw images, the source will invariably be a folder or the selected images in Bridge.

▶ **Destination** lets you control what happens to the processed images. None delivers them as open images in Photoshop; Save and Close saves and closes the processed images; Folder lets you designate a folder in which to save the processed images. It also includes the renaming features offered by Batch Rename.

When you process raw images, you'll always choose either None or, much more commonly, Folder. Save and Close often ends up being a "hurt-me" button, because its normal behavior is to overwrite the source image. With raw files this is usually impossible and always undesirable. Photoshop can't overwrite files in formats it can't write, including most raw image formats; but if you use a camera that records its raw images as .tif, there's a real danger of overwriting your raws if you choose Save and Close, so avoid it!

▶ **Errors** lets you choose whether to stop the entire batch when an error is encountered or log the errors to a file. I usually stop on errors when I'm debugging an action used in Batch and log them to a file when I'm actually running a batch in a production situation. However, when processing raw files, the batch typically either works on all files or fails on all files.

The difficulties that users typically encounter in running Batch are in the way the selections in the Source and Destination sections interact with the action applied by the batch operation. Here are The Rules. (Note: these are my rules, and I swear by them. They don't represent the only possible approach, but by the time you're sufficiently skilled and knowledgeable to violate them with impunity you'll have long outgrown the need for a book like this one!)

Rules for Opening Files in a Batch Operation

To make sure that the raw files get opened and processed the way you want them in a batch operation, you need to record an Open step in the action that will be applied in Batch. In the case of raw images, you'll want to make sure that Camera Raw's Settings menu is set to Image Settings so that it applies the custom-tailored Camera Raw settings you've made for each image, and you'll also want to make sure that Camera Raw's workflow settings—Space, Bit Depth, Size, and Resolution—are set to produce the results you want.

Now comes one of the counterintuitive bits. If you record an Open step in the action, you must check Override Action Open Commands. If you don't, the batch will simply keep opening the image you used to record the Open step in the action. Override Action Open Commands doesn't override everything in the recorded Open command; it just overrides the specific choice of file to open, while ensuring that the Selected Image and workflow settings get honored.

Some people find this set of behaviors so frustrating and counterintuitive that they latch onto the fact that you can run Batch using an action that doesn't contain an Open step and hence doesn't require messing around with the checkbox. The problem with doing so is that you lose control over Camera Raw's workflow settings—the batch will just use the last-used settings. So you may expect a folder full of 6,144 by 4,096-pixel images and get 1,536 by 1,024-pixel ones instead, or wind up with 8-bit sRGB instead of 16-bit ProPhoto RGB. If you simply follow The Rules, you have complete control over the workflow settings—the correct ones get used automatically.

Rules for Saving Files in a Batch Operation

To make sure that the processed files get saved in the format you want, you need to record a Save step in the action that will be applied in Batch. This Save step dictates the file format (.tif, .jpg, .psd) and options that go with that format—TIFF compression options, JPEG quality settings, and so on.

Now comes the second counterintuitive bit. You must check Override Action "Save As" Commands: otherwise the files don't get saved where you want them, don't get saved with the names you want, or possibly even don't get saved at all! When you check Override Action "Save As" Commands, the file format and file format parameters recorder in the action's Save step are applied when saving the file, but the name and destination are overridden by the options you specified in the Batch dialog box.

Rules for Running a Batch Operation

Two other settings commonly trip people up. Unless you check Suppress File Open Options Dialogs, the Camera Raw dialog box pops up whenever the batch opens a file, and waits for you to do something. Checking this option just opens the image directly, bypassing the Camera Raw dialog box. The Camera Raw settings for each image are used, but the batch operation isn't interrupted by the appearance of the dialog box.

If the workflow settings recorded in the action result in an image in a color space other than your Photoshop working space, you should also check Suppress Color Profile Warnings; otherwise the batch may get interrupted by the Profile Mismatch warning—the day always gets off to a bad start when you find that the batch operation you'd set up to generate 2,000 Web-ready JPEGs overnight is stalled on the first image with a warning telling you that the file is sRGB when your working space is ProPhoto RGB! (This feature didn't work in Photoshop CS. Fortunately, it's fixed in Photoshop CS2 and now works as advertised.)

Playing by the Rules

If you follow the relatively simple set of rules I've provided, your batch operations won't fall prey to any of these ills, and they'll execute smoothly with no surprises. If you fail to do so, it's very likely that your computer will labor mightily and then deliver either results that are something other than you desired or, even more frustrating, no results at all!

So with The Rules in mind, let's look first at creating some actions and then at applying them through the Batch command.

Recording Batch Actions

Writing actions for batch-processing raw images is relatively simple. You don't need to worry about making sure that the action can operate on files that already have layers or alpha channels, or that are in a color space other than RGB. You're always dealing with a known quantity.

Bear in mind that if your actions call other actions, the other actions must be loaded in Photoshop's Actions palette, or the calling action will fail when it can't find the action being called. An easy way to handle this is to make sure that any actions on which other actions are dependent are saved in the same set as the actions that depend on them.

I'll start out with simple examples and proceed to more complex ones.

Simple Action—Save as JPEG

I'll start with a very simple action that opens a raw image at its native resolution and saves it as a maximum-quality JPEG in the sRGB color space.

Creating an action and action set. Start out by creating a new action set called "Batch Processing" in which to save the actions you'll create in the rest of this section. So the first step is to create a new action set, which you do by opening the Actions palette and clicking the folder ("Create new set") icon and then entering the appropriate name in the ensuing dialog box and clicking OK to dismiss it. The new set then appears in the Actions palette—see Figure 9-2.

Figure 9-2
Creating an action set

To create a new action set, click the "Create new set" icon, enter a name, then click OK. The new set appears in the Actions palette.

Creating a new action. Before creating the action, select a raw image in Bridge that has already had custom Camera Raw settings applied. That way, once you've created the action, you can start recording immediately without recording any extraneous steps, such as selecting a file, and you can correctly record the Camera Raw Selected Image setting.

Click the "Create new action" icon in the Actions palette, enter the name—"Save as JPEG"—in the ensuing dialog box, and then click Record to dismiss the dialog and start recording the action.

Recording the Open step. The first step is to open the image in Camera Raw, so that you can include the correct Camera Raw settings in the action. When you use the action in Batch, the Camera Raw dialog box won't appear, so it's essential to get these settings right when you record this step. Open the image by pressing Command-O (you must open the image in Camera Raw hosted by Photoshop), and the Camera Raw dialog box appears—see Figure 9-3.

Figure 9-3
Recording the Open step

When you record an Open step, it's critical to make sure that the Settings menu is set to Image Settings and the workflow settings are set the way you want them for the batch operation.

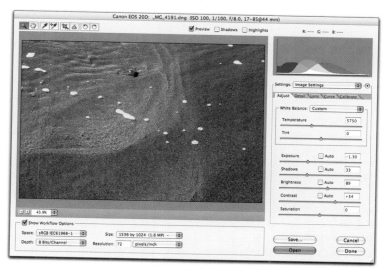

You need to record several key settings for this action in the Camera Raw dialog box.

▶ Set the Settings menu to Image Settings to ensure that each image gets opened using its own custom settings.

▶ Set the Space menu to sRGB to produce a converted image that's already in sRGB, the standard color space for the Web.

▶ Set the Depth menu to 8 bits/channel, because you're simply saving JPEGs (which only support 8-bit channels), and this action won't include any operations that could benefit from a higher bit depth.

► Set the Size menu to the desired size (in this case, I chose 1536 by 1024).

► Set the Resolution field to 72 pixels per inch (to preserve the polite fiction that Web images are 72 ppi).

Then click OK to open the image. (If the Profile Mismatch warning appears, click OK to dismiss it. This doesn't get recorded in the action, and you'll suppress the warning when you use the action in Batch.) The image opens, and the Open step appears on the Actions palette.

Recording the Save step. To record the Save step, choose Save As from the File menu, or press Command-Shift-S. The Save As dialog box appears. The filename and the destination for saving that you enter here has no impact on the batch process—I always enter an obviously silly name such as "foo.jpg" (I'm too lazy to type "throwmeaway.jpg") and choose the Desktop as my destination, to simplify cleanup. See Figure 9-4.

Figure 9-4
Recording the Save step

When you apply the action in a batch operation, the filename and destination will be overridden, but the format options will be applied.

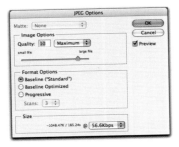

Make sure that the format is set to JPEG, and incorporate any other settings in this dialog box that you want to include in the action. In this case, I'll leave all the options unchecked—any RGB file that I create without an embedded profile can safely be assumed to be sRGB, and I don't care about icons or thumbnails—but if you want any of these options included in your batch-processed files, check them now.

Click Save to proceed to the JPEG Options dialog box, set the desired quality, set the Format Options to Baseline for maximum compatibility with JPEG-reading software, and then click OK. The File is saved on the Desktop as "foo.jpg," and the Save step appears in the Actions palette. Then close the image so that the Close step appears in the Actions palette.

Stop and Save. Click the Stop button in the Actions palette to stop recording. Photoshop doesn't allow you to save individual actions, only action sets; so if you want to save an action as soon as you've written it, you need to select the action set that contains it in the Actions palette and then choose Save Actions from the Actions palette menu—see Figure 9-5.

Figure 9-5
Saving the action set

Note that until you save actions explicitly using the Save Actions command, they exist only in Photoshop's Preferences, and Photoshop's Preferences only get updated when you quit the application "normally" by using the Quit command. If Photoshop crashes, or you suffer a power outage, any unsaved actions will be lost. A simple action like this one probably wouldn't have me running to the Save Actions command, but if you make any actions that are even slightly complex, it's a very good idea to save them before doing anything else. You can save actions anywhere, but if you want them to appear automatically in the Actions palette even after deleting Photoshop's preferences, save them in the Adobe Photoshop CS2/Presets/Photoshop Actions folder.

When you expand the steps in the Actions palette by clicking the triangles beside those that have them, you can see exactly what has been recorded for each step—see Figure 9-6. When you use this action in Batch with the appropriate overrides selected (see "Batch Processing Rules," earlier in this chapter) the filenames and folder locations you recorded will be overridden by the settings in the Batch dialog box, and all the other settings you've recorded here—the Camera Raw workflow settings and the JPEG Save Options—will be honored.

Figure 9-6
Save as JPEG action

Variants. You can create variants of this action by recording different Open or Save steps. For example, you can create larger JPEGs by changing the Size setting in the Camera Raw dialog box to one of the larger sizes, and you can embed thumbnails or create lower-quality JPEGs by making those settings in the Save As and JPEG Options dialog boxes, respectively. To save in a different format, with different options, just choose the desired format and options when you record the Save step.

Complex Action—Save for Edit

The following example is a more complex action that produces 16-bit/channel TIFFs with sharpening applied and adjustment layers set up ready for final editing in Photoshop. It's designed for use on "hero" images that merit individual manual edits in Photoshop. It doesn't actually *do* any of the editing, because the required edits will almost certainly be different for each image in a batch. Instead, it simply does a lot of the repetitive grunt work involved in setting up an image for editing, so that when you open the image, all the necessary adjustment layers are already there, waiting for you to tweak them.

Creating a new action. Record this action in the same set as the previous one, since it's also designed for raw processing. As before, select a raw image that has had custom Camera Raw settings applied before you start recording the new action. Then click the "Create new action" icon in the Actions palette, enter the name "Save for Edit" in the New Action dialog box, and then click Record to start recording.

Recording the Open step. As before, start by launching Camera Raw by double-clicking the selected image. In the Camera Raw dialog box, again make sure that Settings is set to Selected Image. This time, though, you'll make some different workflow settings.

▶ In the Space menu, choose ProPhoto RGB, my preferred working space.

▶ Set the Depth menu to 16/bit channel, because you'll want to make the edits in Photoshop in 16-bit/channel mode.

▶ Set the Size menu to the camera's native resolution.

▶ Enter 240 pixels per inch in the Resolution field, because you'll almost certainly check your edits by printing to an inkjet printer at 240 ppi.

Then click OK to open the image. The image opens, and the Open step appears on the Actions palette.

Adding the edits. This action adds four different editing layers (actually, three layers and one layer set) to the image before saving and closing. First, add sharpening layers using your sharpening tool of choice (mine is PhotoKit Sharpener from Pixel Genius LLC). Then add a Levels adjustment layer, a Curves adjustment layer, and a Hue/Saturation adjustment layer, as follows.

▶ I apply sharpening by choosing PhotoKit Capture Sharpener Expert from Photoshop's File>Automate menu, selecting Digital High-Res Sharpen, Medium Edge Sharpen, and clicking OK. You can substitute your own sharpening routine here, or you can elect to defer sharpening until you've edited the image in Photoshop.

▶ Add a Levels adjustment layer by opening the Layers palette's Adjustment Layers menu, choosing Levels, and then clicking OK to create a Levels adjustment layer that does not as yet apply any adjustments. You'll make the adjustments on an image-by-image basis in Photoshop—the action just does the grunt work of creating the layers.

▶ There's one small issue. PhotoKit Sharpener produces an open (expanded) layer set, and the Levels layer gets created inside the set. There's no way to record closing or expanding a layer set, so you need to record a step that moves the Levels layer to the top of the stack, using the shortcut for Layer>Arrange>Bring to Front (Command-Shift-]).

▶ Add two more adjustment layers—a Curves layer, then a Hue/Saturation layer—in both cases simply clicking OK when the respective adjustment dialog boxes, Curves and Hue/Saturation, appear. These layers are automatically created in the correct positions in the stack, so you don't need to employ any more layer-moving trickery—see Figure 9-7.

Figure 9-7
Adding adjustment layers

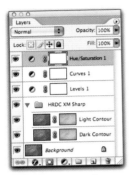

The Layers palette

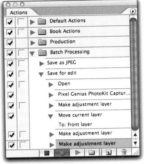

The Actions palette

When you open the resulting images in Photoshop, you can start editing immediately by double-clicking the adjustment icon in each adjustment layer without having to do the work of creating them first. If you don't need all the adjustment layers, you can easily throw the unused ones away. All the edits will be performed in 16-bit/channel mode for the best quality.

Recording the Save step. Record the Save by choosing Save As from the File menu. Again, name the file "foo" and save it on the Desktop for easy disposal. This time, choose TIFF as the format, make sure that the Layers and Embed Color Profile checkboxes are checked (creating untagged ProPhoto RGB files is a Very Bad Idea). Then click Save to advance to the Tiff Options dialog box.

In the TIFF Options dialog box, choose ZIP for both Image Compression and Layer Compression, and then click OK to complete the save—see Figure 9-8.

Finally, close the image (so that the batch operation will do so too), and click the Stop button in the Actions palette to stop recording. Figure 9-9 shows the resulting action in the Actions palette with all the steps expanded.

As with the earlier, simpler action, when you use this action in a batch process with the necessary overrides applied in the Batch dialog box, the filenames and locations will be overridden by the Batch settings, while everything else in the Open and Save steps will be honored.

Figure 9-8
Save as TIFF

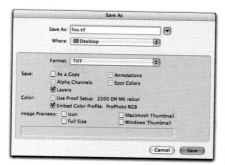 

Figure 9-9
Save for Edit action

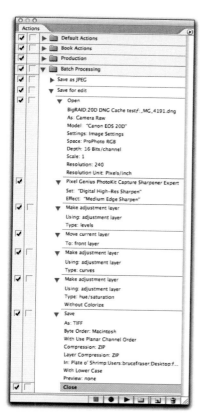

Running Batch

Using the actions I've just shown you in Batch is really very simple—as long as you remember The Rules! (If you need to take another look, refer back to "Batch Processing Rules," earlier in this chapter.) Play by The Rules, and all will go smoothly. Violate them at your peril.

Besides the settings in the Batch dialog box, there are three common situations that can cause a batch operation to fail.

▶ There isn't sufficient space on the destination volume to hold the processed files.

▶ No source files were selected—see "Selecting and Editing" in Chapter 7, *It's All About the Workflow* if you need a reminder on how to select images in Bridge.

▶ Files with the same names as the ones you're creating already exist in the destination folder.

If these points seem blindingly obvious, I apologize. I mention them because they've tripped me up more than once. With those caveats in mind, let's look at setting up the Batch dialog box to run the Save for Edit action you built in the previous section. The key settings in Batch are the overrides in both the Source and Destination sections of the panel.

Source Settings

Whenever you run a batch operation using an action that includes an Open step, you must check Override Action "Open" Commands in the Source section. To process raw images, you also need to check Suppress File Open Options Dialogs—otherwise the Camera Raw dialog will pop up for every image—and whenever you run a batch operation unattended, it's a good idea to check Suppress Color Profile Warnings so that the batch doesn't get stuck on a Profile Mismatch warning.

Destination Settings

Similarly, whenever you run a batch operation using an action that includes a Save As step, you must check Override Action "Save As" Commands in the Destination section; otherwise the files won't get saved. The Destination section also offers the option to rename the files as part of the batch operation. See "Sorting and Renaming" in Chapter 7, *It's All About the Workflow*, for the major caveats on file-naming conventions. Figure 9-10 shows the Batch dialog box set up to run the Save for Edit action you created earlier in this chapter.

Batch is the most flexible command on Bridge's Automate menu, but the menu also includes some automation features that are useful for very specific purposes.

Figure 9-10
Batch

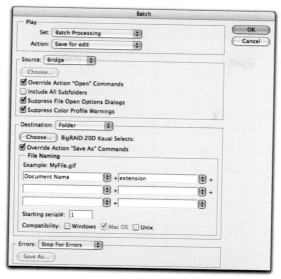

Figure 9-10
Batch

Contact Sheet II

As its name suggests, Contact Sheet II builds virtual contact sheets—pages full of image thumbnails. The contact sheets are built as unsaved Photoshop documents, with a choice to create either a flat file or a layered one with each image (and each image's caption, if included) on a separate layer. Figure 9-11 shows the Contact Sheet II dialog box.

Figure 9-11
Contact Sheet II

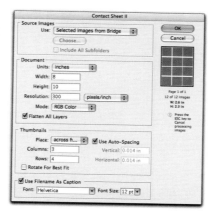

The Source Images section of the dialog box lets you choose the images for the contact sheet—in this workflow, you'd use Selected Images from

Bridge. The Document section lets you set the size, resolution, and color mode for the contact sheet. (The color is converted to the current working space for the selected color mode.) The Flatten All Layers checkbox, when checked, creates a flat file, and when unchecked, creates a layered file with each thumbnail and each caption on a separate layer—handy if you want to fine-tune the layout in Photoshop.

The Thumbnails section lets you control the size of the thumbnails by specifying how many rows and columns the contact sheet will contain. The page mockup underneath the main buttons shows the layout, and the readout underneath it shows the maximum dimensions of each thumbnail. The Rotate For Best Fit checkbox rotates verticals to horizontal to make bigger thumbnails in the available space. Finally, the Use Filename As Caption checkbox does exactly what it says—it adds the filename as a caption for each thumbnail in your chosen font and size. Figure 9-12 shows a contact sheet generated by Contact Sheet II.

Figure 9-12
Contact sheet

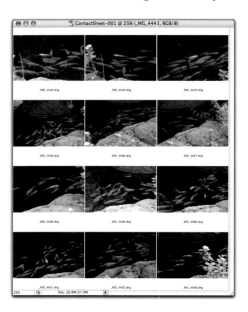

Once the contact sheets are open in Photoshop, you can save or print them just as you would any other Photoshop document.

Image Processor

New to Photoshop CS2, Image Processor offers a quick way of saving up to three versions of the selected images—a JPEG, a TIFF, and a Photoshop file, with each format in a separate subfolder. You can set different sizes for each format, and optionally, run an action and include a copyright notice. Figure 9-13 shows the Image Processor dialog box.

Figure 9-13
Image Processor

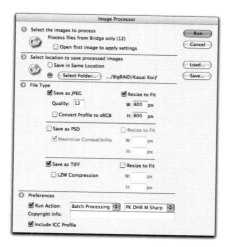

Let's look at the options.

▶ **Open first image to apply settings** is primarily useful for processing unedited images that require approximately the same treatment. When you run Image Processor, the first raw opens in Camera Raw. The settings you make there are applied to all the other images. These settings are used only by Image Processor—they aren't written to the image's metadata.

▶ **Select location to save processed images** lets you save the images either in the same folder, or in one that you designate here. In either case, if you've chosen multiple file formats, a subfolder is created for each file format.

▶ **File Type** lets you save any combination of JPEG, PSD, and TIFF, with the option to resize the image in any of the chosen formats.

▶ **Preferences** lets you choose an action that runs on all the processed images, lets you include copyright info if you haven't done so already, and gives you a choice as to whether or not to include the ICC profile in the images.

The settings shown in Figure 9-13 create a full-resolution TIFF, and a JPEG downsampled to a maximum dimension of 800 pixels—the image's aspect ratio is always maintained. A sharpening action was applied to all the images, and I elected to include the ICC profiles. The images were saved in JPEG and TIFF subfolders inside the "Kauai Koi" subfolder.

One nifty feature of Image Processor is that it takes care of flattening and downsampling to 8-bit/channel automatically for the JPEGs while saving the TIFFs as layered 16-bit/channel images. So it's by far the quickest and easiest way to save a high-resolution TIFF and low-resolution JPEG version of the same image—something many of us need to do often.

Merge to HDR

Merge to HDR is a faceless (when launched from Bridge) automate routine that combines multiple raw exposures into a High Dynamic Range (HDR) file. HDR files use 32-bit floating point values per channel to let you represent an essentially unlimited dynamic range. Since you can't print HDR images, and can display them only with specialized displays that are well outside the mainstream, this is an esoteric routine for most photographers—HDR images are mostly used in the movie industry, and are often rendered synthetically.

For mainstream photography, HDR offers the ability to map a very wide dynamic range captured through multiple exposures through an HDR file to a tone-mapped 16-bit or 8-bit channel image. You need a series of raw exposures of the same scene that differ only in shutter speed. A heavy tripod, a cable release, and mirror lockup are also recommended, particularly with longer focal lengths. Subject movement pretty much kills the process, so considerable planning is needed. If you have a real need for HDR imagery, by all means investigate Photoshop's HDR support further. Otherwise, file under E for Experimental.

PDF Presentation

The PDF Presentation command lets you build very simple slide shows with the Presentation option, or multipage PDFs with the Multi-Page Document option. Both options build a multipage PDF with one image per page, but the Presentation option does a little extra work, setting up a transition between pages and making sure that the PDF opens in full screen mode. I almost always use the Presentation option—see Figure 9-14.

Figure 9-14
PDF Presentation

PDF Presentation is fairly limited. It doesn't let you add captions, or copyright notices, or anything else to the image, and it only lets you set a single transition that's used between all the images. It does, however, do the grunt work of getting all the images into a PDF. If you own Acrobat 7.0 Professional, you can add text there and finesse the transitions on an image-by-image basis. The PDF Presentation dialog box also gives you one last opportunity to change the image order by dragging the items in the list, but this is a task that's better done in Bridge, where you can at least see the thumbnails.

Once you've made your choices in the PDF Presentation dialog box and you've clicked Save, you're prompted for a filename and destination for the PDF; then the PDF Save Options dialog box appears. If you're using PDF Presentation to create a simple slide show, most of these options are irrelevant. It may be conceptually interesting that you can create a multipage PDF/X1a:2001 document directly from raw files, but it's hard to envisage a reason for doing so! Here are the settings that matter for slide show use.

▶ **General tab.** The only useful preset for slide show use is Smallest File Size, which may apply heavier JPEG compression than you want. Otherwise, leave Standard set to None, and choose your desired level of compatibility from the Compatibility menu. If in doubt, choose Acrobat 4 (PDF 1.3)—it's the lowest common denominator.

▶ **Compression tab.** PDF Presentation uses the last-used Camera Raw workflow settings. If you need to downsample, you can choose downsampling options here—the differences for on-screen use between the various downsampling methods are quite subtle. You can also choose a compression method and quality setting in this tab. The option to convert 16-bit/channel images to 8-bit/channel doesn't always seem reliable, so if you want the slide show to be compatible with the largest number of PDF readers, you should probably set the Camera Raw workflow settings to produce 8-bit/channel images before launching PDF presentation.

▶ **Output tab.** The only relevant options in the Output tab are the color ones. Choose No Conversion if you want the PDF in the output space specified in Camera Raw's workflow settings. If you want it in some other space, choose Convert to Destination, then choose the space you want from the Destination menu. I always recommend choosing Include Destination Profile—despite the wording, this option dictates whether or not the PDF contains a profile.

▶ **Security.** The security options only work inside Adobe products. If you set *any* level of security, you need the password to open the document in Photoshop. Once it's open in Photoshop, it's completely editable—the restrictions apply only when the document is opened in Acrobat or Acrobat Reader. Macintosh users can open the PDF in the Mac's Preview application with no restrictions, so the security is largely illusory. (Perhaps the tab should be labeled "False sense of security.")

PDF Presentation tends to emphasize the disconnect in user interface and terminology between Acrobat and The Rest of the Adobe Universe. It has become massively more complex though admittedly more powerful in Photoshop CS2, so if you want to use it to build slide shows (which it does quite well), find the settings that work for you and save them as a preset.

PhotoMerge

PhotoMerge is Photoshop's autostitching routine for creating panoramas. While it's conceptually interesting that you can work directly from raw files, I usually find that it makes more sense to feed converted images to PhotoMerge. Often, one edge of an individual image needs different color balance and tone mapping than the other to create a seamless blend, and you can't do that with a raw image.

Figure 9-15 shows the PhotoMerge dialog box, which appears after PhotoMerge has opened the raw files and, if necessary, has downsampled them to 8-bit/channel mode.

Figure 9-15
PhotoMerge

If you want to try working with PhotoMerge directly from raw files, I recommend checking the "Keep as Layers" option.

Picture Package

Picture Package is quite similar to Contact Sheet II, except it puts multiple copies of a single image on each page. The Source Images section works identically to that of Contact Sheet II. The Document section also works like Contact Sheet II, with the addition of a Layout menu that lets you choose various different layouts. The Label section offers a little more control over captioning than Contact Sheet II, including the ability to enter custom text (but not, unfortunately, different custom text for each image). Figure 9-16 shows the Picture Package dialog box.

Figure 9-16
Picture Package

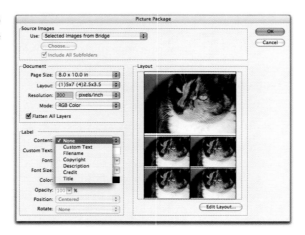

If none of the preset layouts is quite what you need, you can customize the layout by clicking the Edit Layout button to open the Picture Package Edit Layout dialog box—see Figure 9-17.

Figure 9-17
Picture Package
Edit Layout

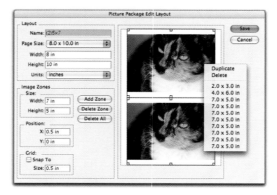

You can edit the layout either by clicking on the thumbnails and dragging the sizing handles to change size, or by dragging the entire thumbnail to move, or by entering numbers in the appropriate fields. The Add Zone and Delete Zone buttons let you add and delete thumbnails to the layout. One slightly odd feature is that if you Option-click on a thumbnail, a menu pops up when you release the mouse button, with commands to duplicate or delete the current thumbnail or add a zone using any of the preset sizes.

Like Contact Sheet II, Picture Package creates unsaved documents that are opened in Photoshop, ready for you to save or print.

Web Photo Gallery

Web Photo Gallery is a surprisingly deep feature. It creates a home page with thumbnail images and a gallery page for each image, or a frame-based page that combines scrolling thumbnails with a single larger gallery image. Some of the styles offer a feedback option where visitors to the page can check Approved or Other, or email feedback. Figure 9-18 shows the different sections of the Web Photo Gallery dialog box.

Figure 9-18
Web Photo Gallery

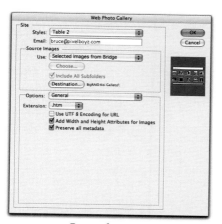

General settings

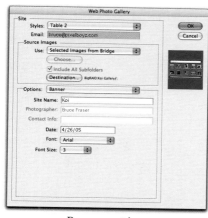

Banner settings

Large image settings

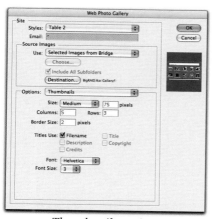

Thumbnails settings

Figure 9-18
Web Photo Gallery,
continued

Custom colors settings

Security settings

The Site section lets you choose a style for the gallery from the Style menu (the appearance of each style is reflected in the thumbnail that appears below the main control buttons) and enter an email address for receiving feedback.

The Source Images section lets you choose a folder or Selected Images from File Browser as source. It's also, somewhat confusingly, where you specify the destination folder.

All the styles produce the following:

▶ An index file

▶ A photos.js JavaScript

▶ An Images folder that contains the large images and the graphic page elements

▶ A Pages folder that contains an .htm or .html file for each image

▶ A Thumbnails folder that contains the thumbnail JPEGs

▶ A UserSelections.txt file

The files and folders produced by Web Photo Gallery *always* have these names, so the only way to differentiate between different galleries is by the enclosing folder name. Hence it's always a good idea to create a new, empty folder and use it as the destination.

The remainder of the dialog box is devoted to the Options panels, of which there are six.

▶ The **General** options let you choose between an .htm or .html extension, use UTF 8 encoding (a Unicode encoding that offers backward compatibility with ASCII-based systems) for the URL, include width and height attributes for the images to speed downloading, and choose the option to preserve or strip all the metadata. (If you only want to strip some metadata, you'll need to edit it using the techniques discussed in Chapter 8, *Mastering Metadata*, before running the automation.)

▶ The **Banner** options let you enter a site name, Photographer, contact info, and date. These entries appear in the banner on each page.

▶ The **Large Images** options let you set the pixel size of the images and the amount of JPEG compression, apply a border, and use selected metadata for titles—the available options vary depending on which style you've selected.

▶ The **Thumbnails** options let you choose the thumbnail size and, in some styles, layout, apply a border, and use selected metadata for titles. As with the Large Image options, the available options vary from style to style.

▶ The **Custom Colors** options let you choose colors for the background, banner, text, links, active links, and visited links. Again, the available options vary from style to style.

▶ The **Security** options let you place text on the images to prevent people from stealing them. You can choose from various metadata selections or enter custom text, with control over the font, size, opacity, position in the image, and rotation.

Not only do the options that are actually available vary depending on the style chosen, sometimes options that seem to be available don't actually do anything. Pages created with Web Photo Gallery probably won't win any design awards, but the feature does provide an easy way to make simple web galleries. Figure 9-19 shows the thumbnail page and an image page created using the settings shown in Figure 9-18.

Figure 9-18
Web Photo Gallery result

The index page

An image page

If the preset layouts don't do what you need, you can create custom layouts using the presets as templates. You'll need to be comfortable editing HTML, which I confess I am not. But if you are, you'll find a folder corresponding to each of the preset styles in Applications/Adobe Photoshop CS/Presets/Web Photo Gallery (Mac) or Program Files\Adobe\Photoshop CS\Presets\Web Photo Gallery (Windows). Inside each folder you'll find five .htm files.

▶ **Caption.htm** determines the layout of the captions that appear below the thumbnails on the home page.

▶ **FrameSet.htm** dictates the layout of the frame set for displaying pages.

▶ **IndexPage.htm** dictates the layout of the home page.

▶ **SubPage.htm** determines the layout of the gallery pages.

► **Thumbnail.htm** dictates the layout of the thumbnails that appear on the home page.

None of these filenames can be changed, so if you want to edit an existing style, duplicate the entire folder of the style you want to edit and work on the files in the duplicate folder. When you're done, rename the duplicate folder to the style name you want.

Advanced Automation

You can accomplish a great deal through the combination of Photoshop actions and the built-in features on Bridge's Tools menu, but actions do have some limitations. You can build amazingly complex actions, but the editing environment is a nightmare once you get beyond a dozen or so action steps, and debugging can be a serious chore.

Some operations can't be recorded in an action, and others must be recorded in very specific ways—earlier in this chapter, I showed you the problems that can occur when you add an adjustment layer to an image with an open layer set, for example. Usually you can come up with a work-around if you invest enough ingenuity, but sometimes you'll run into the wall. So I'll conclude by pointing out that Bridge is completely scriptable using JavaScript, and Photoshop is quite scriptable using either Apple-Script (Mac), Visual Basic (Windows), or JavaScript (cross-platform).

Inside the Photoshop CS2 application folder, you'll find a Scripting Guide folder. It contains comprehensive documentation on AppleScript, JavaScript, and Visual Basic scripting for Photoshop; some sample scripts that you can deconstruct; and a plug-in called ScriptingListener that, when loaded, dumps everything you do in Photoshop to a JavaScript log file. (So you only want to load it when you need that data—otherwise you'll make Photoshop run very slowly and create some very large log files!)

For a good example of the power of scripting, just look at Image Processor. It's actually a JavaScript that lives in the Presets>Scripts folder (or just search for Image Processor.jsx). Bridge shows some signs of being a version 1.0 application—it's a great start, but it certainly has some omissions. Expect to see many of the gaps being filled by scripts from enterprising third parties or from Adobe.

If I were to attempt to cover scripting in any depth at all, this book would instantly double in length, so I'll content myself with making you aware of the resources that Adobe supplies. Scripting is most certainly not for everyone, but if you've completely digested, implemented, and exhausted all the techniques in this book, and you want more automation, it's the next world to conquer.

If scripting is something you place in the same category as root canal therapy without the benefit of anaesthesia, you're far from alone. But Bridge's scriptability presents huge opportunities for those who actually enjoy such things, and I fully expect to see a plethora of scripted solutions, some free, some commercial, that will extend Bridge's functionality in all sorts of useful ways.

Right now, Bridge is where Photoshop was before the days of third-party plug-ins (yes, I go back that far), but this is not a situation that will last long. So keep an eye out for useful third-party solutions that plug some of the gaps in Bridge—a good place to start is the new Bridge Forum on Adobe's User-to-User Forum. Who knows, the market for Bridge scripts may actually turn out to be bigger than the Photoshop plug-in market.

The more you automate your workflow, the more time you'll have to actually practice photography, which presumably is what drew you to this book in the first place, and is certainly what motivated me to write it.

Good shooting!

Index